ETHNOGRAPHIC SURVEY OF AFRICA

Volume 4

THE NILOTES OF THE SUDAN AND UGANDA

THE NILOTES OF THE SUDAN AND UGANDA

East Central Africa
Part IV

AUDREY BUTT

Routledge
Taylor & Francis Group

LONDON AND NEW YORK

First published in 1952 by the International African Institute. Reprinted (unrevised) with supplementary bibliography 1964.

This edition first published in 2017
by Routledge
2 Park Square, Milton Park, Abingdon, Oxon OX14 4RN

and by Routledge
711 Third Avenue, New York, NY 10017

Routledge is an imprint of the Taylor & Francis Group, an informa business

© 1952, 1964 International African Institute

British Library Cataloguing in Publication Data
A catalogue record for this book is available from the British Library

ISBN: 978-1-138-23217-4 (Set)
ISBN: 978-1-315-30463-2 (Set) (ebk)
ISBN: 978-1-138-23198-6 (Volume 4) (hbk)
ISBN: 978-1-138-23200-6 (Volume 4) (pbk)
ISBN: 978-1-315-31381-8 (Volume 4) (ebk)

Publisher's Note
The publisher has gone to great lengths to ensure the quality of this reprint but points out that some imperfections in the original copies may be apparent.

Disclaimer
The publisher has made every effort to trace copyright holders and would welcome correspondence from those they have been unable to trace.

Publisher's note

Due to modern production methods, it has not been possible to reproduce all the charts which appeared in the original book. Please go to www.routledge.com/Ethnographic-Survey-of-Africa/Forde/p/book/9781138232174 to view them.

ETHNOGRAPHIC SURVEY OF AFRICA

EDITED BY DARYLL FORDE

EAST CENTRAL AFRICA

PART IV

THE NILOTES

OF THE

SUDAN AND UGANDA

by

AUDREY BUTT

INTERNATIONAL AFRICAN INSTITUTE

LONDON

This study is one part of the Ethnographic Survey
of Africa which the International African Institute
is preparing with the aid of a grant made by the
Secretary of State under the Colonial Development
and Welfare Acts, on the recommendation of the
Colonial Social Science Research Council

First published 1952
Reprinted (unrevised) with
supplementary bibliography 1964

REPRINTED IN ENGLAND BY
STONE & COX LTD.
LONDON AND WATFORD.

ETHNOGRAPHIC SURVEY OF AFRICA

FOREWORD

The preparation of a comprehensive survey of the tribal societies of
Africa was discussed by the Executive Council of the Institute as far·
back as 1937, but the interruption and restricting of its activities
caused by the war resulted in the postponement of the project.   Events
and developments during recent years, however, have led to a wider recognition of the need for collating and making more generally available·the
wealth of existing but uncoordinated material on the ethnic groupings and
social conditions of African peoples, particularly in connection with
plans for economic and social development.   Moreover, it appeared that
the International African Institute, as an international body which has
received support from and performed services for the different Colonial
governments, was in a very favourable situation for undertaking such a
task.

The Institute, therefore, in 1944 worked out a scheme for the preparation of an Ethnographic Survey of Africa.   A committee, under the
chairmanship of Professor Radcliffe-Brown, was appointed to consider the
scope and form of the Survey (the Editor's name appears on each volume)
and collaboration was established with research institutions in South
Africa, Rhodesia, East Africa, French West Africa, Belgium and the Belgian
Congo.   In addition to a grant from the British Colonial Development and
Welfare Fund, awarded on the recommendation of the Colonial Science
Research Council, the Institute has received a grant from the Government
of the Anglo-Egyptian Sudan to assist in the preparation and publication
of sections relevant to that territory, and this assistance is gratefully
acknowledged in connection with the present study.

The aim of the Ethnographic Survey is to present a concise, critical,
and accurate account of our present knowledge of the tribal groupings,
distribution, physical environment, social conditions, political and
economic structure, religious beliefs and cult practices, technology and
art of the African peoples.   The material is to be presented as briefly
and on as consistent a plan as possible, and the text will be supplemented
by maps and comprehensive bibliographies.

The Ethnographic Survey is being published as a series of separate,
self-contained studies, each devoted to one particular people or cluster
of peoples.   It is hoped that publication in this form will make the results more quickly and readily available to those interested in specific
areas or groups.   A list of the sections which have already appeared is
given on the cover of this volume.

Since the unequal value and the generally unsystematic nature of the
available information constituted a chief reason for undertaking this
survey, it will be obvious that the material here presented can make no
claim to be complete or definitive.   Every effort has been made, however,
to scrutinise all available literature and to check it by reference to unpublished sources and to workers actually in the field;   thus it is

intended to present a clear picture of our existing knowledge and to point out the directions in which the need for further studies is most pressing. Any assistance from those who are in a position to remedy deficiencies and correct inaccuracies by providing supplementary material will be greatly appreciated.

The International African Institute expresses its thanks to the many scholars, research workers, administrative officers and missionaries in Europe and Africa who have generously responded to our requests for information, and who have spared time to correct and supplement drafts. Personal communications are acknowledged in footnotes. Our thanks are especially due to Professor Evans-Pritchard for assistance in supervising the work on this section of the Survey and for providing his bibliography of the Nilotes.

DARYLL FORDE,
Director.

Acknowledgements

Ethnological and social anthropological studies in the Anglo-Egyptian Sudan and in East Africa generally have been built up over the last fifty years by a number of eminent scholars and contributors from other professions. In writing this survey I have been greatly indebted to them all. In particular, I wish to thank Professor E.E. Evans-Pritchard under whose guidance this survey has been written, and whose numerous and excellent studies of the Nilotic peoples have been freely drawn upon. His bibliography of the most important works on the Nilotes in here published for the first time. I also wish to thank Mlle. Boone, Mr. Breugelmans and Mr. Jansen-Smith for advance information on official population figures and for other unpublished material incorporated in this study.

Audrey Butt.

CONTENTS

PART I.   GENERAL

PART II.   THE   SOCIAL   ORGANISATION, POLITICAL   STRUCTURE   AND   MAIN CULTURAL   FEATURES   OF   THE   NILOTES

THE SHILLUK

Part I

GENERAL

The designation 'Nilotic' has, for a great number of years, been
applied indiscriminately by explorers, traders, government officials and
travellers to all those peoples who live in the Upper Nile Valley, along
the banks and in close vicinity to the great river and its tributaries.

As with most old terms, applied in the first instance to little-known
areas and people, it later became necessary to redefine and limit its
scope.   The term Nilotic has come to have a specialised meaning for anthropologists.   It refers only to certain groups of people in the Nile
valley - and to some further south in Uganda, Kenya and Tanganyika - who
have closely related physical, linguistic and other cultural characteristics as well as traditions and myths suggesting common origin.   It is
these features, together with certain characteristic types of social
structure and organisation, which have led anthropologists to feel themselves justified in including all such groups under one common title -
'Nilotes' - and to recognise the Nilotic peoples as a unique ethnic group.
Other groups of people living in the same area have been greatly affected
by the Nilotes, through intermarriage, warfare, and constant borrowing
over many generations of close, and sometimes intimate contact.   In turn,
the Nilotes have been greatly modified, physically, linguistically and
culturally, by their neighbours and in several cases it has been difficult
to determine, often with the slightest and most inadequate ethnographic
material, whether a certain group of people should be assigned to the
Nilotic peoples or to some other ethnic group, such as the Nilo-Hamitic
peoples of East Africa.

The classification of the lesser known tribes of the Upper Nile basin
is still controversial, even where language has been acknowledged as the
chief criterion of affinity to one or another ethnic group.   It may be
that some groups will never be classified with certainty owing to extensive
mingling with neighbours;   in other cases further research will determine
the peoples they most closely resemble.   For the purpose of this survey
only those which can be classified with certainty, and for which we possess
adequate information for comparative purposes, will be considered in full.

LOCATION,   POPULATION   AND
NOMENCLATURE

The Nilotic tribal groups are contained approximately within the
limits of Lat. 12°N. - Lat. 4°S. and Long. 36°E. - Long. 22°E.   The southern half of the Anglo-Egyptian Sudan is the present homeland of the majority of the Nilotes, who are found in the Provinces of Darfur, Kordofan,
White Nile, Fung, Upper Nile, Bahr el Ghazal and Equatoria.   Certain
Nilotic groups, however, are situated in the western borderland areas of
Abyssinia, in the northern regions of Uganda, and in Eastern Kenya, while
in two instances they overlap into the Belgian Congo and Tanganyika.   The

Nilotes do not occupy one continuous stretch of territory.   In the north
there is the block consisting of the Dinka, Nuer, Shilluk and Anuak;
separated from these are the Pari, Burun-speaking people, Atwot and scattered groups of the Bahr el Ghazal.   The central Nilotes (Acholi, Lango,
Alur and Jo-Paluo) are separated from the northern block by Sudanic and
Nilo-Hamitic peoples, and the southernmost Nilotic groups are further
separated from each other and from the central block by Nilo-Hamites and
Bantu.   At a broad estimate they number about two and a half millions.

A more detailed account of the location, population, nomenclature and
neighbouring tribes of the Nilotic groups follows the list of tribal groups
given below:

1. Dinka	6. Lango	11. Shilluk Luo tribes of
2. Nuer	7. Luo	the Bahr el Ghazal
3. Shilluk	8. Burun	12. Pari
4. Anuak	9. The Bor Belanda	13. Alur (a) Jo Padhola
5. Acholi	10. Jo Luo (Jur)	(b) Jo Paluo

The official population figures given below are in many cases only approxi-
mate owing to the difficulties of carrying out an adequate census in remote
and often inaccessible areas.

THE DINKA

LOCATION

The Dinka extend over a vast area from 12° - 6°N. Lat., from Renk in
the north to Malek and Tombe in the south, only about 160 miles from the
Uganda border.   There is a wide extension to the west so that the people
occupy much of the Bahr el Ghazal province and also the most southern part
of Kordofan province, immediately north of the Bahr el Arab river.   There
is a long intervening wedge of Nuer about the Bahr el Ghazal, Bahr el
Zeraf and main Nile rivers.   The Dinka tribes are usually divided into
geographical sections as follows:- (1)

(a)   *The Northern Dinka*, situated mainly in the Upper Nile Province;
they extend south to the Bahr el Zeraf, Lake No and the Bahr el Ghazal.
The main Dinka tribes inhabiting this area are known as the Padang Dinka.

(b)   *The Eastern Dinka*, situated on the right bank of the Nile from
south east of Ayod to Malek.

(c)   *The Central Dinka*, inhabiting the area on the left bank of the
Nile, extending west to Tonj.

(d)   *The Western Dinka*, situated west of the Nuer about the Jur river
area from Tonj in the south and the Bahr el Arab in the north and westwards
of Aweil.   This area is inhabited by the Malual Dinka and other lesser
tribes.   In addition the Manangier live in the swamps among the Rek Dinka
between the rivers Jur and Lol.   The Manangeir are Jo Luo people who took

(1)   Bryan and Tucker, *Distribution of the Nilotic and Nilo-Hamitic Languages*,
1948, p.7.

refuge among the Western Dinka to avoid the Arab slave raids and, later, the conflict between the Dinka and Azande. They are rapidly being absorbed by the Dinka and are consequently losing their Jo Luo customs and dialect. They are said to number 1,000 - 2,000 souls approximately.

NEIGHBOURS

The neighbours of the Dinka include the Nuer. There has been conflict between the two for a long time and relations have been predominently war-like and marked by interminable cattle raiding. In the north east the Dinka are in contact with the Shilluk while, in the south west, in the Bahr el Ghazal province, there is the confusion of tribes in the neighbourhood of Wau. Among the Wau district tribes there is the Nilotic Jo Luo (Jur) who have been in immediate contact with their Dinka neighbours for a number of generations and have been subordinate to them to a certain extent.

POPULATION

Total population has been estimated at 500,000 souls approximately.

NOMENCLATURE

The Dinka name for themselves is *Jien*. Dinka is believed to be the anglicized form of the Arabic *Denkawi*, from *Jien*.

THE NUER

LOCATION

The Nuer inhabit the savannah stretching on both sides of the Nile south of its junction with the Sobat and Bahr el Ghazal rivers and on both banks of the two tributaries. The Nile divides the Nuer country into two parts, Eastern and Western Nuerland. According to Evans-Pritchard the most important tribal groups of the Western Nuer are: the Bul, Jagei, Lek, Nuong and Dok. The most important tribes of the Eastern Nuer are: the Thiang, Lak, Gaweir and Lou.[1] The Jekany tribes are found on the west bank of the Nile and also far to the east of the Sobat river where they extend over the Anglo-Egyptian border into Abyssinia.

NEIGHBOURS

The western parts of Nuerland are in direct contact, and usually conflict, with their Dinka neighbours. Nuer expansion has been at the expense of their Dinka neighbours and it is generally recognised that much of present day Nuer country was Dinka in the middle of the 19th century. Relations between Nuer and Dinka will be discussed in the account of the Nuer political structure. The Shilluk are separated from the Nuer by the Dinka, except in a small area, and there has been little contact between the two groups, perhaps owing to the more highly organised society of the Shilluk which renders them difficult to raid with impunity. The Nuer give the

(1) Evans-Pritchard, *The Nuer*, 1940, p.8 (map).

reason that the Shilluk have no cattle and they only raid people with cattle.(1)   Although in direct contact with the Anuak in the far eastern parts of Nuer territory, tsetse fly and absence of cattle make the area unsuitable for encroachment and the Anuak were only occasionally raided by the Nuer.   When rifles were introduced and the Anuak could defend them-selves they retaliated with raids on the Nuer.   The Burun were occasion-ally raided by the Nuer for captives.   Other communities, Arab and those of the Nuba mountains, were raided only occasionally.   Except for the Beir whom the Nuer appear to have respected, and the Dinka whom they fought, most foreign peoples were classed by the Nuer as *Bar*, that is, cattle-less folk, or people possessing few cattle.   Another category was *Jur*, cattle-less people whom the Nuer regarded as lying on the outskirts of their world;   these included the Azande, Europeans, and the Bongo etc., although the Nuer have differentiating terms for most of them.

POPULATION

Official estimate of population is 260,000.   Estimates for the various tribes are given approximately as follows by Evans-Pritchard.(2)

THE   EASTERN   NUER

The Sobat Nuer				The Zeraf Nuer		
Gaajak	Gaawang	Gaajok	Lou	Lak	Thiang	Gaawar
42,000	7,000	42,000	33,000	24,000	9,000	20,000

THE   WESTERN   NUER

Bul	Leek	3 Western Jikany Tribes	Jagei Tribes	Dok	Nuong
17,000	11,000	11,000	10,000	12,000	9,000

NOMENCLATURE

The Nuer call themselves *Naath*, (sing. *Ran*).   The Shilluk, Arabs and Dinka call them *Nuer*.   The Nuer also speak of the tribes west of the Bahr el Jebel as *Nuth cieng* - 'the homeland Nuer', and of those east of the river as *Nath Doar* - 'Bush Nuer'.(3)

THE ATWOT

These appear to be a Nuer tribe, speaking a Nuer dialect, but having adopted many Dinka habits.   They are situated in the Lakes district south west of Yirrol, south of the Dinka;   they number 31,600 approximately. Little is known of them.

(1)   Evans-Pritchard, *The Nuer*, 1940, p.132.
(2)   Ibid. p.117.
(3)   Seligman, *Pagan Tribes of the Nilotic Sudan*, 1932, p.207.

THE SHILLUK

LOCATION

The Shilluk are the northernmost group of the Nilotic peoples. They occupy a narrow strip of country in the Upper Nile province and are settled mainly along the west bank of the White Nile from near Lake No in the south to approximately 11°N. Lat. - 300 miles south of Khartoum. They also have a number of settlements on the east bank of the Nile and along the lower reaches of the Sobat. In former times their country was larger, extending further north up the river towards Khartoum.

NEIGHBOURS

East of the Shilluk are the Dinka with whom they have little real contact; south west are the Nuer, and, in the north, the Arab Baggara. It was Arab pressure which forced the North Shilluk to retire to their present settlements further south.

POPULATION

It is estimated that there are 100,000 souls approximately.

NOMENCLATURE

According to Howell and Thomson and other authorities, the name Shilluk is most probably an Arabic version of the word *Colo* which is the name used by the Shilluk to refer to themselves. They are called *Teat* by the Nuer.

THE ANUAK

LOCATION

A riverain people, the Anuak are distributed along the Baro, Aluro, Obela, Gila and Akobo rivers and their tributaries in Abyssinia, and on the Akobo, Oboth, Agwei and Pibor rivers of the Anglo-Egyptian Sudan.

There are indications that the Anuak formerly occupied a wider territory than at present. They were probably in possession of part of what is now East Jikany Nuer country, north and south of the Sobat river. South of the Oboth river the country was once occupied by Anuak. Evans-Pritchard writes, "Further eastwards the whole country for a considerable distance to the south of the Oboth river was once occupied by Anuak. According to their traditions the noble clan was centred here and a century ago the people whose descendants formed the extensive village Utalo in the time of Akwei - wa - Cam were living to the south of the Oboth on sites which are being reoccupied today.[1]

NEIGHBOURS

North and west are the Nuer neighbours of the Anuak. To the south and south east are the Beir and Beir-speaking peoples and in the south west

---

(1) Evans-Pritchard, *The Political System of the Anuak*, 1940, p.8.

the Galla.   In the past, hostility and war marked relations between Anuak
and Nuer and Beir, and the Anuak people suffered considerably from raids.
They were unable to meet the cattle raids of the Nuer owing to their isolation in independent villages which rendered combination for defence virtually impossible.   Beir raids were not so severe and occasional friendly
relations were established.   Towards the end of the 19th century the
Anuak obtained rifles from Ethiopia and were then able not only to defend
themselves but also to carry out extensive counter raids into Nuerland
until the Anglo-Egyptian government compelled them to live in peace.

POPULATION

Evans-Pritchard estimates a total population of approximately 45,000
souls, of which about 10,000 live in the Anglo-Egyptian Sudan.(1)

NOMENCLATURE

The Anuak call themselves *Jo Anywa* or *Anyuaa*.   The designation *Yambo*
is used by the Ethiopians.   *Nuro, Shakko* or *K'orio* are the other names by
which they are known.(2)

THE ACHOLI

LOCATION

The Acholi district is situated in the north of Uganda and on the
borderlands of the Sudan.   A small section of the Acholi are situated in
the Opari district of the Sudan.

NEIGHBOURS

In the past there was a close relationship between the Acholi and
Lango and this intimate contact is indicated by certain common features.
The Acholi were also in close contact with the Alur, the Madi and Lotuko.

POPULATION

There are various estimates ranging from 180,000 - 340,000.
Crazzolara gives a total of 215,655.

NOMENCLATURE

The Acholi call themselves *Acoli*.   They have been known by the nickname *Gang* or *Gaŋ*.   They call the Jie *Lango Dyaŋ* ("the cattle people"),
which the Jie (and Turkana) reciprocate by calling the Acholi *ŋkatap*
(lit. "the porridge people").(3)

(1) Evans-Pritchard, *S.N.R.* XXVIII, 1947, pp.64-5.
(2) Bryan and Tucker, 1948, p.13.
(3) Personal communication from P.H. Gulliver, 1951.

THE LANGO

LOCATION

The Lango are situated in northern Uganda; their country is bounded in the west by the Victoria Nile and in the south by Lake Kioga and adjacent swamps. In the north the Moroto or Aswa river forms part of the boundary line.

NEIGHBOURS

The Lango are bounded on the south west by the Baganda (Bantu); to the east are the Teso and Karamojong (Nilo-Hamites), and in the north the Acholi. The Lango inspired the surrounding tribes with fear and respect. They lent military assistance to warring factions in Bunyoro but otherwise they had few dealings with their neighbours. Warfare with the Acholi was of the border variety and similarly with the Kumam. In 1911 the Lango came under British administration

POPULATION

Tucker records an official estimate of 276,119.[1]

NOMENCLATURE

The Lango call themselves *Laŋo*. The name Lango is of Nilo-Hamitic origin and these people, according to Driberg, seem formerly to have been known as *Langodyang*. They distinguish themselves by referring to a person of another tribe or race as *mo*, a foreigner. The Lango are known to the Teso as *Emirut* and to the Acholi as *Umiru*. The Jie and the Karamojong call the Lango *Ŋimiriono* and do not recognise the name Lango at all.[2] The Lango call both Jie and Karamojong *Olok*, a word meaning a head ornament popular among these tribes.

THE LUO

LOCATION

The Luo inhabit the Central and South Kavirondo districts bordering the north east shores of Lake Victoria to the north and south of Kavirondo Gulf. The southern section of the people stretches into Tanganyika.

NEIGHBOURS

The Luo are surrounded, on the land side, by Bantu tribes. A wedge of Bantu peoples separates them in the north from the Lango. The Luo have indirect contact with some of the Nilo-Hamitic people, the Nandi and the Masai. There is much intermarriage between the Luo of pure descent and assimilated or partly assimilated Bantu. At the present day there is also some intermarriage with the Kisii Bantu.

---

(1) Bryan and Tucker, 1948, p.17. (1945-7 official estimate)
(2) Personal communication from P.H. Gulliver, 1951.

POPULATION

Estimates are various;   perhaps the most likely is between 400,000 - 600,000 souls.

NOMENCLATURE

They are known as the Nilotic Kavirondo or Luo to Europeans;   the people call themselves *Joluo*.   The Bantu Kavirondo call them *Abanyoro* and they are also known as *Nyifwa*.[1]

The above seven tribal groups, Dinka, Nuer, Shilluk, Anuak, Acholi, Lango and Luo are those about which we know most and which will form the basis for comparison and discussion in Part II.

The Nilotic tribal groups set out below are little known and recorded information concerning them is both controversial and scanty.

THE BURUN

LOCATION

The Burun-speaking people inhabit the country between the White and Blue Niles in Dar Fung Province, on the borders of the Sudan and Abyssinia. Evans-Pritchard[2] divides them into:

> (a) The Northern Burun.
> (b) The Southern Burun.

The Northern Burun live on rocky hills which rise out of the flat open plain.   These include hills Maiak, Surkum, Kudul, Ragreig, Abuldugu, Mughaja and Tullok.   The Southern, or plains Burun occupy the forest or marsh country in the extreme south of Dar Fung.   The Northern Burun-speaking peoples are divided into a number of distinct hill communities.   The Southern Burun-speaking peoples are divided into the Meban (Burun of the Southern Plain) and the Jumjum, situated south west of the Northern Burun and north west of the Meban of the South.

NEIGHBOURS

The Burun are in contact with the Dinka and Nuer to the west and south west, and also with the Shilluk.   The Ingassana people of the Tabi mountains border them and also the Uduk and Berta-speaking groups.   The Southern Burun (Meban) suffered from Nuer raids and the slave raids of the Fung of Gule, while the Arabs, particularly the Baggara of the White Nile, used to supply themselves with slaves from the Meban on a large scale.   The Burun-speaking people have suffered from a series of invasions and conquests.

POPULATION

The Northern (hill) Burun are estimated at 1,600.   The Meban are estimated at 20,000 and the Jumjum at 4,500 souls.

(1) Bryan and Tucker, 1948, p.18.
(2) Evans-Pritchard, *S.N.R.* 1932, Vol.XV, Pt.1, p.53.

NOMENCLATURE

Burun is a linguistic term primarily and is applied by Europeans to a number of tribes in Dar Fung Province. The term *Burun*, or *Barun*, was originally used by the Arabs. The hill Burun in the north are called *'Laŋɛ'* by the Acholi and *Cai* by the Nuer.[1] They do not have one term applicable to themselves but each hill community and district has a separate name. Evans-Pritchard records that the people of Kurmuk call themselves *Tarak* or *Boit* and are called *Mekormuk* by the people of Jebel Ulu.[2] The people of Mughaja call themselves *Mumugadja*. The people of Mugwa are called *Mopo* by those of Kurmuk, while the people of Abuldugu are called *Bogon* by those of Jebel Ulu and *Mugomborkoina* by those of Mughaja.

The Meban of the Southern Burun are called *Guru* by the Berta, *Tungan* by the people of Kurmuk, *Barga* by those of Ulu, *Tonko* by the Jumjum.

The Jumjum are called *Berin* by the Kurmuk people and *Olga* by those of Ulu.

Little is known about the Burun people and their immediate neighbours and a hasty survey by Evans-Pritchard is as yet the main source of information.

THE BOR BELANDA[3]

LOCATION

The majority of the Belanda occupy the country in the triangle formed by the rivers Wau, Sueh and Bo of the Bahr el Ghazal Province. They are also found in some numbers on the east bank of the river Sueh; others live in the neighbourhood of Deim Zubeir and some live under Azande rule in the country between the rivers Bo and Tembura.

NEIGHBOURS

Evans-Pritchard aptly remarks that, "The tribes of the Bahr el Ghazal present the appearance of a routed army."[4] There are numerous tribal units which often consist of a few families isolated from the main body. Hybrid cultures have resulted from the various combinations due to the Zande invasions which carried many tribes before them. The whole area is a puzzle of names and groups, many of which have not been placed or in any way sorted out. South of the Belanda main group (in the triangle formed by the Bo, Wau and Sueh rivers) are the Azande who have in the past exerted considerable pressure on the Belanda and absorbed a part of them. A section of the Bongo people and some of the Bukuru are found in the neighbourhood. In addition, there are the Luo (Jo Luo or Jur) group north of Wau, and the Dembo and Shatt (or Thuri) who are all predominant in the Bahr el Ghazal Province and are of the same stock as the Bor section of the Belanda. There are also related Ndogo groups who have influenced the Bor in the past, chiefly through the Biri.

(1) Bryan and Tucker, 1948, p.14.
(2) Evans-Pritchard, *S.N.R.* 1932, Vol.XV, Pt.1, p.35.
(3) A term which includes the Biri of the Ndogo Sere group, who are not considered here, and the Bor of the Nilotic group.
(4) Evans, Pritchard, *S.N.R.* 1931, Vol.XIV, Pt.1, p.15.

POPULATION

It is difficult to give accurate numbers owing to the scattered settlements and the fact that many of the Bor Belanda still live in Zande country and the majority are very close to the Ndogo Biri. Santandrea estimates 3,000 approximately in the area south of the Bo river.

NOMENCLATURE

It was as late as 1923 that M.J. Wheatley's article recorded the fact that the Belanda consist of two separate tribes of quite different origins, whose languages and cultures were being grouped together under the same name - Belanda. There have been considerable arguments over the names which should be applied to the separate tribal divisions covered by this common term.

The term Belanda has been applied by the Arabs. It was stated by various authors to be a Bongo name meaning 'hill dwellers' and Santandrea maintains that the Bongo call all the Luo-speaking people *Ber* or *Beer*, so that *Beer-landa*, meaning 'the Beer of the Hills', was gradually contracted into Belanda by the Arabs and other neighbouring tribes.[1]

Wheatley states, "In reality the term covers two distinct tribes, the Amberidi and Ambegumba".[2] Tucker and Santandrea have come to the conclusion that the Luo-speaking Belanda call themselves *Bor*, or *Jo-Bor*, while the Ndogo-speaking Belanda, who are not Nilotes, claim *Biri* as their own real name. The Bor Belanda are also called *Mve-Rodi*. The Biri, Ndogo and Dembo peoples call them *Rodi*, which is changed into *(A)Mbe-rcdi* by the Azande. There is thus a considerable variation in spelling and nomenclature. In this survey the Nilotic group will be referred to as Bor and if there is any occasion to mention the non-Nilotic, Ndogo, group with whom they are closely allied and from whom they have adopted many cultural features, they will be referred to as Biri.

THE JO LUO

LOCATION

The Jo Luo are situated north of Wau in the direction of Aweil and south as far as Tonj in the Bahr el Ghazal Province.

NEIGHBOURS

The tribes around Wau are small and diverse and form a complexity which has not yet been satisfactorily sorted out by ethnologists. The Jo Luo are in contact with the Shatt, the Shilluk of the Bahr el Ghazal - both of Nilotic origin - and also with the Bongo, Ndogo and other groups around Wau. The Dinka to the north and east of them have exerted the greatest influence, however, and the recent history of the two groups has been closely intertwined.

(1) Santandrea, *S.N.R.* 1933, Vol.XVI, Pt.2, p.161.
(2) M.J. Wheatley, *S.N.R.* 1923, Vol.VI, Pt.2, p.251.

POPULATION

According to Santandrea and Tucker they number 16,000 souls approximately.

NOMENCLATURE

The people call themselves the *Jo Luo* - the Luo people.   Both Arabic-speaking people and Europeans call them the *Jur* - a nickname meaning 'foreigner' which was originally applied to them by the Dinka.   All the other Luo-speaking groups in the area - Shatt, Dembo and Shilluk Luo - name them *Abai*.

Two other nicknames exist;   the Jo Luo living on the right bank of the river Jur call those on the left bank *Ya-Gony*, the meaning of which is not known;   the people on the left bank refer to those on the right as *Ya Kuak*, meaning   people of the leopard'.

THE SHILLUK LUO TRIBES OF THE BAHR EL GHAZAL.
DEMBO, SHATT AND SHILLUK LUO

LOCATION

These tribes are found in scattered groups in the area immediately north west of Wau.

NEIGHBOURS

The main peoples in the vicinity are the Dinka, Jo Luo and non-Nilotic Ndogo groups and the confused mixture of tribes in the area.

POPULATION

There are no accurate estimates available.   From the records of tax-payers the Shatt may be reckoned at 1,400 souls.   The Dembo may be similarly estimated at 800 and the Shilluk Luo at 1,600 souls.

NOMENCLATURE

The Shatt or Thuri call themselves *Jo-Turi* according to Tucker.[1]   The Dembo or Bodho call themselves *Jo Bodo*.   They are known as *Bwodo* by some of the Jo Luo.   According to Santandrea the Shilluk Luo of the Bahr el Ghazal are known as Luo, but Tucker states that they call themselves *Jo Colo*.

THE PARI

LOCATION

The Pari occupy Lafon Hill to the east of the Nile in Equatoria Province of the Sudan.   The hill is known locally as Lepul and is a small rocky outcrop rising abruptly out of the surrounding plain, and completely

---

(1) Bryan and Tucker, 1948, p.15.

covered with terraced villages.[1]

NEIGHBOURS

Somewhat isolated from other Nilotic tribal groups the Pari are more closely in contact with the Nilo-Hamitic groups, the Bari and Lokoiya.

POPULATION

Estimates vary from 1,800 to 6,000. Figures derived from tax payers' estimates given by Bryan place the population at 7,000 approximately.[2]

NOMENCLATURE

They are known as the Pari, Feri and Lokoro.

THE ALUR

LOCATION

They are situated in the extreme north-east of the Belgian Congo and extend into Uganda, along the north-west shores of Lake Albert and south and west of Mahagi.

NEIGHBOURS

Their western neighbours are the Acholi, with whom they are believed to have much in common. To the north are the Madi, to the west and south the Lugbara and Lendu.

POPULATION

There are various estimates. According to the official sources quoted by Bryan and Tucker they number 92,987 in the Mahagi territories.[3] Belgian Congo Alur number 100,563 souls.[4]

NOMENCLATURE

The people call themselves the *Jo Alur*.

The Burun, Bor Belanda, Jo Luo, Shatt, Dembo, Shilluk Luo, Alur and the Pari will not be considered in any detail in this survey since the available information is not sufficiently reliable to enable any useful comparisons with them to be made. A brief summary of the material recorded for each group will be given.

A few remaining groups, generally classified as Nilotic, are mentioned here to complete the list but are not further discussed owing to an almost complete lack of literature on them. They are as follows:-

(1) Driberg, *S.N.R.*, 1925, Vol.VIII, p.47.
(2) Bryan and Tucker, 1948, p.13.
(3) Ibid., p.17.
(4) Figures given by Mlle. Boone.

(a) *THE JO PADHOLA*

Situated south-west of Mount Elgon on the Kenya-Uganda border in Mbale District, they are separated from the Luo in the south-east by a narrow wedge of Bantu.   They border on the Nilo-Hamitic Teso in the north.   The Jo Padhola were estimated at the Uganda Census of 1931 to be 49,683 souls. The people refer to themselves as *Jo Padhola* but they are called *Budama* by their Bantu neighbours.[1]

(b) *THE JO-PALUO*

Situated in Uganda in the northern part of Bunyoro district, the Jo-Paluo are found on the south-west border of the Acholi and on the west border of the Lango - the Victoria Nile forming a boundary for both groups. Crazzolara estimates the population at 6,000.   Nicknamed the *Chopi* they call themselves the *Jo-Paluo* and are called *Loloka* by the Acholi.   Virtually nothing is known of them.

There are certain other groups which have been classed as Nilotic in origin or are today predominently Nilotic in culture and language.   Among these Crazzolara includes the Barabaig, a people numbering about 9,000 and living south-east of Lake Eyasi in the Arusha Province of Tanganyika territory.   Their language, however, is undoubtedly Nilo-Hamitic and related to Nandi.[2]   There has been some uncertainty as to whether the Kuman, consisting of about 50,000 souls, living north of Lake Kioga between the Lango and Nilo-Hamitic Teso, should be classified as Nilotic or Nilo-Hamitic, but they are now generally regarded as Nilo-Hamitic.   The Labwor people, about 30,000 souls, living on the western border of Karamoja district, are considered by some authorities to speak a Nilotic language.

All the tribal groups which have been mentioned, and about which we have a certain amount of information, have a number of basic and important features in common.   Consideration of these will not only justify the inclusion of these groups under one common term, as forming a distinct and unique ethnic group, but will also serve as a framework into which a more detailed consideration of the social structure and organisation of the main groups may be fitted in later sections of the survey.

THE NILOTIC LANGUAGES

The chief criterion in the classification of tribes in the Anglo-Egyptian Sudan and East Africa generally has been that of language.   In spite of efforts to substitute physical type or common origin as the deciding factor, language still remains the most important feature, in spite of cultural differences which might tend to deny its evidence.

It has long been recognised that certain groups of tribes in the Upper Nile valley speak languages which are similar in essential features and which are genetically related.   Westermann's classification of the

(1) Bryan and Tucker, 1948, pp.17-18.
(2) Information from G.W.B. Huntingford, 1951.

languages of the Nile valley in general includes the Shilluk, Anuak, Jur, Dembo, Belanda, Acholi, Lango, Alur, Luo and Jo-Paluo in one group, and the Dinka and Nuer in another related group.(1)   These he distinguishes from the Nilo-Hamitic, Arab and other languages.   Later evidence has indicated that Westermann's work is in most respects sound and, by consulting a Nilotic word list, the similarities between words of the same meaning may be seen - although the words may be drawn from different tribal groups living, today, many hundreds of miles from each other.   In most cases the differentiation in grammar and vocabulary which has taken place makes communication between the representatives of two different groups very difficult or even impossible.   Nevertheless, the basic common features are still clearly discernible.   A.N. Tucker, in his "Linguistic Survey of the Nilotic Languages", gives a full list of the characteristics of the Nilotic languages which differentiate them from others, and starts off with the assertion that "the Nilotic languages have a peculiar pronunciation of their own which at once distinguishes them from most other sorts of languages." (2)

Tucker divides the Nilotic languages into two groups: the Dinka group, consisting of the Nuer and Dinka dialects, and the Luo group, consisting of the remaining Nilotic tribal groups.   The Luo language group has previously been known as the Shilluk-speaking group, but recent research by Tucker and information supplied by Crazzolara and other investigators indicate that the term Luo, or Lwo, is more appropriate.(3)   The name is used by many tribes and is acknowledged by them as the original tribal name.

According to Crazzolara individuals from the furthest extremities of the Nuer group can understand each other without difficulty.   In the Dinka tribal group individuals can understand each other with little difficulty. In the Luo group dispersion has caused more divergence.   The various languages are obviously dialects of one original language and are much closer to each other than to either Nuer or Dinka.   He reckons that for the Luo language dialects nine distinct grammars are needed.(4)

Tucker lists a number of specifically Luo traits and further subdivides the language group into two:

(a) The Northern Luo dialects.   These consist of Shilluk, Anuak Burun, Jo Luo, Bor etc.

(b) The Southern Luo dialects.   These consist of Acholi, Lango, Alur, Luo etc.

"The two subdivisions are separated geographically by a belt of Moru - Madi and Bari languages.   Northern Lwo has more in common with the Dinka - Nuer than has the Southern Lwo, which seems to have come under Eastern Sudanic influence." (5)

(1)   Westermann, *The Shilluk People*, 1912, pp.30-31.
(2)   Bryan and Tucker, 1948, p.19.
(3)   The spelling 'Luo', being more generally used in the literature, is used throughout this study except where direct reference is made to an authority using the form 'Lwo'.
(4)   See Crazzolara, *The Lwoo*, Part I. *Lwoo Migrations*, pp.5-6. He includes in his list of Nilotic tribal groups the debated Barabaig of Tanganyika and he also separates the Kuman from the Lango, claiming Teso origin for them.
(5)   Bryan and Tucker, 1948, p.23.

DINKA LANGUAGE GROUP	LUO LANGUAGE GROUP	
	(a) *Northern Luo*	(b) *Southern Luo*
Dinka	Shilluk	Acholi
Nuer	Anuak	Lango
	Burun	Alur
	Jo Luo	Luo
	Bor	etc.
	etc.	

TUCKER'S NILOTIC LANGUAGE CLASSIFICATION

Tucker makes a further linguistic division of the Southern Luo on the grounds of differences in pronunciation. Apart from local dialects.and differences due to isolation and development of regional peculiarities, there are clearly perceived differences which are due to the absorption of some parts of the languages of neighbouring non-Nilotic groups, and these Tucker has taken into account in his analysis. In the case of the Lango, for example, the language spoken by them today is very similar to that of the Acholi and has therefore been classified as belonging to the Nilotic group. Tarantino points out, however, that a considerable number of nouns have Karamojong roots and he does not hesitate to affirm that the original language of the Lango was that of the Karamojong - Teso group.[1]

In the case of the Belanda, linguistic affinities have been very important, particularly in helping to place the Bor section of the two Belanda tribes and linking them to larger groups of people. Santandrea says that the Bor have lost the original purity and structure of the language. The vocabulary is largely a Luo type of vocabulary and has presumably remained unaltered, but the grammatical structure is substantially different from the Luo and related dialects.[2] This is due to the influence of the Ndogo-speaking Biri, the other section of the Belanda with whom the Bor have had a long and most intimate contact.

In some cases it has been difficult to decide from linguistic evidence whether a people is of Nilotic origin or has adopted many Nilotic linguistic characteristics although of a very different type fundamentally. Such an instance is provided by the Burun-speaking people about whom Evans-Pritchard has said, "The grammatical evidence is insufficient to say whether the Burun languages have borrowed extensively from Nilotic languages or whether they should themselves be classed as Nilotic tongues ..... at least the vocabularies give us basis for an hypothesis of strong and prolonged contact between the Burun and Nilotic nations."[3] In spite of this obvious drawback in the linguistic mode of classification it has at least, as Evans-Pritchard has stated, enabled the Burun to be linked with the Nilotic peoples and has assisted in differentiating the various groups from the rest of the Dar Fung people.

It may be said that the criterion of language in classification is an especially useful one, for the Nilotes have certain unique linguistic characteristics in common which serve to identify the various tribal groups with each other and to differentiate the whole from neighbouring peoples. Nevertheless, in spite of the obvious value of using language as a basis

(1) Tarantino, *Uganda Journal*, 1946, Vol.X, No.1, p.15.
(2) Santandrea, *Anthropos*, 1942, p.235.
(3) Evans-Pritchard, *S.N.R.* 1932, Vol.XV, Pt.1, p.55.

for ethnic classifications and inter-relationships, there are certain disadvantages due to inter-mingling with, and borrowing from, originally
different groups of people. It is therefore clear that linguistic
evidence should be supplemented by other data - physical, cultural and,
where possible, historical and structural.

THE   NILOTIC   PHYSICAL   TYPE

Except where they have most obviously intermarried with other stocks,
the Nilotic peoples show a remarkable physical uniformity. The difference in type from other negro peoples of Africa was noted by the earliest
travellers who penetrated the Upper Nile valley regions and Northern
Uganda and Kenya. Since then physical anthropologists have speculated
on the nature of these physical differences without coming to a satisfactory conclusion. Seligman's theories concerning the Hamitic influence in
East Africa is one of the main solutions which have been proposed. In his
own words his theory is as follows: "Wherever they (i.e. the Hamites)
originated, there is no doubt that they entered Negroland in a succession
of waves, of which the earliest may have been as far back as the end of
the pluvial period, and so gave rise ..... to numerous groups of hamiticised Negroes. The manner of origin of the Negro-Hamitic peoples will
be understood when it is realized that the incoming Hamites were pastoral
Caucasians, arriving wave after wave, better armed and of sterner character than the agricultural Negroes. Diagrammatically we may picture the
process somewhat as follows. At first the Hamites, or at least their
aristocracy, would endeavour to marry Hamitic women, but it cannot have
been long before a series of peoples combining Negro and Hamitic blood
arose; these, superior to the pure Negro, would be regarded as inferiors
by the next incoming wave of Hamites and be pushed further inland to play
the part of an incoming aristocracy *vis a vis* the Negroes on whom they
impinged, and this process was repeated with minor modifications over a
long period of time....."[1]

Whatever may be thought of this proposition, it is generally agreed
among ethnologists and physical anthropologists that the pastoral peoples
of the Sudan and East Africa have characteristics which can only be explained in terms of Caucasian affinities. Seligman classified the
hamiticised Negroes of the Sudan into two great groups, the Nilotes and
Nilo-Hamites.[2] This provides a generally accepted terminology for
anthropologists, whether speaking in physical or in cultural and other
terms, though as 'hamitic' is properly employed as a linguistic term we
should beware of confusion in its use. Both groups have certain physical
characteristics in common, such as tall stature and dolichocephaly, but
these are more marked in the Nilotes, while the Nilotic group is more uniform in type than the Nilo-Hamitic. General characteristics of the
Nilotic type are summarised as follows:-

(a) They are very tall, averaging 5ft. 10ins. or more; many individuals are over 6ft. 5ins. and this is particularly the case among the

(1) Seligman, *Pagan Tribes of the Nilotic Sudan*, 1932, p.4.
(2) *Ibid.*

Nuer and Dinka.   The Nilotes have been characterised as the tallest people in the world on average.

(b) In figure they are generally slight and lithe with narrow hips, thin calves and extraordinarily long legs.   They have slender bones and are not muscular.

(c) Their hair is frizzy like that of the African negro.   They have little body hair and their complexions are dark brown verging on black, although there is considerable variation ranging from black and very dark brown to light bronze shades.

(d) In features they have the broad nose, everted lips and prognathous profile which approximates to the negro type.   Nevertheless, some individuals are met with aquiline noses, thin lips and long finely shaped faces.   There is considerable variation between two extreme types.

(e) The Nilotes are markedly dolichocephalic.   They have long heads and an average cephalic index of approximately 72.   The following figures are given by Seligman and they are approximated by Tucker and Myres in their article in J.R.A.I. 1910.   ("A contribution to the Anthropology of the Sudan.") and other researches.[1]

	Cephalic Index	Nasal Index	Facial Index	Stature
Shilluk	71.3	93.3	83.2	1.77 m.
Dinka	72.7	91.6	86.0	1.78 m.
Nuer	73.5	100.0	83.1	1.79 m.

These five features, dominant among the Nilotic peoples and characteristic of them, are modified in some of the regions where there has been intermarriage and mingling with non-Nilotic neighbours.   It is remarked, for example, that the Acholi are mesaticephalic, that the Jo Luo, while similar to other Nilotes, are large boned, muscular and not so tall.   The Bor, through intermarriage with the Biri of Ndogo stock, have lost many Nilotic characteristics.   Both Bor and Biri have in fact modified what must have been their original pronounced racial characteristics.   Evans-Pritchard, having taken specific measurements of the Bor, states that they are considerably shorter in stature than the Shilluk Luo of the Bahr el Ghazal and they show a tendency towards mesaticephaly.[2]

The most outstanding example of the Nilotic physical type is the Dinka; they have, to a marked degree, all the general characteristics outlined above, as have their neighbours the Nuer.

A characteristic pose of the Nilotes has caused much comment from those who are acquainted with them.   This is the habit they have of standing on one foot, with the sole of the other pressed close against the inner surface of the knee, while the whole body is balanced by leaning on a spear or stick.   This pose is not, however, peculiar to the Nilotes, although it may be assumed by them more frequently than by other peoples.

(1) Seligman, *Pagun Tribes of the Nilotic Sudan*, 1932, p.13.
(2) Evans-Pritchard, *S.N.R.*, 1931, Vol.XIV, Pt.1, p.14.

In summarising the data on the Nilotic physical type we may say that the Nilotes have a number of physical characteristics which, in combination, serve to separate them from other peoples as a unique racial group.   Although there is a generally recognised standard physical type there are many deviations from it, indicating that there has been considerable inter-mingling with different neighbouring groups in some parts.   In general, physical and linguistic deviations go together, as among the Belanda and the Burun, and this is because they are due to the same cause.

HISTORY

The history of the Nilotes, in the sense of their discovery and ex-ploration and the beginning of documented knowledge concerning them, begins as late as the early 19th century.

THE EGYPTIANS IN THE SUDAN

The Egyptians invaded the Sudan in 1821 at the command of Mohammed Ali Pasha who sent his son, Ismail, south from Egypt into the Sudan so that, through conquest, these regions might provide the Egyptians with soldiers, slaves and wealth.   The period of Egyptian maladministration which followed the conquest was marked by extortion and rapine.   Most of the Nilotic tribes were too far south to feel the full brunt of the evils which ensued, but slave raids occurred and heavy taxation was extorted from the less inaccessible tribes.   By 1850 the trade monopoly, which had at first been exercised by the government, was allowed to lapse and Arab traders from the northern districts were enabled to obtain, for a consideration, concessions to procure slaves by whatever means they pleased.   By 1869 the power of the slave traders had become so great that they were practically independent kings.   A number of efforts were made at reform, notably by Sir Samual Baker who, in 1869, was made Governor-General of the Equatoria Provinces by the Khedive and was told to annexe the Nile basin southwards from Gondokoro.   He was succeeded by Gordon in 1874.   Between them they effected the opening of communications with the Great Lakes and Uganda.[1]

Thus it was that in the first half of the 19th century western civil-isation first came into real contact with the Sudan.   During this time there was a succession of great explorers; Speke and Grant, Marno, Schweinfurth, Junker Schnitzer (Emin Pasha), Beltrame, Petherick, Poncet, Baker and Heuglin and others, penetrate the region and a certain amount of reliable information on the character of the various Upper Nile tribes began to be assimilated, although anthropologically the value of their accounts is slight.

THE MAHDI

The efforts at reform did not sufficiently mitigate the evils of the Egyptian administration and when, in 1881, the Mahdist revolt against

(1) Macmichael, *The Anglo-Egyptian Sudan*, 1934, p.37.

Egypt was inaugurated by Mohammed Ahmed who proclaimed himself the divine saviour, the prevailing discontent concentrated itself in religious fervour. The followers of the Mahdi, the Dervishes, reconquered the Sudan from the Egyptians over a period of several years culminating in the disaster at Khartoum and the assassination of General Gordon in 1885. The Sudan remained in the hands of the Dervishes until 1898 and their administration proved no more beneficial than that of the Egyptians. In 1891 there were outbreaks in the provinces of Darfur and Kordofan. On the White Nile first the Shilluk and then the Nuer took up arms, while the Dinka destroyed forces which had been sent against them for raiding purposes.

The Dervish power came to an end when the European countries began to close in on the Sudan with the object of establishing an effective administration and ending the period of extortion which had existed for so long. The Abyssinians threatened in the east, the Belgians in the Congo, the Italians in Eritrea, and the British in Uganda and on the Egyptian border. The Anglo-Egyptian army under Lord Kitchener invaded the Sudan and the decisive defeat of the Dervish Empire was achieved at the battle of Omdurman in 1898. A reconnoitre in the south afterwards found the Shilluk and Dinka friendly and the Nuer shy and apprehensive.[1] The whole of the Sudan was gradually occupied, its international status established and the Condominium agreement made. It was now that the first organised government of both the Northern and Southern Sudan began and this soon affected the Nilotic tribes which had, up to then, except for the slave raids and Egyptian and Arab extortions, largely followed their own local interests, enmities and independent pursuits.

THE ANGLO-EGYPTIAN SUDAN GOVERNMENT

From 1900 - 1930 the Sudan government was troubled by occasional revolts in the south which were largely due to a natural mistrust of northern government and a spirit of extreme independence and hatred of interference and encroachment in their own spheres of life. Incitement by prophets (in the case of the Nuer) and the zeal of young warriors provided the means of causing trouble. Expeditions were sent against the Nuer for raiding the Burun and Dinka, against the Anuak for raiding the Nuer and against the Nuer, Dinka and Anuak for flouting the government.

By 1928 the Dinka had largely become accustomed to the authority of the government and the Anuak were fairly peaceful. The Nuer, however, remained truculent and year by year one section or another raided the Beir or Anuak or attacked a government outpost. No real effort was made to stop this until 1928 when the matter was brought to a head by the murder, in the previous year, of the District Commissioner, Fergusson, by the consistent hostility of the Nuer prophets towards the government and by further raids on the Dinka. Forces were sent and by 1930 the Nuer were subdued and the activities of the prophets ended.

After 1930 the military activities of the Sudan government were mostly confined to the frontier districts, especially those bordering on Abyssinia. From 1900 onwards the Southern Sudan had been gradually opened up. Further exploration became possible and ethnological work began on more scientific

(1) Macmichael, *The Anglo-Egyptian Sudan*, 1934, p.59.

lines.   The anthropological researches of Professor and Mrs. Seligman, undertaken in 1909 and 1910 and again in 1921 and 1922, provided the first systematic studies of the Nilotic and neighbouring peoples and laid the foundation for more intensive research.

AGENCIES   OF   MODERN   DEVELOPMENT RELATING   TO   THE   SOUTHERN   SUDAN

THE GOVERNMENT

After 1898 the Provinces were each put in charge of a Provincial Governor who was answerable to the Governor General of the Sudan for the state of his province.   There was an allocation of duties to a staff of District Commissioners, and a number of police, a clerical staff and other officials were appointed.   The District Commissioner was responsible for the administration of the law and the fair distribution of taxation.   As the local representative of the Governor in his district he heard cases, supervised the police, settled feuds, caused roads to be built and dealt with economic matters.   He was called on to deal with any type of trouble and with all aspects of native life.

It was from 1900 - 1905 that the foundations of the Sudan Political Service were laid for the purpose of administering the native peoples. Young university men, civilians, were enrolled to form the nucleus of a Civil Service - the disadvantages of using military personnel being that an officer was liable to be called away at short notice and this tended to dislocate the machinery of government.[1]   It was the policy of the Sudan government, even before 1921, to admit, in certain cases, the indigenous peoples to a share in the management of affairs in their locality.   Native people of the Sudan were appointed to certain governmental posts carrying direct administrative duties and legislation was passed regularising the exercise by native chiefs of powers over members of their own tribes.[2] This was speeded up after 1921.

This policy of native administration worked fairly successfully with the more centralised Nilotic people, such as the Shilluk and Anuak, but not so well with the independent Nuer and Dinka to whom chiefs and central-ised governments, even of a symbolic and ritual nature, were foreign.

MISSIONS

The policy of the newly established Sudan government was to give no financial aid to the missions which were established in the country after the conquest and to avoid interference as far as possible.   South of about 10°N. Lat. a system of missionary spheres of influence was establish-ed to avoid competition and quarrelling between the various Churches repre-sented.   This system of mission spheres has been maintained to the present. Only four types of missions were allowed to work in the Sudan:

(1) Macmichael, *The Anglo-Egyptian Sudan*, 1934, p.83.
(2) *Ibid.*, p.247.

The American Methodist Mission was established on the Sobat.

The Roman Catholics established stations in the Shilluk area near Fashoda. In 1903 the Catholics were allowed to start work again in the Bahr el Ghazal area, the missions previously established in the 19th century having been destroyed by the Mahdia.

The Church Missionary Society (Anglican) started work in 1905 in the areas of east Bahr el Ghazal and Mongalla.

The Sudan United Mission (Australian) in 1913 opened a station at Melut for work among the Dinka living on the east side of the White Nile below Malakal.

SCHOOLS

Education proceeded in the Northern Sudan with considerable vigour immediately after 1898. Gordon College was founded, as well as several technical and other schools in the towns and villages. In the South nothing serious was at first attempted in education which was left entirely in the hands of the missionaries. In 1922, however, a system of small annual subsidies to missionary bodies was instituted for the first time in the Southern Sudan, to assist their educational activities. In 1926 a serious effort was made to provide a systematic educational organisation in collaboration with the missionaries, granting larger subsidies for educational and medical work and making provision for inspection by appointing a resident, Inspector of Education for the South. In 1927 two types of schools were adopted: one elementary, which provided a simple, practical four year course of study carried out in a vernacular language; the other intermediate, offering a six year course in which English was spoken. The second type of school, fewer in number, was designed to train teachers and clerical staff to meet the needs of the South.

From 1928 an annual conference was held at Rejaf, attended by representatives of the Sudan, Uganda and Congo governments and of the missionary bodies at work in those countries, to consider questions of language and education.

The question of a *lingua franca* is a very difficult one in the Southern Sudan owing to the number of different language groups and dialects spoken in any given area. Generally only their own vernacular is spoken by the people and the 'bush schools' of the missionaries are conducted in the local dialect. A debased form of Arabic is used throughout many of the regions and English is taught at the higher levels.

MEDICAL SERVICES

Medical work in the most inaccessible areas remained in the hands of the medical officers of the Egyptian army for some years after the reoccupation. Hospitals were established in the towns but lack of funds prevented the organisation of adequate medical services in the country districts. In 1904 **the** first steps were taken towards a civil medical organisation. In 1909 epidemics of sleeping sickness began to spread from the Belgian Congo and special clearing operations were instituted.

As more money became available after the 1914-18 war the medical

services began to expand.   In each province a British doctor was in charge.
Each province had a medical headquarters with a well equipped hospital.   A
number of dispensaries were established so that less serious cases could be
treated locally.   By 1935 there had been instituted a service of tribal
dressers based on and controlled by the dispensaries.   The men were
selected by chiefs, had a medical refresher course every year, and reported
at fixed intervals.   Only the most elementary ills were treated by them
but the system was nevertheless useful in remote areas.

AGRICULTURE

The southern provinces of the Anglo-Egyptian Sudan are not an economic
asset but a drain on the resources of the rest of the country.   The supply
of ivory diminished rapidly after the reconquest.   Rinderpest and other
cattle diseases have greatly reduced the herds while it is the custom of
the Nilotic people to cultivate only for their own immediate needs.   They
are suspicious of the introduction of any cash crops and, as the wants of
the people are few, they are satisfied with their own traditional mode of
life.   Cost and difficulties of transport and the attitudes of cattle-
loving people have meant that economic advancement on any large scale has
not so far been practicable.   A number of all weather roads have been
built linking important points and villages in the south.

The known and recorded history of the Nilotes has to be studied
against a background of events affecting the rest of the Sudan and involving European and Egyptian power.   For nearly three-quarters of a century
before the establishment of the present government the southern tribes were
raided for slaves and ivory.   Slave stations were established in the territories of the people who were either sold and sent away or made to work
as serfs for their captors.   The Shilluk were sufficiently organised to
deter many of the raiders, while the warlike qualities of the Nuer and the
Dinka, and their ability to escape into the almost inaccessible swamps and
marshes of their country meant that they were luckier than many of the non-
Nilotic peoples near them.   Apart from the horrors of slave-raiding, the
Nilotes were little affected by foreign rule.   Under the present Anglo-
Egyptian administration their entire way of life has been affected.   Missionary activities, medical services, development schemes, irrigation,
road-making and public works have all had some effect, though not, in many
instances, so much as in the North.   The imposition of peace and the introduction of a European type of government have led to great changes in
the indigenous modes of organisation.

Their known history gives no indication of a former unity among the
Nilotic people; during the 120 or so years they have been known, the
various tribal groups have, so far as can be ascertained, been in independent occupation of their present territories, except for very limited
movements such as the expansion of the Nuer from west to east and their
conquest of eastern Dinka territory, which occurred during the 19th century.

For indications of earlier contacts it is necessary to consider evidence concerning the pre-European era, an era for which there is no history
in the true sense of the word, but for which the various tribal groups retain traditions and myths of earlier activities, inter-relations and migrations.

TRADITIONS AND MYTHS OF THE
RELATIONS AMONG NILOTIC TRIBAL GROUPS

Speculations concerning the origin, former movements and inter-relationships of the various Nilotic tribal groups have long occupied ethnologists. The sole information is provided by the myths and traditions related by the Nilotic peoples themselves. Crazzolara remarks, "Tradition is a popular narrative which tells of events, real events of the past".[1] The myths of the Nilotes are, in part, histories of the people, but expressed in terms of personalities and symbolic events and very difficult to interpret. Transmission by word of mouth from generation to generation is not a satisfactory mode of recording history if accuracy rather than artistic effect is desired.

Interpretations of Nilotic myths of origin have been limited. Westermann considered that the Shilluk reached their present territory about the end of the 15th century. Seligman writes that it may be assumed that the Nilotic cradleland lay somewhere to the east of the Great Lakes; that from the homeland emerged two great waves which were in reality composed of a series of movements to the North. The two waves may be called those of the Dinka and the Shilluk, the former giving rise to the Dinka and Nuer, the latter to the Shilluk, Luo, Anuak, Acholi and others less characteristically Nilotic, to be accounted for by contact with a different people pressing forward from the Nile-Congo divide.[2]

Crazzolara, in his *Lwoo Migrations*, has ingeniously fitted together the recorded traditions and presents a full picture of how, in his view, the dispersal of the 'Lwoo' people into their present territories must have occurred. His conclusions are, briefly, as follows: *Jii*, meaning human beings, is a collective name for the Nilotes as opposed to the Bantu and other racial groups. There are three Jii groups - the *Naadh* (Nuer), *Jiaan* (Dinka) and *Lwoo* (Shilluk, etc.).

The area around and to the south of Lake No is the common cradleland. The Nuer have moved least for they still show the place, south of Lake No, where Kwoth (God) created man, but they have pushed into Dinka country.

The Lwoo, according to Crazzolara, were a border group south of the central Jii group and their former home was around Rumbek. ·This group grew in numbers and herds and started differentiating itself; for some reason, possibly overpopulation, the Lwoo began to migrate. A small group remained behind - the forebears of the Atwot, Crazzolara infers - but the rest moved away. Shilluk tradition relates that their original home was called Lwo-wo or Dowaat. Nyikang quarrelled with his elder half-brother Dowaat because the latter had been made chief. Disappointed, Nyikang and a large group of Lwoo decided to leave the country and did so, proceeding in a northerly direction. The first great split occurred when a group, headed by Boor, moved west and then south and finally settled on the Sueh river to become the Bor Belanda. A tradition held by both the Shilluk and

---

(1) Crazzolara, *The Lwoo*, Part I, The Lwoo Migrations, p.10.
(2) See Seligman, *Pagan Tribes of the Nilotic Sudan*, 1932, p.18.

the Jo Luo states that quarrelling now broke out between Dimo and Nyikang.
(Dimo is sometimes said to be Nyikang's brother.)   Followers of Dimo went
south, eventually settled on the Jur river and gave rise to the Jo Luo.

The main Luo group, continuing to move north east, reached Lake No
and, after a period of delay, came to the present Shilluk country which
they conquered and occupied under Nyikang's guidance.   Shilluk tradition
has it that Giilo, a brother of Nyikang, now sought to be *reth* but Nyikang
and his son Dak objected.   Giilo's party was victorious in the fighting
which followed but they abandoned the country, crossed the Nile and proceeded east up the Sobat river, thus entering Anuak country.   From Anuakland some of the Luo migrated yet further.   Unsuitable environment in the
north meant that the direction of Luo movements changed and a southward
trend began.   The Luo occupied Lafon Hill for a time and another split
led to treks through Bariland and the occupation of Acholi country.   At
Pubunu, Crazzolara states, the group split again.   Some stayed and
colonised Alur country and Acholiland, the third migrating group, under
Oluum or one of his sons, went south to Bunyoro.   From Acholiland and
Bunyoro the Uganda Nilotes spread and the Jo Luo and Jo Padhola originated.   The Lango-Omiru are explained in terms of an original Nilo-Hamitic
group, allied to the Bari, Teso etc., which was largely assimilated by an
invading Luo people so that they have become mainly Nilotic and comparable
to the other tribal groups.

The detailed design worked out so ingeniously by Crazzolara is both
interesting and valuable and, as a full scale interpretation of Nilotic .
traditions of origin, is particularly notable.   On the other hand, many
of his conclusions are necessarily hypothetical at present, as the Nilotic
traditions are often contradictory, misleading and open to many and
various interpretations.   Nevertheless, Nilotic myths, as Crazzolara's
publication particularly shows, undeniably point to a former close interrelationship between the Nilotes if not to a common origin in two related
groups.   This is clearly shown in myths relating to the founding ancestors of various Nilotic sections, for it is a common practice among
primitive peoples to conceptualise groups and both present and historical
relationships in terms of personalities.   Thus, we get Nyikang, the
ancestor and founder of the Shilluk, whose brother, Giilo, is recognised
as the forefather of the Jo Luo.   A mass of traditions, varying in detail
from tribal group to tribal group, but in principle consistent, indicates
a genetic relationship between Jo Luo, Dembo, Shatt, the Shilluk of the
Bahr el Ghazal and the Bor Belanda.   One tradition says that Dimo, Maggi,
and Uto, the respective forefathers of the Jur, Dembo and Belanda, were
brothers of Nyikang.   Traditions of both Dembo and Bor relate that the
Bor resulted from a later break-away: it is perhaps for this reason that
the Jo Luo do not recognise any connection with the Bor, although they do
with the Dembo.   Another tradition states that Boor led his people from
the main Luo group, thus causing the first split from the main body.   The
Shilluk-Luo group of the Bahr el.Ghazal are acknowledged to be connected
with Jo Luo, Dembo and Shatt.   Evans-Pritchard, in his article on the
Mberindi and Mbegumba of the Bahr el Ghazal writes, "...what little information we possess points to successive waves of Shilluk southwards, each
representing a typical Nilotic break-away from the amalgam of Shilluk-
speaking tribes."(1)

(1) Evans-Pritchard, *S.N.R.*, 1931, Vol.XIV, Pt.1, p.20.

The Pari of Lafon Hill, for the most part, claim that they came from the Anuak in the north.   Tables set forth by Driberg, tracing the leaders of the three Pari sections, indicate that two of the sections trace themselves back to the mythological ancestor Ochudho, who rose from a river or lake and brought herds of sheep, goats and cattle with him, but returned to the water owing to the disobedience of his people.   He left behind him a wife who bore a son called Eno, the founder of the Boi and Kor sections, which were originally one but quarrelled and separated.   In Anuak tradition Ucudhu was the father of Gilo, the progenitor of the Anuak noble house.   Ucudhu similarly arose from a river and the details of the myths are identical as regards the cattle brought out and the wife left pregnant. Thus the Anuak say that he left Koori pregnant and she gave birth to Gilo, the first noble;   the Pari say that he left Achala pregnant and that she bore Eno, the ancestor of the Boi and Kor lineages.   Evans-Pritchard writes, "The similarity between the Shilluk royal house and the Anuak nobility may now be viewed in relation to the fact that there are lineages at Lafon hill which trace their descent from the same ancestor as the Anuak nobles."(1)

With regard to the remaining Luo tribal groups, there is little information concerning traditions of origin.   The Luo relate that they came from the north west under one chief.   The Acholi do not connect themselves with other Nilotic tribal groups but recognise a Luo origin.   The Payera, the most important Acholi tribe, have a myth of origin relating that Luo, the first man, sprang from the union of the earth and Jok and also that Luo's grandchild, Labongo, became the first *rwot* of the Payera.   Although closely bound up with the Acholi in the past, the Lango do not claim genetic relationship with them but with the Nilo-Hamitic groups, the Teso and Lango group of tribes.   It is possible that they were mainly Nilo-Hamitic in origin but have become predominantly Nilotic through absorption and borrowing of Nilotic elements.

The Jie say that the Lango are of one "clan" *(ateger)* with themselves,(2) and that long ago the Lango lived in what is now central Jieland.   They moved westwards and lived in the Labwor Hills before the Jie themselves moved west to their present location.   On the flanks of the Lango, and somewhere in between them and the Jie, lived the Labwor.   When the Lango were in the Labwor Hills the Labwor lived on the Dopeth river (10 miles west of Kotido).   Jie and Labwor have "always" been firm friends and have never fought each other.   It seems probable that Jie and Lango did not fight each other either, though this is less certain.   The Jie also tell a story that the Lango and a people who may be identified with the Teso moved from their country south-westwards together and split up near Otukwe, south west of the Labwor Hills.(3)

There remains to be considered the other Nilotic group, the Nuer and Dinka.   The Nuer claim a common ancestry with the Shilluk, Anuak and Dinka.

(1) Evans-Pritchard, *Man*, 1940, No.62.
(2) Gulliver, personal communication, 1951;   but he also states that there is no considerable correspondence between clan-names in Jie and Lango, as Tarantino suggests, and that clan structure appears to be essentially dissimilar.   In addition civil war between clans or other groups was not uncommon in Lango but never occurred in Jie-land, which appears to indicate a radical difference in tribal ethos.   (3) *Ibid.*

Shilluk recognise a relationship with the Dinka but deny any such connection with the Nuer. One Shilluk tradition of origin states that Nyikang and Deng (ancestor of the Dinka) were cousins, Deng being the son of Abuk, sister of Nyikaia, the mother of Nyikang. Other traditions mention only friendship and appear to deny blood relationship. In general, however, relationship between the Dinka and Shilluk is generally admitted by both groups. In the same way Nuer and Dinka claim descent from a common stock; in view of the Shilluk denial of relationship with the Nuer, it may be that the Dinka and Shilluk are older and the Nuer are an offshoot of the former. A legend relating the common ancestry states that in the past Dengdit, the great spirit of the Dinka, married a woman called Alyet in Dinka dialect and Lit in that of Nuer. Alyet gave birth to Akol who married Garung from whom were descended Deng and Nuer, brothers and ancestors of the Dinka and Nuer tribes respectively. When Garung died he left behind a cow and a calf, the former being bequeathed to Deng and the latter to Nuer. Deng stole the calf of Nuer and Nuer resorted to raiding Deng - just as today the Nuer raid Dinka cattle.

Such, then, are the assertions of interrelationship and common origin in the traditions of the people themselves. According to these there is a genetic relationship between Dinka and Nuer and of both (through the Dinka) with the Shilluk. The Shilluk, Anuak, Feri and all the tribes of the Bahr el Ghazal are linked together and the Acholi and other southern-most groups still retain traditions of Luo origin. Thus, through a maze of individual tribal traditions of relationship the majority of the Nilotes themselves proclaim their common origin. Former genetic relations have become personalised in terms of founding ancestors who are assumed to have been related to each other by kinship ties; such a conception of social relationships is, in fact, characteristic of many primitive peoples and of the Nilotes in particular. That these elaborations are not merely expressions of present day conditions and relationships - though to some degree they are this as well - is indicated by the fact that in many cases the tribal groups concerned have lost contact over a period of generations. How can we interpret these traditions of origin save in terms of a surviving remembrance of past history? They are the fragmentary records, embellished and somewhat confused as a result of the transition from history to tradition, myth and folklore, of the migrations and dispersions of the various Nilotic tribal groups which exist today.

DRESS, ORNAMENTATION AND TRIBAL MARKS

In these aspects of their culture the Nilotes have much in common.

DRESS

Men, for the most part, go naked. Even when they are not naked the genitals are left uncovered, except on the occasions of visits to mothers-in-law, when it is insisted that a small leather apron or such like covering should be worn. Among the Luo a piece of goat-skin is worn by a man who has children, and this is very important as a point of etiquette. Among the Dinka, we are told, the men are usually naked but sometimes wear

a strip of sheepskin suspended from a string band. The Anuak men, when
hunting and away from their homes, go naked, but on other occasions they
wear a loin-cloth or a skin or piece of cloth knotted over one shoulder.
The Nuer leopard-skin chief wears a similar form of dress and formerly the
Shilluk also wore a skin knotted on the left shoulder and slung round the
right hip.

For women a distinction must be made between young unmarried girls and
married women. Unmarried girls are usually quite naked except for ornaments, but among the Lango, who are a notable exception to this rule, girls
from the age of five wear a few strings to cover the pudenda and these
strings increase in number with the age of the wearer. They are attached
to a thin leather girdle which is fastened behind and twisted into a stick-
like leather continuation *(achudi)* which projects backwards. If the girl
is of a prosperous family she may wear an *ariko* (apron) of small metal
chains in place of strings. This is reminiscent of a similar custom in
dress among certain Nilo-Hamitic groups, from which it may be derived.

Married women generally wear leather aprons, back and front, composed
of two pieces of skin suspended from the waist, as among the Shilluk,
Anuak, Dinka, Nuer and Jo Luo. Among the Anuak married women usually also
wear a skin or cloth suspended from the shoulder or tied round the waist.
Among the Lango a woman who has borne a child wears a strip of leather
about 2-3 inches wide, which hangs down behind from a girdle to below the
knees; this is given to her by the father of her child; formerly a broad
leather tail was worn. In a similar way the Luo married woman wears a
tail of strings behind and, in addition, dons a goat-skin which is slung
from the shoulder when visiting. An Acholi woman wears a *cip*, which consists of a string of beads worn round the waist, from which hangs a tiny
fringe of grass string, with the *ceno*, a similar but larger fringe hanging
down at the back like a tail. Among the Alur a tail *(chieno)* is also the
particular mark of a married woman although it is not donned immediately
after marriage.(1) All available information suggests that among the
Nilotes there is a general dislike of clothing and, except for the married
woman's small leather skirts, no clothes are worn regularly.

ORNAMENTATION

What the Nilotes lack in clothing they make up for in ornamentation of
every kind. Bangles, strings of beads and coils of wire are worn by the
young people in particular. After marriage the older people tend to
abandon all but a few favourite ornaments. Nuer youths wear anklets,
spiked wristlets and ornaments for the hair, ears, neck, wrists, loins and
ankles, while beads are worn round the waist.

Ivory and sometimes wooden bracelets, worn by men at the wrists and on
the upper arms above the biceps, are favourite ornaments among the Nilotes.
The Lango are reported to be particularly fond of ornaments and wear coils
of brass wire on arms, neck and as ear-rings and nose ornaments. Among
the Acholi the lower lip is sometimes pierced and a plug inserted. Among
the Dinka girls wear a light metal ring in a hole in the centre of the
upper lip, while Nuer women sometimes fix a piece of stick in the upper or

(1) Breugelmans, *Les Alur*, p.74.

lower lip.[1]   A very distinctive form of decorating the ear is practised
by the Luo who insert flattened rings of brass in as many as 15 holes
which may be made in the outer rim.

A form of ornamentation which is widely practised and which seems to
have little or no ritual purpose is the raising of cicatrices on the forehead or on the upper parts of the body.   Nuer cicatrisation for example,
is done by experts on the chest and back.[2]   The Alur are reported to
have cicatrices forming elaborate patterns, the designs on the chest being
always the same regardless of sex.   In the case of the Alur the ornamentation is carried out at the age of 8-9 years.[3]   Painting the body with
red earth, chalk and ashes and similar preparations is common.

Hair styles adopted by youths are often most elaborate, and mud,
grease and red clay are used to produce striking designs.   The Jo Luo are
particularly famous for braiding their hair.   Nuer hair is dressed with a
preparation of cow dung and often shaped into a horn-like prominence pointing either to the front or the back of the head.   Before marriage Dinka
girls grow the bride's coiffure of ringlets down to the neck, with cover-
ings of grease and red ash;   after marriage their hair is kept shaved in
front.   As men and women grow older and are settled with families they
tend to keep their heads shaved.

Although there is a certain uniformity in their modes of ornamentation,
the styles followed are not peculiar to the Nilotes.   In their tribal
markings, however, some unique features of a common culture may be seen.

TRIBAL MARKS

In nearly every tribe of Nilotic origin, the incisor teeth of both
sexes are extracted before puberty.   The Jo Luo children of 10-12 years
have six lower incisors knocked out;   the Luo, Anuak, Shilluk, Dinka and
Nuer likewise have these removed, mostly at ages varying from 8-10 years.
Among the Shilluk the royal family alone keep their teeth intact.   The
Shilluk-Luo of the Bahr el Ghazal and the Alur have the four lower incisors
removed, without any ritual.   (Among the Alur this is done at a later age,
10-12.)   The Bor Belanda and Acholi, the Lango and Burun-speaking Jumjum
have two central lower incisors levered out.   Only the Shatt and Dembo do
not knock out any teeth.   Various reasons for this practice are given by
each tribal group.   Among the Nuer the object is said to be to distinguish
a human being from the carnivora.   The Shilluk believe that if it were
not done sickness would result.   The Lango believe that without it children would not grow up.   It is obvious that these explanations of so widespread a practice cannot be taken seriously.   Its origin and purpose we
cannot pretend to know for certain;   it appears to be some kind of tribal
mark, differentiating the Nilotes from other peoples, but today it is a
feature common to a number of closely related cultures.

A less widespread but important type of tribal mark is that which is
made on the forehead.   Shilluk men and women have 3 to 5 rows of dots or

(1)   Jackson, *S.N.R.*, 1923, Vol.VI, No.2, p.133.
(2)   *Ibid.*, p.134.
(3). Breuglemans, *Les Alur*, p.43.

scars (called *tai*) on their foreheads.   At the time when initiation ceremonies are held, and as part of the proceedings, Nuer boys have six (or,
more rarely, seven) deep cuts made across their foreheads extending from
ear to ear.   The Dinka and Jo Luo boys have cuts made on the forehead at
initiation.   Unlike the extraction of incisor teeth the practice of scar-
ring the forehead seems mainly confined to the Dinka-Nuer group.

PHYSICAL ENVIRONMENT

In all studies of people who live entirely by the direct and simple
use of the natural resources around them the conditions of the physical
environment are of the utmost importance.   The ecological relationship -
that intimate connection between a society and the country it inhabits and
exploits - is a primary relationship upon which the social structure and
organisation are built.   The precise relationship between the Nilotic
societies and their environment is considered in the sections on political
organisation;   here, it is proposed to give a brief outline of the type of
countryside and the chief products by which the Nilotic peoples live.

THE COUNTRYSIDE -
SOIL, CLIMATE AND VEGETATION

In general all the Nilotic tribes occupy a similar type of country and
are familiar with similar types of climate and vegetation.   There are, of
course, local variations of the utmost importance to the process of adjust-
ment to surroundings, but they do not invalidate the general statements set
out below.

Taken as a whole the Southern Sudan forms a wide shallow basin bounded
by the plateau of the Nile-Congo watershed in the west and south-west, by
the mountains of the Uganda border in the south and by the Abyssinian highlands in the east.   Every part of this vast basin drains into the Nile and
its numerous tributaries;   in the centre of the basin, particularly around
Lake No, there is an extensive swamp zone.   The highest land in the swamp
areas is nowhere more than 1,300 feet above sea level.   To the west and
south the edge of the swamp zone is bordered by the rising ground of the
iron-stone ridge which forms the fringe of the central African iron-stone
plateau.   In general the majority of the Nilotes may be said to inhabit
the black clay plains, the swamp area, or the outskirts of the iron-stone
plateau with its red soil and frequent outcrops of stone.

The following features are characteristic of Nilotic countryside and
affect their way of life considerably.

(a) *Land Surface*.   The Southern Sudan and the other regions in East
Africa occupied by Nilotic tribal groups are largely savannah country - a
vast flat plain with occasional slight elevations, ridges and small rocky
outcrops.   Occasionally, as in the case of Lafon Hill and in the Burun
country of Dar Fur province, a number of large rocky hills or Jebels rise
out of the plain and provide some variations in the landscape;   otherwise
there are few striking features to relieve the flat or gently rolling
plains.

(b) *Soil*.   The soil of the savannah country is generally dark clay, commonly known as cotton soil, and along the banks of the Nile and its tributaries is particularly black and fertile.   On the ridges and crests of the more elevated tracts the soil is lighter and more sandy and drains well.   South and west of the belt of dark clay soils iron-stone begins to prevail below the surface, and in the western region of the Dinka country the iron-stone plateau begins and the soil becomes red and sandy.

The clay soil typical of the low-lying regions of the Sudan is extremely sticky in the wet season and, because of its property of retaining water rather than letting it drain away, large tracts of country quickly become waterlogged in the rainy season.   In the lowest parts of the countryside and where the network of water-courses is particularly intricate, there is permanent swamp and bog even in the dry season.   This is especially the case over large tracts of the Nuer, Dinka, Anuak and Lango country, and also that of the Luo in Kenya.   In the dry season, on the other hand, the clay soil becomes hard and baked and is fissured by large cracks.   It is only because the soil is heavy clay and holds water that the grasses are able to survive the dry season and the burnings which are then practised by the inhabitants.

(c) *Hydrological Conditions*.   Hydrological conditions are of the utmost importance in determining the type of vegetation of these areas.   The year is, in this respect, divided into one wet and one dry season.   The rains begin in April and have set in by the end of May.   The maximum falls are in July and August, when the temperature is cool and the sun overcast for much of the time.   Showers become less frequent in October and cease in November when the dry season begins.   The temperature rises as the surface water evaporates until, in March and April, the heat is intense. This division of the year into two on account of climatic, and particularly hydrological conditions, applies to the whole of the Southern Sudan and is an important factor in the life of the tribal groups, from the Shilluk in the north to the Luo of Kenya in the south.

In the Sudan surface water comes from rainfall and the flooding of the numerous rivers and water-courses.   The main river is the Nile, into which many of the larger rivers discharge their waters.   The chief tributaries of the Nile have been divided into the Blue Nile system, the Sobat system, the Bahr el Ghazal system and the Jur system.   These numerous water-courses, lakes and streams are very important and greatly affect the people who live along or in the vicinity of their banks.   Nearly all the rivers and lakes flood in the time of the rains and overflow their banks, which are in any case very shallow.   The whole of the surrounding countryside, except for a few elevated spots, is then turned into a vast weed-choked swamp and man and beast alike have to retreat to the high ground.   During this period travelling is very difficult and often impossible and groups of people, perched above the flood level on a few miles of high ridged land, are cut off from the rest of the country during the height of the floods. In the height of the dry season, on the other hand, the rivers, lakes and ponds shrink almost to nothing, the smaller ones dry up altogether except for a few muddy pools strung out along the bed.   People have to resort to the edges of the permanent swamps and to the banks of the larger rivers and lakes and abandon their elevated resorts of the rainy season.   In the higher regions on the rising ground of the iron-stone plateau there is little flooding and few swamps in comparison with the lower regions of the Nile basin.

The flatness of the land, the predominantly clay soil and the alternation of a very wet followed by a very dry season determine the characteristic vegetation of this type of country.

(d) *Vegetation*. There are three main variations in vegetation in the country occupied by the Nilotes. In the Southern Sudan, south of Khartoum, the sandy, desert type of country gradually gives way to thorny savannah, and it is this type of country which is occupied by the Shilluk and Northern Dinka. South of the thorny savannah is a belt of open savannah and this is the countryside occupied by the Dinka and Nuer. To the west and south lies savannah forest and also in the approaches to the Ethiopian highlands.

The thorny savannah, besides having all the characteristic features described above, has the luxuriant vegetation of tropical savannah. Grasses grow high, thick and coarse during the rains and the country is dotted with small thorny trees and acacia shrubs.

In the open savannah country there are level and almost treeless plains. During the rains high coarse grass covers the countryside, replaced in the dry season by tracts of brown stubble with patches of green, tender grass growing in the damp hollows. There are few patches of thornwood forest, such as are widespread in thorny savannah, and no broad-leaved trees except where a belt of forest sometimes lines a river bank. It is good cattle country and suitable for crops which survive plenty of water.

In the savannah forest areas the tall grasses of the wet season are characteristic, but scrub, bushes and trees are numerous enough in some places to form open forest, although the trees are only of medium height. These areas provide some of the most fertile land for crop growing, but are not suitable for cattle owing to the breeding of the tsetse fly in the forest shade. Where there is particularly thick forest, as in the most easterly areas of Anuakland, on the fringes of the Ethiopian rain forest region, not even sheep, goats and dogs can be kept. Vegetation on the iron-stone plateau in the west, and consequently tsetse fly, likewise render pastoralism impossible although cultivation of the soil yields good results.

The countryside occupied by the majority of the Nilotic tribal groups, both in the Southern Sudan as described above and in Kenya and Uganda, may be described as consisting in general of flat land with a clay soil, covered with high grasses in the rains and only thinly wooded. It is subject to heavy rainfall for one half of the year and to drought during the other half. It is traversed by numerous rivers which flood annually and which, in the more swampy areas, cause the people to remain in wet-season villages on the higher land. The drought, on the other hand, causes them to abandon the high ground and to spend the dry season in camps on the edge of permanent swamp or on some water-course which does not completely dry up.

MAIN FEATURES OF ECONOMY

CATTLE

The Nilotes are essentially pastoralists.   Although they cultivate
the ground in order to procure an adequate food supply, this is done from
necessity in most cases and not out of devotion.   At heart they are a
cattle people and their love of herds is a fundamental social reality.
Cattle are not just an economic asset.

The importance of their herds to the Nilotes is stressed in the
sources available, but it is only for the Nuer tribal groups that we have
a full and detailed account of the relationship between a man and his
cattle and between the whole of a society and its herds.[1]   An outline of
the economic importance of cattle to the Nuer, followed by brief mention of
the main social spheres into which the 'cattle complex' enters is given
below (p.136).

Among the other Nilotes cattle are similarly important.   The Shilluk,
we are told, regard their cattle as almost sacred and give them every care.
The Luo consider cattle as the principal form of wealth and they use oxen
for riding to funerals.[2]   Like the Nuer, the Dinka live for their cattle
and are only happy when watching, tending and talking about cattle.   The
southern Burun and the Pari of Lafon Hill likewise have considerable herds.
For the Acholi there is little information.   Authorities agree that they
are primarily a cultivating people but hold conflicting views concerning
Acholi fondness for cattle.   Kitching reports, however, that they will pay
high prices for cows and this is in itself an indication of the social as
well as the economic value of cattle.   Details concerning the Alur care
for their cattle would suggest an affection for their herds similar to that
of the Northern Nilotes.   The Alur chiefs possess large herds.[3]   The
Jo Luo have had no cattle in recent times; there is a tradition that,
formerly, their cattle were seized by Dinka.   Prosperous men keep goats
and occasionally sheep.   Nowadays cows are met within chiefs' compounds
while others keep them with Dinka friends and use them for bridewealth.

Among the main Nilotic tribal groups and those for which we have adequate information on this subject, only the Anuak may be reckoned as a
people who do.not care for cattle.   The tsetse fly prevents them from keeping cattle in the east, but, in fact, they do not greatly care for them and
slaughter animals for meat much more readily than do the other Nilotic
groups.   Cattle have little ritual significance and are not used for bridewealth among the Anuak.   The interest which the other Nilotes focus on
cattle the Anuak tend to focus on beads.   They say themselves that they
are a bead people and it is certainly the case that beads and other articles
are nowadays used for bridewealth.   The extensive list of cattle-names and
ox-names which is found in their language suggests, however, that at one
time the Anuak were predominantly pastoral and a cattle people in the Nilotic sense.

(1) E.E. Evans-Pritchard, *The Nuer*, Chapter I.
(2) Odede, *JEAUNHS*, 1942, Vol.XVI, p.128.
(3) Breugelmans, *Les Alur*, p.61.

Although cattle provide the main interest, all the Nilotes keep herds of goats and very often sheep. Chickens are kept in some of the tribal groups, but in several instances, as among the Nuer, they tend to be regarded as scavengers and as unclean. The Nuer are not fond of eating birds of any kind, a fact which they explain in mystic terms as they consider that there is a close connection between birds and twins.

CULTIVATION OF THE SOIL

With the exception of the Anuak, the Nilotes prefer a purely pastoral life to one of cultivation. Cultivation is forced on them, however, by the prevalence of cattle diseases which have greatly reduced the herds, and by the falling off of milk supplies at certain periods of the year owing to insufficient pastures and to climatic conditions. The structural and organisational implications of a need to practise both pastoralism and cultivation is considered in Part II and also the interaction of events in the yearly ecological cycle. Here, it is proposed to outline the type of cultivation and its economic importance.

Cultivation is carried on in the vicinity of the village in most cases. Among the Nuer each homestead has its gardens in the village and also plots at a distance from the houses and from the river banks. The Jo Luo prefer to cultivate in the bush but sufficiently near the homestead for the birds to be frightened away and the gardens easily cared for. Among the Anuak the people of a village sow in contiguous gardens, different plots being demarcated by a line of plants of a particular sort. The area cultivated by a village is often considerable, and in most cases is cultivated year after year until the land is exhausted. Then the entire village will move to a nearby site, stay there for perhaps 5-10 years, and move again. Among the Jo Luo, on the other hand, fields are cultivated only 2-3 years in succession and at the end of that time another plot is cleared. This can only occur without a general move, if there is surplus land available near the village. Stubbs and Morison give a detailed account of cultivation by the Western Dinka on the alluvial terraces in the flood plain of the Lol river. These people cultivate intensely and successfully owing to their use of animal manure, obtained by tethering their animals on the garden plots at the beginning of the wet season; this keeps the land sufficiently fertile for crops to be grown indefinitely on the same soil. This method appears to be exceptional among Nilotes.

The Horticultural Year begins at the end of March, when the ground is cleared, rubbish burned and the soil dug. This preparation is followed by sowing from May to July. Two main crops are harvested, usually at the end of the rains, from September to November. Local climatic conditions, the varieties of plants grown and the degree of intensity with which cultivation is carried on, determine the actual planting and harvesting times in the different tribal groups. Among the Shilluk, for example, the plots near the village are sown in May and the harvest is gathered in October; the inland crops, away from the village, are planted in June and harvested in November. Among the Acholi a late millet crop is sown which is harvested the following April. There is no information that other Nilotic groups do likewise.

The horticultural calendar, as produced by Evans-Pritchard in *The Nuer* (page 78) gives the best idea of the Nilotic sowing and harvesting activities and is reproduced here:-

April	May	June	July	August	Sept.	Oct.	Nov.	Dec.	Jan.
Sow Maize			Harvest Maize						
Sow 1st. Millet					Harvest 1st. Millet				
	Sow beans						Harvest beans		
			Sow jaak Millet				Harvest jaak Millet		
			Sow tobacco			Harvest tobacco			
				Sow 2nd. Millet					Harvest 2nd. Millet

Crops.   The staple crop is millet, of which there are several varieties, and usually two harvests are reaped.   It is a hardy plant, can take a great deal of rain and matures quickly.   It is an ideal crop for the Southern Sudan climate and is an extremely important part of the food supply, as from it the people make beer and porridge, two of the staples in their domestic economy.   Maize is grown to a smaller extent but is important because it is the first crop harvested and therefore relieves the famine which sometimes prevails during the rainy season.   Beans, peas, squashes, sesame, groundnuts, sweet potatoes, semsem, and sorghum are some of the main crops.   A little tobacco is usually grown for chewing, for smoking and for use as snuff.   Gourds are grown for eating or to provide household utensils.

Production of Food.   No Nilotic tribal group exists on vegetable produce alone, but the degree of enthusiasm with which cultivation proceeds from year to year varies considerably.   The Nuer cultivate enough to grow an important part of their diet and to enable them to survive cattle plagues and the deficiencies in their pastoral economy due to climate.   They consider cultivation to be an unfortunate necessity.   The Dinka regard cultivation in the same light as do the Nuer but appear to take more care and to show considerable skill.   The Acholi, Jo Luo and Luo may be said to be predominantly cultivators owing to their lack of cattle.   In the case of the Lango and Pari, cultivations are diligently worked and the surplus produce is disposed of to neighbours in exchange for cattle to increase the beloved herds.   Driberg goes so far as to suggest that it may have been the desire for cattle and the wish to replace stocks after disease which led the Lango to the industrious pursuit of horticulture, "For there is a recognised currency of grain and livestock, by which so many bundles of millet equal one goat, and so many goats equal one bull or cow".[1]

The Anuak are more than diligent cultivators; they appear to enjoy it and to prefer it to other methods of obtaining food.   The black soil of the forest area is particularly fertile and in some areas maize and tobacco are grown all the year round.   Evans-Pritchard mentions that on the Gilo river the gardens were exceptionally large and that... " in

(1) Driberg, *The Lango*, 1923, p.68.

addition to their own needs these villages produced a supply adequate to
feed some hundreds of Italian irregulars who lived on the country".[1]
There is no evidence that the surplus is used to buy cattle and it appears
unlikely that the Anuak would wish to do this.   With this one exception
we may sum up Nilotic cultivation as being very necessary to them but in
general opposed to their whole-hearted passion for cattle and the pastoral
life.

The Nuer and Dinka are particularly fortunate in that the ecological
bias fits in with their own cultural bias, and increased horticultural
activities would be unprofitable.

HUNTING, FISHING, AND COLLECTING

Hunting.   The Southern Sudan and neighbouring countries are very
rich in game, ranging from elephants, lions and hippopotami, to wart-hog,
gazelle, giraffe and bush-pig.   In spite of these opportunities to augment the food supply, the northernmost Nilotic tribes do not much care for
hunting.   The Nuer seldom go out to hunt except when gazelle and giraffe
approach their villages, or to secure hippo-meat, which is much sought
after.   Their herds provide meat and the people tend to look down on
hunting as an inferior occupation.   Dinka are not keen hunters but they
use traps considerably.

It is among the Lango and Acholi that hunting is pursued with skill
and eagerness.   Large numbers of people participate in the highly organised annual hunts.   The Lango countryside is divided into hunting areas
each called an *arum*.   The Lango maintain that this division was made when
they first entered the country.   The leaders who first occupied a locality claimed it as their *arum*, and each *arum* has remained the property of
the clan in occupation.   The *won arum*, as the 'owner' is called, has magical and administrative functions.   He is not necessarily a chief, but there
can be no hunting on his property without his permission.   He is responsible for the upkeep of the *arum* and is compensated for his labour (an *arum*
may be over 100 sq. miles in size) by his right to certain parts of all the
animals slaughtered.   He uses these as a medium of exchange for grain and
other food.   He is not the absolute owner of the *arum* in the sense that he
can stop people from building there, although they ask his permission first.
He seems to be the caretaker for the rest of the tribe.

In Acholiland we find a similar organisation for hunting.   Each tract
has an owner, the *won tim* ('owner of the bush') who is the descendant of
the head of the clan which had in the past settled in the area.   The
country is divided up into these hunting tracts and the hereditary owners
have certain ritual functions (to ensure successful hunting and avert
danger from large fierce animals) as well as the task of organising the
communal hunts.   Both Acholi and Lango have a number of special forms of
hunting suitable to specific conditions and times of the year.

Fishing.   Fishing is a particularly important activity in every
Nilotic tribal group.   The numerous rivers and lakes of the country are
well stocked with many varieties of fish and, except during the height of

(1)   Evans-Pritchard, *S.N.R.*, Vol.XXVIII, 1947, p.72.

the rainy season, they are fairly easy to obtain.   Fish is often the main standby in times of scarcity and large quantities are eaten.   The Shilluk are exceptionally skilled fishermen with a high reputation among their Nilotic neighbours.   They often engage in fishing parties at night, holding burning torches over the water to entice the fish and then spearing them.   Among the Dinka and Nuer those who are cattle-less or have few cattle and can leave them in the care of friends, will devote the dry season to fishing, living in camps along the banks of rivers.   The two best seasons of the year for fishing are November and December, when the floods are falling rapidly, and at the beginning of the rains when they are rising again.   In the former period streams and rivers can be dammed at suitable points and the fish, unable to escape into the main steam as the water level falls, are easily speared in the shallows.   At night there is fishing at the dams.   In the latter period, as the water rises, the fish are speared in the new ponds and streams which begin to form. As the water continues to rise, however, fishing by these means becomes virtually impossible owing to the great expanse of water and the weed-choked swamps.   Fishing from canoes is occasionally practised in this period.   During the dry season, however, the fish supplies keep at a steady level.

In conclusion it may be said that the fishing activities of the Nilotes provide an important part of their food supply during the greater part of the year and particularly during the period of the early rains, when the grain stocks are low or exhausted and the new harvest has not yet begun.

Collecting.   Except when food is extremely short, most of the Nilotes pay little attention to the wild fruits, seeds and roots which are available to them.   These are usually eaten by the children and men disdain to be seen picking or devouring them and will do so only in private and if driven by hunger.   Among the Nuer the one exception to this rule is their liking for the roots and seeds of water-lilies.   The Lango, on the other hand, are reported to gather roots and berries and to eat them with fair regularity.

STAPLE FOODS AND THE FOOD SUPPLY

In the majority of cases the two staple foods among the Nilotes are milk and millet.   Fish, meat, and vegetables form the next most important and regular additions to the diet, while wild fruits, roots and birds are only seriously resorted to in times of famine.   Beer, made from millet, is drunk universally.   On the whole the Nilotic diet is well balanced, owing to the considerable variety of foodstuffs available, but the quantity is insufficient, supplies are unreliable, and diseases or climatic severities may cause famine.   Among the Lango in 1918 there were several deaths from starvation, in spite of the fact that normally their herds and cultivated plots produce a sufficiency and sometimes a surplus.   The period of danger for all the Nilotes seems to be at the beginning of the rains, when the grain stocks from the previous harvest are small or exhausted and the new crops are not ready for harvesting; at this time the milk supply also is low.   Fortunately fishing is particularly productive at this period and in cases of necessity people will live for a few weeks on nothing but fish eked out with wild fruits and what

milk can be obtained.   In extremity cattle may be killed.   When rinderpest and the failure of the crops occur together people die of starvation.

Evans-Pritchard, writing on the Nuer, states that meat of domestic-
ated animals is mainly eaten after the harvest when sacrifices and feasts
occur.   Meat consumption, in fact, follows grain consumption, both gradually growing less at the end of the dry season and in the early rains.
Fish then takes the place of grain and meat as the principal food from
January to June - the hungry months being from May to August when the
maize is ripening, the fish supplies begin to diminish and the milk supplies are low.   September to mid December are the months of plenty when
there is much millet, meat and milk.

In general the problems of food supply seem to be similar for all the
Nilotes, though for those who have few or no cattle circumstances are
slightly different.   It seems that only the Eastern Anuak have a really
good, as well as a varied, food supply, and thus do not have to fear
periods of famine.

DIVISION OF LABOUR AND
ECONOMIC CO-OPERATION

Division of labour is related to the natural differences of age and
sex.   Certain types of work are traditionally performed by women, others
by men, but the determining factors in most cases seem to be suitability
and convenience.   Thus, the women do the cooking and look after the children and the home.   They cultivate their gardens, weeding, planting, and
harvesting and doing all the lighter tasks.   They help in the fishing and
gather wild fruits.

The men, on the other hand, hunt, fish and do the heavier tasks in
cultivation.   They clear the ground of bush, grass, and trees and sometimes dig the surface of the soil ready for sowing.   In polygynous households each wife has her own field and the husband helps each in turn.   The
harvest belongs to the woman who owns the field, and to her husband and
children, but not to the other wives and their children.   In practice
there is a good deal of sharing of food both within the polygynous family
and between different homesteads of a village.

With regard to cattle and the tasks connected with the herds, the
general principles concerning division of labour in other spheres do not
hold.   To the pastoral Nilotes cattle are something more than economic
assets.   Except among the Nuer, women after maturity are kept strictly
away from anything concerning cattle, which are herded by men and boys who
look after their every want.   The one exception is milking which, at
least among the Nuer, is performed by women, girls and uninitiated boys.
Men are forbidden to milk except on journeys or war expeditions when there
are no women or boys present, but this rule is relaxed when they grow older.
Among the Shilluk only small boys milk the cattle.[1]

The only division of labour among men, which is economically and not

---

(1)   Seligman, *Pagan Tribes of the Nilotic Sudan*, 1932, p.73.

ritually determined, occurs in certain cases of specialisation. Certain families and individuals have developed special skills, such as canoe-building, making of musical instrument, and so forth, but only among the iron-smiths do any specialists rely on their craft for obtaining the basic necessities of life. Iron-smiths may barter iron for food and use it for bridewealth. All other craftsmen live like the rest of the people, practising their craft only in their spare time and in addition to every-day activities. Thus every family is capable of providing for its wants and performing nearly all necessary work by the general activities of its members based on a traditional allotment of tasks founded on the capabilities of sex and age.

There is a good deal of mutual assistance between families of the same village in spite of the high degree self-sufficiency of every family. In most cases it is spontaneous, unorganised assistance based on kinship ties. The village herds, for example, may be led to pasture by only a few of the owners. Among the Lango, however, there are the *jo awi dyang*, the people who keep their cattle in one kraal. The *won awi dyang* is the person who first made the kraal, or his heir. He is in charge and anyone is allowed to keep cattle in his kraal provided his permission is asked first. All who make use of the kraal help in building it. The *won awi dyang* settles disputes involving cattle. According to Hayley, the *jo awi dyang* is a stock-raising group and achieves economy in herding.[1]

There are two reported instances of organised working parties in connection with cultivation. Among the Southern Burun (the Meban), we are informed, parties of men up to 30 in number combine to work together on each cultivation in turn and the owner provides free beer and a pig for his assistants. Among the Lango the *wang tich*, reported by Driberg and Hayley, is a group or association of men which may act as a working party on the cultivations of members. Only in cases of extreme poverty does a man cultivate without the assistance of his neighbours which is obtained in return for food and drink after the day's work. The extent of the assistance is determined by the reward. A *wang tich* group is a permanent body, numbering about 20-40, and may embrace a whole village. The chief member is the *won wang tich* (guardian of the *wang tich*) and, according to Hayley, he is responsible for keeping order at the beer party after work in the fields. Each member of the group helps to dig the fields of every other member in turn. Two or more *wang tich* may combine to do a particular piece of work, and any member can call his *wang tich* by brewing beer. Digging and weeding are the usual tasks. The *wang tich* provides a co-operative form of labour which enables more work to be done than could be achieved by the separate efforts of a man or a family.

CRAFTS

The resources available for craftsmanship vary from region to region but are in no case abundant. Among the Nuer, for example, there is a complete lack of iron and stone and of wood suitable for carving. Vegetable materials and animal products are the only materials ready at hand and technology revolves entirely round such natural products. The forest

(1) Hayley, *The Lango*, 1923, p.60.

savannah people and those on the iron-stone plateau have the advantage of wood and iron ore respectively.

Houses. Housing materials consist of thorn-wood and millet stalks for framework and thatching. Houses are built with mud walls and are plastered with dung on the inside and on the floor. The style varies but there is a generally recognised Nilotic pattern which is seen to perfection in the huts made by the Shilluk, which have round mud walls with conical thatched roofs cut in flounces. The houses last from three to four years until the inroads of termites and the weather make it necessary to rebuild. Repairs are carried out every year. Some of the Western Dinka, the Dembo, and the Shilluk-Luo of the Bahr el Ghazal build houses on piles. The Lango *otogo*, which is built by a youth on reaching the age of puberty, is a small hut raised on piles some feet above the ground. It is reached by a log ladder and has a round hole as an entrance. No particular reason is given for this type of construction and it is not typical of the Nilotes in general.

Among the Dinka and Nuer special dwellings are erected in the dry season camps. They are 'beehives' made of sticks and grass and given a coat of mud; they are merely temporary structures and collapse after a storm or two. In the Dinka wet season camps (situated in the vicinity of the village when the crops are growing) shelters consisting of a strong convex roof of wood and grass with a foot of earth on top are built - the whole construction being supported on thick posts and having no sides other than stiff hides which may be hung up to keep out the rain. Calves, sheep, dogs and men huddle over a fire in the middle. Both men and women help in building the huts. Cattle byres, granaries and the bachelor's hut, where it exists, are all built in a manner similar to that used in building living-huts, but they vary in size.

Various implements and articles. Gourds are used as containers. Pottery is made by women, occasionally with the assistance of men. Skins are widely used for sleeping on and for containers of all types. Baskets are everywhere made from grasses. Wooden articles are few, comprising head-rests, rough dug-out canoes, clubs, spear handles, drum frames and miscellaneous implements. There is no decorative art and no carving of the human figure. Among the Dinka and Nuer little clay models of cattle are made for children to play with and perhaps as an expression of the maker's affection for his favourite ox.

Weapons include clubs, spears and shields, although some of the Western Dinka, the Alur, and the Jo Luo use bows and arrows, a practice which is thought to have been adopted from neighbouring non-Nilotic tribes. The spear is the typical Nilotic weapon and certain consecrated spears have a ritual significance.

Iron-working. The art of iron-working is subject to considerable variations among the Nilotic tribal groups. The Luo do not smelt iron but obtain it in pig form from the Bantu Kavirondo. Likewise the Lango smith, the *atet*, is ignorant of the art of smelting the iron ore which is abundant in parts of the country. If anyone wants spears or knives or iron ornaments the metal has to be supplied in the form of iron hoes. The fee is regulated according to the amount of work required.

Among the Nuer there is no knowledge of smelting and little of the blacksmith's art. Spears are beaten out cold and all pieces of iron rings, bells and spears are greatly cherished by the owning families. In contrast to these elementary efforts, the Jo Luo are widely famed for their skill as iron-workers. They smelt iron from ore in kilns, using a special sort of clay mixed with wood to help in the smelting. Pig-iron is beaten and worked, then fired a second time and beaten out to two smiths into the intended shape. A bellows is used for the fire. The smiths are paid by the people who dig out the iron ore, the fees being fixed in percentages of pieces of iron. The Dinka likewise smelt iron. The ore is collected from the hills in the west and the smelting is done in a cylindrical furnace. The bellows are two spouted earthenware pots with goatskin tied over their mouths. These are placed on either side of the fire and a toggle is attached to the centre of the skin and worked up and down, thus producing draught through the spouts. Charcoal is used in the furnace. The anvil is an iron wedge driven into a log of wood.

The implements in greatest demand among the Nilotes are spear-heads, iron hoes, knives, adzes, bill-hooks and similar tools. Among the Lango there are two classes of iron-workers; the smith who manufactures all iron instruments and ornaments, except the *ariko* the intricate chain apron worn by girls, and a second type of smith who confines himself to making these.

It seems that the blacksmith's craft is always in the hands of certain families or clans and the techniques are inherited or passed on to apprentices who are usually relatives. There is one mention of discrimination and prejudice against iron-workers occurring among the Luo. According to Hobley and Johnston they are called *yothetth*; among some of the tribes they constitute a separate caste called *uvino* and there is considerable prejudice against them. It seems that iron-working is not regarded as quite an ordinary manufacturing process, and even if there is in general no such prejudice against it as is found elsewhere in Africa, there appears to be a ritual significance attached to it. Among the Jo Luo, during the time of ore digging and smelting, people are bound by special taboos and are not allowed to eat porridge or meat cooked in the ordinary way. Seligman states that the Cic Dinka had only two clans practising the craft, Nyonker and Gumbel, spoken of as *adjong*. They have no cattle and do not make pots, but receive pots, sheep and hippo-flesh in exchange for their iron-work. Owing to the fact that they pay lumps of iron for bridewealth instead of cattle they find it difficult to intermarry with the other clans. They are despised as being cattle-less but there are no indications that they are regarded as having special magical powers.

In general it may be said that technology among the Nilotes is in every way meagre. This is no doubt due to the scarcity of natural resources available for craftmanship and also to the overwhelming interest in cattle.

TRADE

Trade is not very important among the Nilotes as, in general, they feel little need for other people's products. Most of the tribal groups consider cattle as wealth and, as Evans-Pritchard has written about the

Nuer, they have nothing to trade except their cattle and all they desire is more cattle.(1)   The Lango do exchange surplus produce and ivory for cattle with Arab traders.   Internally, the Nilotes are too self-sufficient for there to be more than an occasional exchange of articles.   Some people make better pots, baskets and so forth than others, while only smiths can provide iron objects.   People who want things from them either ask in the name of kinship or friendship or give some equivalent in the form of millet or garden produce in exchange.   There is no third person acting as intermediary.   There is little inequality of wealth, for these is no ob- ject in acquiring more than can be used by a family.   There may be some exchange of goods between the Nilotic groups bordering on each other.   The Jo Luo, being superior iron-workers, supply the Dinka with spear-heads. The Anuak supply their neighbours with canoes.   All this exchange is very elementary and scanty and it may be said that, apart from a limited exchange of material goods among themselves, the concept of trade scarcely exists among the Nilotes.

THE CHARACTER OF THE NILOTIC PEOPLES

All who have come into contact with the Nilotes have remarked on the proud, individualistic and truculent behaviour which they display towards each other and particularly towards foreigners.   They consider their coun- try the best in the world and everyone inferior to themselves.   For this reason they despise clothing, scorn European and Arab cultures, and are con- temptuous and reserved with foreigners, so that it is difficult to get to know them.   Their attitude towards any authority that would coerce them is one of touchiness, pride, and reckless disobedience.   Each determines to go his own way as much as possible, has a hatred of submission, and is ready to defend himself and his property from the inroads of others.   They are thus self-reliant, brave fighters, turbulent and agressive, and are extreme- ly conservative in their aversion from innovation and interference.

Once their suspicions have been overcome, however, they are hospitable to strangers.   They admire those who, like themselves, are independent and capable of fighting for themselves and they are said to be chivalrous in their treatment of women.   Such is the 'Nilotic temperament' which has been recorded by authorities on the Sudan.   In many ways it is typical of the independence and aloofness and of the fighting qualities that are found in association with a predominantly pastoral mode of life.   Among the Nilotes it is perhaps a product of the loosely organised social and political en- vironment in which they live.   This is particularly so among the Nuer and Dinka, who had no conception of a centralised authority or a sovereign power before European intervention.   Even among the Shilluk, who are highly organised in comparison, there is little in the way of 'government', for the king is primarily a symbolic representation of the Shilluk people and has ritual rather than regulative and executive powers.   Living in the type of society in which the coercive, administrative and regulative powers of state re unknown, the individual, supported by his kin, has to fend for himself nd look after his possessions.   This being the traditional mode of

l) Evans-Pritchard, *The Nuer*, 1940, p.88.

organisation it is difficult to see how anyone could hold a respected place among his fellows, or continue in possession of property, without this hardy, rebellious and individualistic attitude.

CONCLUSION

The more general ethnological aspects of the Nilotic tribal groups taken together justify beyond doubt the inclusion of a number of separate territorial and social entities under one designation in anthropological classifications. Linguistically, physically, and in their traditions of origin, the various groups are still closely connected and must have experienced the most intimate contact in the past. Perhaps they are genetically related, as their physical characteristics and their own traditions suggest, but we shall never know their past history for certain. The evidence of their mode of life, their material culture, the reaction to their environment, their economy, mode of dress, ornamentation and tribal marks, supports the main conclusions reached through the chief criteria of classification first considered, but cannot in itself be taken as indicative of a unique ethnic group. This is because the characteristics of the Nilotes are very similar to those of other pastoralists and especially those who inhabit adjacent territories - the Masai and others of the Nilo-Hamitic group. Moreover, the Nilo-Hamites are somewhat similar in physical type and have to some extent mingled with the southernmost Nilotes, such as the Lango and Acholi, so that it has sometimes been difficult to decide, on present evidence, whether a people is to be reckoned in one ethnic group or another. It is for this reason that language has been the deciding factor in classification although, as previously pointed out, this is not always a satisfactory one. It is probably better to take as many factors into account as possible in the process of classification and for this a full and adequate knowledge of all aspects of the life and organisation of the people is necessary.

A modified chart, similar to that produced by Evans-Pritchard in *The Nuer* (page 3) indicates what seems to be the position of the Nilotes in relation to the other East African ethnic groups.

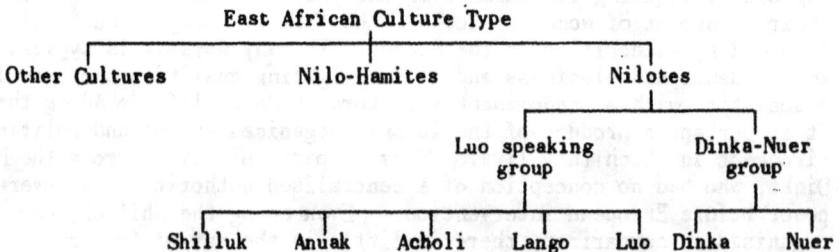

East African Culture Type

Other Cultures   Nilo-Hamites   Nilotes

Luo speaking   Dinka-Nuer
group   group

Shilluk   Anuak   Acholi   Lango   Luo   Dinka   Nuer

The structural and organisational aspects of the Nilotic tribal groups, their religious, magical, and ritual beliefs and actions must also be examined for purposes of classification and will be considered in as much detail as the literature allows. To the social anthropologist these are the most interesting and most rewarding of all the approaches which may be made in the study and comparison of societies. This general outline will provide a framework into which may **be** fitted the account of the relations between groups and individuals, the patterns of behaviour and the methods of organisation which each tribal group has developed over a long period of time through constant interaction between its members within a certain environmental and historical context.

———————————

Part II

THE SOCIAL ORGANISATION, POLITICAL STRUCTURE AND MAIN CULTURAL FEATURES OF THE NILOTES

INTRODUCTION

The structure and organisation of the Nilotic tribal groups, though showing similarities in many respects and suggesting a certain degree of progressive variation from one or two structural types, cannot be considered in one descriptive whole owing to the complexity of the subject. It is therefore proposed to consider the main Nilotic groups in turn and in conclusion to point out some of the features common to all.

Except where specifically mentioned, the information relating to a people applies to their indigenous organisation.

THE SHILLUK

GENERAL

The Shilluk live in a number of hamlets and settlements which, almost without a break, line the west bank of the White Nile from about 11°N. Lat. to Lake No in the south. There are also a few settlements on the east bank and along the lower reaches of the Sobat river.

They are predominantly agricultural and sedentary, owning comparatively few cattle. The long river frontage of their habitat gives them adequate water and grazing in the dry season for the few cattle they do possess. There are no large scale transhumant movements in the dry season to find cattle pastures. Only youths go into dry season cattle camps which are situated mainly on islands in the river or in dry water-courses near it. The cultivations are likewise nearby, either in the settlement area or inland a short distance away. Ecological conditions therefore enable the people to remain in the same place all the year round and render the settlement areas self-contained economically.

SOCIAL ORGANISATION AND POLITICAL STRUCTURE

TERRITORIAL DIVISIONS AND KINSHIP UNITS

The Homestead (gol)

The *gol* is the smallest social unit in the tribe and usually consists of about two huts encircled by a fence. Every married man has a *gol* which he occupies with his wife, or wives, and children. In addition

there may be a dependent relative or friend. A man's sons live in his
homestead until they get married; if their father is dead, they live in
the *gol* of their eldest brother or in that of their father's married
brother. The owner of the homestead is the head of the *gol*; he holds the
cattle belonging to the unit and is responsible for the behaviour of the
members of his *gol*. He has to pay cattle in compensation for any wrong
which may be committed by any of the members.

The Hamlet (pac)

Hamlets are built about 100 yards apart on high ground parallel to the
river. They vary considerably in size according to the number of homesteads which compose them. The homesteads of a hamlet are grouped round a
cattle kraal containing a hut which shelters all the herds in the rainy
season. The byre and hut are used as the general meeting-places and
social centres for the inhabitants at all times and guests are entertained
there. There is often a *geu*, a hut with no surrounding fence, which is
used as a dormitory by the unmarried men. The hamlet is a homogeneous
unit being an extended family group, or a small lineage.

The Settlement (podh)

The settlement consists of a number of hamlets, occupied by different
lineages. There are several hundred settlements, often not spacially
distinct from one another. There is, however, a structural division which
is recognised by the people themselves in referring to the settlement
units. In spite of lineage differentiations within each settlement, all
unite to defend the whole, all take part in the ritual of the age-set
organisation, all participate in the settlement's relations with other
settlements and all acknowledge a common chief.

The lineage organisation within a settlement revolves round two recognised types of lineages: the *dyil* and the *wedh*. It is said that Nyikang,
the Shilluk culture hero and founder of the present Shilluk tribe, originally granted each settlement to a clan. The surviving descendants of the
grantees are considered the 'owners of the soil' and are termed *dyil* to
distinguish them from lineages which settled on their land later and which
are called *wedh*. If the original owners of the land are extinct, the
wedh lineage next in importance takes their place and becomes *dyil*. The
members of the *dyil* lineage are closely associated with the land they
occupy and are accorded considerable prestige and authority in virtue of
their position and this association. The *dyil* form the core of the
settlement and political activities revolve round them. The *wedh* lineage
members are not socially inferior, but the *dyil* lineages have greater prestige and are expected to be the leaders in important matters in the settlement. For this reason the *dyil* of a settlement is the 'dominant lineage'.

The chief of the settlement, the *jago*, is taken from the *dyil* lineage.
In practice, it occasionally happens that the dominant position of the
dyil lineage is taken over by a stronger, wealthier, and more numerous
lineage but, even if dispossessed of political power and the chieftainship,
the original *dyil* lineage retains its ritual connection with the soil and
also much of its local prestige. This ritual relationship remains so long
as any living representatives of the original *dyil* lineage remain.

The Shilluk settlement is open, on the other hand, to certain structural weaknesses which follow from its internal organisation. These are pointed out by Pumphrey.[1] Each *wedh* kinship group has a dual loyalty to its own lineage and to the settlement as represented by the *jago* and the dominant lineage. Only if the settlement chief and his lineage are strong are the loyalties of the hamlet lineages submerged in the larger unit. The cohesion of the settlement is, however, favoured in the rainy season owing to the fact that travelling is difficult and the community tends to be isolated. At such times the influence of the Shilluk *reth* is diminished and he has to rely on the loyalty of the settlement chief; isolation also increases the feeling of unity and the Shilluk clans, being dispersed and without territorial cohesion, are placed at a disadvantage.

Each lineage represented within a settlement has its original hamlet, the *pan dwong*, founded by the original immigrant who started the lineage in the settlement, and this is at the head of all hamlets of the lineage which have subsequently been formed in the settlement. The lineage head is the chief of the *pan dwong* and represents his lineage in the administration of the settlement unit. New hamlets are continually being founded by ambitious young men - usually in the same settlement as the parent hamlet and subservient to it, but occasionally they are started in another part of the country. The offshoots from the original hamlet *(pan dwong)* in the same settlement are called *nyole myer* and are included under the name of the original hamlet, but if some grow important and large they will acquire separate names. Some originally powerful hamlets may eventually disintegrate altogether.

The lineages, and therefore the hamlets within a settlement, are closely related through kinship ties of one sort and another. A common feature in many lineage systems, and one which is also found among the Shilluk, is that the descendants of a man who has settled with his wife's people trace their descent through the female link to the lineage in whose home they live. Howell quotes specific instances in which this occurred in a settlement.[2]

The *wedh* lineages are thus grafted on to the dominant lineages of a settlement. Intermarriage occurs between members and relationship is traced through female links, the *wedh* lineage becoming 'sister's sons', and thus the structural differentiation within a settlement is greatly mitigated. The settlement is an integrated unit bound together by territorial unity, common economic and legal interests, allegiance to one chief and to a dominant lineage to which all are connected in some way, and finally, bound by the necessity of mutual co-operation during the rainy season and in times of danger from outside sources. To counterbalance this, there are lineage loyalties and lines of structural cleavage within the settlement. These, in certain circumstances, such as weak leadership and dissatisfaction with their representation by the chief to the central authority, may cause the settlement unit to be rent by internal feuds and fissions.

Divisions

There are 11 divisions as follows:-[3]

(1) Pumphrey, *S.N.R.* 1941, Vol.XXIV, p.7.   (2) Howell, *S.N.R.* 1941, Vol.XXIV, p.55.
(3) Howell and Thompson, *S:N.R.* 1946, Vol.XXVII, Fig.2.

NORTHERN PROVINCE (GERR)

Muomo   Delalajak   Athodwoi   Detwok   Golbany   Fashoda

SOUTHERN PROVINCE (LUAK)

Wau   Malakal   Detim   Fanyikang   Tung

These have little political importance though they are said to have been made by the order of Nyikang. They have the tradition of co-operation when necessary to meet a common danger or a difficult situation. This tendency of contiguous settlements to combine for warfare was utilised by the Turkish government and is now used by the Anglo-Egyptian government to form administrative units. Originally, the associations were not permanent enough to be regarded as politically important.

The Provinces

Shilluk country is divided into two great provinces, Gerr and Luak (Northern Shillukland and Southern Shillukland), which are ritually important but have little administrative significance. The boundary dividing the two provinces is a water-course called Khor Arepajur, just south of Fashoda. The chief of Debalo Kwom, just south of Arepajur, is, through his office, the chief of Luak. The chief of the settlement of Golban, north of Khor Arepajur, is chief of Gerr.

Apart from these, only two other chiefs and divisions counted. These were the chiefs of the settlements forming the northernmost and southernmost regions of Shillukland, the chiefs of Muomo and Tonga.[1] Fashoda, the capital of Shillukland, occupied by the *reth*, is the focal point of the structure of the Shilluk people and this is clearly seen, not only in administrative matters but in ritual and myth and in the circumstances surrounding the installation of the *reth*.

SOCIAL DIVISIONS

The Shilluk people are divided into four main classes or groups of clans:

The Kwareth

This is the royal clan, the largest of all clans and, like the others, is spread through all parts of the country. All members trace their descent, in the male line, from Nyikang and only a member of the royal clan and one whose father has been a *reth* is eligible for election to the kingship. Within the *kwareth* are four main titles.

    (a) *Reth*   - The reigning king.
    (b) *Nyireth* - The son or daughter of a *reth* - whether reigning or dead.

(1) See Evans-Pritchard, *The Divine Kingship of the Shilluk*, 1948, p.9.

(c) *Nyareth*   - The son of a *Nyireth*.
(d) *Kwanyireth* - The grandson of a *Nyireth*.

In some regions the members of the royal clan have become more numerous
than commoners and have supplanted them in the chieftainship of the settlements.   This has been possible because the members of the royal clan are
richer and tend to marry more wives, and also because of the system whereby
the offspring of a *reth* are planted out in various settlements away from
Fashoda.   When one of the *reth*'s wives is about to give birth to a child
she leaves Fashoda and goes to her own village.   As soon as the *nyireth*
is weaned he is placed in charge of some trustworthy settlement chief,
often the mother's brother, and is brought up among his mother's people.
When the child grows up and marries he builds a separate hamlet called *pa
nyireth* (unless he is called on to become *reth*), and thus becomes the
founder of a local lineage branch of the royal clan which may eventually
grow powerful enough to overthrow the dominant lineage and assume the
political aspects of its position in the settlement.

Daughters of a *reth* are not allowed to marry and therefore cannot
start lineages which would count as sister's sons to the royal house.

The Ororo

This clan is separate from the royal clan and consists of the descendants of a disinherited branch.   They are few in number and may intermarry
with the royal clan.   It is said that the *reth* still has the right to dis-
inherit lineages of the royal clan but, apart from one traditional instance,
it is not certain whether the right has been exercised.   The *ororo* are indistinguishable from the commoner clans except for the special functions
they perform for the *reth* at his investiture and at the time of his funeral.
Traditionally, the *ororo* always smother the *reth* when he is ritually killed.
The *reth* always takes some of his wives from the *ororo*.

The Bang Reth

The *bang reth* are the personal attendants of the *reth*.   Originally they
were captives from other tribes but later, volunteers from the commoner clans
in Shillukland, if they were poverty stricken, might leave their own clans and
become the *reth*'s retainers.   In return for receiving cattle to marry with,
they tended animals, engaged in building and cultivation and performed all
the duties connected with the upkeep of the royal household.   Apart from
these and their descendants, the *bang reth* also included all those who were
enslaved because their brothers were homicides and those who became possessed
by the spirit of Nyikang.

The *bang reth* are a fictitious clan; they cannot intermarry even though
there is often no blood relationship among them.   The *reth* never marries
into the *bang reth* clan and, as an indication of the impossibility of this,
he calls the daughter of a retainer *kwara*, 'my grand-daughter'.

The *bang reth* live in a hamlet of their own near the capital in which
the *reth* resides.   When he dies they, together with his elderly widows, go
and live near his shrine and look after it.   When a *nyireth* is planted out,
his father sends some of his retainers to live with him; these become *bang*

nyireth and their descendants continue to live near those of the *nyireth* as a fictitious lineage.

The Colo

The *colo* consists of the main body of Shilluk clans, of which there are about a hundred. They are patrilineal clans tracing descent from the original followers of Nyikang, and also from those who have since migrated into and settled in Shillukland or were in occupation when the Shilluk immigrants arrived under Nyikang's leadership. Their origins are obscured in myth.

The *colo* clans like the *kwareth* are patrilineal and exogamous and marriage occurs between them. The difference is that the *kwareth*, through their connection with the founder of the present Shilluk regime and their ritual importance to the people as a whole, are treated with special respect and have special privileges.

CENTRAL AND LOCAL ORGANISATION

The Reth

The Shilluk people recognise one supreme head, the *reth*, who represents the country as a whole, regardless of territorial, social or kinship divisions. According to Shilluk tradition the present *reth* is thirty-first of the royal line which began with Nyikang, who led the Shilluk into their territory, conquered it, and established the social order. The spirit of Nyikang is thought to reside in every *reth* and to be passed from one to another down the line of his successors.[1]

The Settlement Chief

The settlement chief is traditionally directly responsible to the *reth* and executes his orders. He has certain religious obligations to the *reth*, such as building a house at Fashoda or maintaining the local shrine of Nyikang. The chief settles disputes in his territory, endeavours to keep order and harmony and to lead in community matters. He is selected by the lineage heads of the settlement and not by the *reth* who merely recognises his authority and position by investing him with the *lau*, personally knotting this robe over the *jago*'s shoulder.

The Headman of the Hamlet

The *jal dwong pac* has a status which varies according to whether he is headman of the principal hamlet of a lineage - in which case he is also a representative of his lineage within the settlement - or whether he is the headman of a subsidiary hamlet, in which case he is hamlet headman only and merely the senior member of a group of homesteads. The headman of a principal hamlet often receives a *lau*, sometimes directly from the *reth*, in other cases from the settlement chief. This, however, is only in confirmation and recognition of his status and there is no question of appointment by the *reth* or the *jago*. The headman of a principal hamlet represents

(1) Evans-Pritchard, *The Divine Kingship of the Shilluk*, 1948, p.9.

his lineage in the settlement and, if he is a representative of the *dyil* lineage, he will have a special status as representing the owners of the land and the *jago* will treat him tactfully. The hamlet headman has charge of affairs within his unit and represents his people in external affairs.

The Gol Leader

The owner of a homestead is responsible for the unmarried members of his *gol*, but has no special status. The correspondence between territorial divisions and their representatives may be charted as below. (After Pumphrey, *S.N.R.* 1941, Vol.XXIV, p.7.)

TERRITORIAL DIVISIONS	REPRESENTATIVE AUTHORITY
Shilluk Tribe	The *Reth*
Luak & Gerr Provinces	Chiefs of Gol Nyikang & Gol Dhiang
Northern & Southern Marches	Chiefs of Muomo & Tonga
·····Division *(Luak)*··············	·Division or Court Chief·····
Settlement *(Podh)*	*Jago*
Hamlet *(Pac)*	*Jal dwong pac*
Homestead *(Gol)*	*Jal Gol*

(Dotted line indicates permanent administrative divisions with chiefs made by the Anglo-Egyptian Government. Previously, there were no permanent intermediate territorial units between the two provinces and marches and the settlements.)

THE RETH'S POLITICAL POWER

The actual degree of power possessed by the *reth* has been a matter for dispute among anthropologists. The majority of the early writers stressed his power and authority. Seligman writes, "The Shilluk king is absolute Head temporal and spiritual.."[1] Westermann and others have said likewise. Evans-Pritchard and other recent writers suggest that in administrative matters, the *reth* is not so powerful.

The chiefs of settlements and the hamlet heads are confirmed in their offices by the *reth*. In no case, however, does he nominate them, for they are elected by the people of the units they represent in virtue of their positions as heads of lineages dominant in the area. Likewise the chiefs of the provinces and of the northern and southern marches are traditionally determined and persons who are eligible cannot be passed over for reasons of political expediency. On the other hand, the chiefs owe their *reth* certain duties and are responsible to him for the state of their districts and their inhabitants, for defence of the settlement area and for the collection of tribute. If there is a choice of candidates for any position, each having the necessary ability and lineage qualifications, it is conceivable that the *reth* might use his influence to have as chief the man most amenable to his wishes; otherwise he appears to have little chance of exerting influence on the choice of his local officials.

(1) Seligman, *Pagan Tribes of the Nilotic Sudan*, 1932, p.39.

LEGAL PROCEDURE

According to Hofmayr, Shilluk law "...is a law of tradition based on decisions of Nyikang and of previous kings."[1]   He maintains that justice is very arbitrary and depends much on individual interpretation and custom. The settlement chief has a court to which are brought cases which the *gol* leaders and the hamlet headmen feel unable to settle or which are too serious for them to judge.   The accuser and accused appear before the settlement chief and the headman is often called as witness, while the elders assist.   In major disputes, or if the settlement chief's decision is appealed against, the matter is brought before the *reth*.   Hofmayr further states that important cases are treated by him and his judgement is final.[2]

In the courts compensation is awarded for homicide and fines in cattle or goats, according to the seriousness of the offence, are imposed for disputing the *reth*'s judgement, refusing to pay royal tribute, wounding a royal prince or princess, for theft, robbery and sexual offences.   Apart from minor offences it would appear that offenders were brought to court and tried, not so much for private wrongs as for public delicts or crimes coming under the general category of breaking the *reth*'s peace, disputing the *reth*'s judgement, breaking the *reth*'s and Nyikang's laws.

Information suggests that in practice in the past the *reth*'s judicial authority was by no means undisputed.   Hofmayr maintains that an order or judgement of the *reth*'s court was executed by the *reth*'s bodyguard, which consisted of a number of youths who followed the king everywhere.   According to the same authority "blood revenge is well known among the Shilluk and feuds do exist between persons, between families and also between villages."[3]   The fine for homicide is 10 head of cattle;   formerly a girl was taken instead of cattle.   According to both Seligman and Hofmayr, the *reth* kept the cattle but might give two or three cows to the family of the deceased as compensation.   This practice is comparable to similar legal procedures in communities in which feuds still flourish and the central authority does not exercise very extensive political powers.

Intervention in a serious feud between two districts probably took the form of the *reth* supporting one side against the other, and self-help, sometimes back by the *reth*'s intervention, was possibly the means of obtaining compensation and settling disputes which were not willingly submitted by the two quarrelling parties to arbitration and the judgement of a court. On the other hand, a description of the settlement of a feud by Oyler suggests that the role of the *reth* is essentially that of peacemaker, but that his functions can only be exercised if the disputants are willing to make peace.[4]   In this respect it would appear that the role of the *reth* is comparable to that of other ritual and peacemaking functionaries among the Nilotes, such as the leopard-skin chief of the Nuer and the Dinka spear-chiefs.

(1) Hofmayr, *Die Schilluk*, 1925, p. 157.
(2) *Ibid.*
(3) *Ibid.*, p. 162.
(4) Oyler, *S.N.R.* 1920, Vol. III, No. 3, pp. 296-99.

It would appear, therefore, that in judicial and administrative matters the Shilluk *reth* is far from being an over-riding or autocratic political authority.   Local chiefs seem to be free to follow their own traditional courses without much interference.   In actual powers of government and administration, and in personal prerogative, the *reth* may be little more than a mediator in disputes and perhaps the balancing force which decides a quarrel one way or another.   It is in ritual matters that his real position and powers are indicated.

THE RITUAL SIGNIFICANCE OF THE RETH

Evans-Pritchard writes: "Both his functions and his status are primarily of a ritual order.   He makes sacrifices on important occasions, especially for rain and for victory in war, and it is his duty to provide cattle for the sacred herds of Nyikang at Nyilual and Wau and a canoe for Nyikang's shrine at Nyibodho.[1]

.It is noticeable that everywhere there is the closest connection between the political structure and the religious cult.

(a) The territorial segments and their association with certain dominant lineages are explained in terms of the myth of Nyikang's division of the country among his followers who became the founding ancestors of many of the Shilluk clans.

(b) The lineage heads who are chiefs of settlements have ritual duties to the kingship.   They perform ceremonial services at the time of the *reth*'s investiture, are responsible for building huts in Fashoda and for the upkeep of Nyikang's shrines and those of past *reths*.·   The tombs of the dead kings are indistinguishable from the shrines of Nyikang and have the same ceremonial importance in rain-making ceremonies, harvest rituals and so forth.

(c) The traditional customs of the people and the organisation of society in every way are considered to be the work of Nyikang directly or acting in the line of *reths*.

(d) The identification of Nyikang with the king is the central point of the Shilluk political, ritual and moral system.   The people believe that Nyikang reigns and manifests himself in the *reth*.   Nyikang is also the medium between the Shilluk and Juok - their chief spirit.   The Shilluk consider the *reth* to be in close communication with the mystic forces of life, and Nyikang is the connecting link, participating in Juok as he does in the *reth*.[2]

The *reth* is considered to come under the category of Divine Kings, as described by Frazer in *The Golden Bough*.   This is clear from the mode of his death and succession as well as from the duties he performs during his lifetime.

Succession of the Reth

Only the son of a *reth* who has reigned is eligible, and a *nyireth* may

[1] Evans-Pritchard, *The Divine Kingship of the Shilluk,* 1948, pp. 16-17.
[2] *Ibid.*, p. 19.

attempt to usurp the throne any time after killing the *reth*.   The *reth's*
sons and the sons of previous *reths* are potential rivals and are not
allowed within Fashoda at night.   The *reth* takes precautions to avoid
this danger.   It is not known in which hut he sleeps and he is said to
wander round at night looking for intruders.   This practice of regicide
no doubt accounts for the planting out of the *reth's* sons from the time of
their birth.

The Death of a Reth

The *reth* is considered to have some mystic connection with the world
of nature, and the state of his health has an effect on the fertility of
the land, on the rains, the harvests and on the general material and
spiritual welfare of the people.   If the *reth* becomes weak, the people
suffer and he must be killed.   If he were allowed to die naturally the
spirit of Nyikang might be lost to the Shilluk for ever.   There are a
number of traditions relating to the traditional mode of death suffered by
the *reth*.   One maintains that the *reth* is strangled or suffocated by his
wives if he shows signs of senility;   another that he was walled up alive
in a hut.   The *reth* may be killed by a rival claimant to the throne at
any time.   Evans-Pritchard considers that the ceremonial putting to death
of kings is probably a fiction;   there is no historical evidence for it
and some Shilluk kings seem to have reigned until they were quite old.
Both Howell and Evans-Pritchard consider that there is a close connection
between the tradition of killing the king, because of the bad effects of
his waning vitality, and the tradition that a rival claimant should seize
the throne " .... we must interpret Shilluk statements about the matter as
indicating not that any prince may slay the king on his own initiative, as
has been suggested, but that any prince may lead a rebellion as the candidate of discontent, particularly of the part of the kingdom to which the
prince belongs.   If the king has lost support in the part to which he
belongs he will probably lose also both the resulting contest and his life
in it."[1]   If this is so, the traditions of king-killing are perhaps an
interpretation, couched in symbolic terms, of the actual course of events
following a rebellion against the *reth*.

ELECTION AND INSTALLATION OF THE RETH

Detailed descriptions of the installation of a new *reth* have been
given - apart from information by Nornol - by Howell and Thomson who were
in Shillukland at the election of King Fafiti Yor in 1943 and of his successor, King Anei in 1944.   In the events described by them the political,
ritual and symbolic nature of the *reth* and the importance of the Nyikang
myths may be clearly seen.   In addition, the relationships between the
various social divisions and between the territorial and kinship segments
may be perceived in action.   The whole tribe participates in some degree,
for a series of ceremonies is carried out by the clans, in which each has
a special traditional role to play.

The interregnum is a period of danger, owing to the war which may
break out over the choice of a successor and owing to the absence of the

(1) Evans-Pritchard, *The Divine Kingship of the Shilluk*, 1948, pp.34-5.

symbol of unity and cohesion.   The main events are as follows:-

The funeral of the dead *reth* is carried out and is followed, a
year later, by mortuary ceremonies and funeral dances.   These events
are chiefly a family affair and are organised by the *ororo* and the
kwareth.

The election of the *reth* concerns the whole of the Shilluk people
who are represented by the chiefs of the North and South Provinces.
The *reth* is chosen from among the *nyireth* by an electoral college,
composed of the descendants of the men who were, traditionally, made
chiefs of the first degree by Nyikang when he parcelled out the
country between eleven of his followers.[1]   Three representatives
from the *kwareth* are also included, but the *ororo* and *bang reth* have
no representatives and take no part in the election although they are
important in the ceremonies of installation.

Just as Shillukland is divided into two territorial divisions, Gerr and
Luak, so for ritual purposes this structure is represented in special ritual
terms.   The Northern province becomes *Gol Dhiang*, the Southern province
becomes *Gol Nyikang*.   There is a rough correspondence between the two political and the two ritual divisions.   The chiefs of the ritual divisions are
the political chiefs of Golbany and Kwom, the two settlements just north and
south of Fashoda.

The election of a particular *reth* must have the backing of the whole
country, although at first sight it may appear that the choice lies with the
chiefs of Gol Dhiang and Gol Nyikang.   The election cannot take place unless they agree and this does not involve their own personal opinions solely.
The other chiefs all take part and represent the views of each section of the
country and if there is disagreement between the two provinces civil war may
follow.   Agreement is usually reached before the electoral college sits and
formally proposes and elects the new *reth*.   During the interval between the
death of a *reth* and the election of his successor custom requires that all
potential claimants should stay in their villages.   This is the chance to
seize the *reth*ship by force, if a candidate wishes to do so and has the
necessary backing.   Co-operation between the candidate and his settlement
chief is essential for only the latter has the necessary force and only a
reth's son is eligible for the *reth*ship.   Other chiefs join the rebels and
fighting will begin.   Until one side is defeated, or the *nyireth* is killed
there will be civil war.

The Installation Ceremonies

Skins, ostrich feathers and the various trappings for the pageantry of
the ceremonies are provided traditionally by certain clans and settlements.
The principal shrine of Nyikang is at Akurwa, where he is believed to have
disappeared in a storm.   At his shrine are kept effigies of Nyikang and
his son Dak.   Into these effigies the spirits of Nyikang and Dak may enter
at any time.   On the death of a *reth* new images are made, for it is believed that Nyikang's spirit, formerly in the *reth*, transfers itself to the
new effigy and remains there during the inter-regnum.   At the installation

(1) Howell and Thomson, *S.N.R.*, 1946, Vol.XXVII, p.29.

of the newly elected *reth* Nyikang and Dak are brought in procession from Akurwa to Fashoda with their priests to test the new *reth*.

The conventional opposition between northern and southern divisions now becomes apparent. The forces of the southern province flock to support the *reth*-elect and wait at Debalo settlement while Nyikang and his supporters assemble at Adodo. The two armies then march to Khor Arepajur and a mock battle takes place with millet stalks instead of spears. Nyikang captures the *reth*-elect and there is a procession to the shrine of Nyikang at Fashoda. Certain ceremonies of a mystic nature follow, which are not participated in by the whole people, as are the procession and battle. The image of Nyikang is placed on the royal stool, then the king-elect sits on it and the spirit of Nyikang is believed to enter into him, and possess him causing him to tremble.

A few days later a second mock battle occurs between the king's supporters and Nyikang. The *reth* is victorious, for Nyikang has taken possession of him and the effigy is now merely the symbol of Nyikang and no longer the repository of his spirit. In a final ceremony all the important chiefs and elders from all parts of Shillukland declare their allegiance to the new *reth*.

The installation ceremonies of the *reth* and the traditions relating to Nyikang show how, at every point, the structure and political organisation of the Shilluk people is confirmed by ritual and by mystic symbols.

All rebellions and revolts are directed against the king in person and not against the kingship itself. The unity of the Shilluk is such that the various segments of the country can be represented by the common symbol of the *reth*-ship. Nevertheless, there are powerful tendencies towards fission within the structure. As has been shown, the kingship is the subject of competition on the part of the *nyireth* candidates supported by chiefs and forces available from their territories.

Of all the Nilotic groups for which there is any considerable information, the Shilluk alone form a single political unit, or nation, as opposed to a number of separate tribes or tribal groups which are culturally similar but not politically unified. At the same time, the principles of their political structure and social organisation are similar in many respects to those of the rest of the Nilotes, in particular the Anuak.

AGE SETS

Apart from a brief mention by Hofmayr, the only information concerning the Shilluk age sets is contained in Howell's article in *Sudan Notes and Records*, 1941, Vol.XXIV.

On reaching puberty a Shilluk boy is initiated into the age-set organisation. A Shilluk age set is known as *ric* and is made up of three or more subdivisions each consisting of men of approximately the same age, who have herded cattle together as boys. A man always remains in the subdivision into which he has been initiated, but a periodical shuffling of the subdivisions alters their respective positions in an age set and the whole age-set organisation. A reorganisation of the groups of subdivision thus occurs periodically.   The subdivisions of any age set are known as 'head', 'neck' and 'middle'.

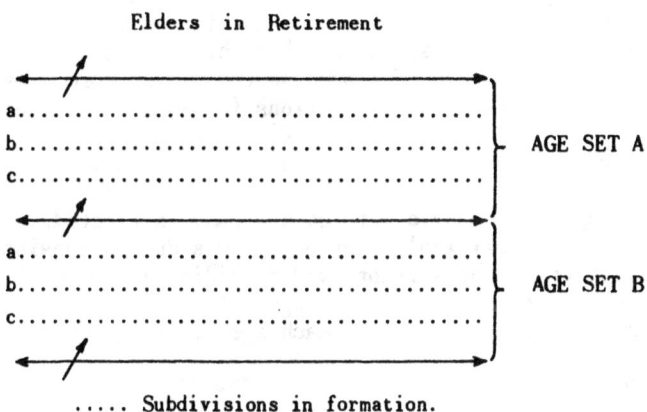

Elders   in   Retirement

a..
b.. — AGE SET A
c..

a..
b.. — AGE SET B
c..

..... Subdivisions in formation.

As new subdivisions are continually being formed by initiated youths the immediate age set into which they enter grows too large.   In addition the oldest subdivisions of the age set, comprising the married men and fathers, begin to die out or are ready for retirement.   A new grouping of all the subdivisions is achieved by the *ngol* or cutting ceremony, when age sets are ceremonially divided into distinct units.   The process is shown in the diagram.   Surviving members of age set A (the older subdivisions) pass completely out of the age organisation into retirement.   Older subdivisions of age set B pass into age set A to replace those retiring, while the' most recently formed subdivisions pass for the first time into age set B.   Thus, room is made for the formation of new subdivisions and there is a moving of subdivisions through the age sets or the formation of newly constituted age sets.

The retired age sets take no part in fighting or in ceremonies connected with the age-set organisation.   The reshuffling occurs at the induction of the very young subdivisions, the members of which are anxious to have further privileges and a higher status.   On ceremonial occasions the age sets have special parts of the animals killed, the highest age set eats the back and chest, the lower will eat the hump and legs only.   According to Howell the regrouping of subdivisions is often the subject of much dispute, particularly between the two subdivisions which will be separated by the new line of division.

There are few occasions when the age set functions.   At funerals the men are organised according to age sets as also at beer feasts when each sits in a special place and sings its own song.

Age sets emphasize the solidarity of the settlement by organising the generations within it.   Each settlement unit has its own age-set organisation and there is no connection between the age sets of different settlements, though they all have similar forms and play similar parts in the settlement units.   The age sets have little political importance, save that they constitute a bond of unity within the settlement, and this is clear

from the fact that the *jago*, elders of the *dyil* clan, and other lineage representatives, hold political authority quite apart from the age organisation. The age sets take no part in disputes within the settlement, but
when the settlement as a whole goes to war the warriors " ... are mobilised
into age sets."(1) Howell suggests that formerly the age organisation had
special military functions, but whether this was so or not, the age sets
seem to fulfil a more peaceful purpose today, and form a useful basis for
organising the relations of generations for social purposes.

The Ngol Ceremony

At the *ngol* ceremony a war leader *(ban)* is elected. The *ban* has no
administrative or political functions. His duties consist in organising
the mobilisation of the warriors and presiding at communal feasts at which
people assemble in age sets. His age mates may assist him in his cultivations. After the *ngol* ceremony each age set is given a new name.

Initiation

There are no elaborate rites of initiation among the Shilluk. Participation in a dance, the *cong bul* marks the initiation of a youth in the
age organisation. The *cong bul* is a social affair which is arranged
periodically with the permission of the *jago* of the settlement. It is not
a ceremony of initiation in the normal sense but merely a formal recognition
by the community that a lad has reached adult status and can take part in a
man's obligations and privileges. Previous to the *cong bul* a youth is
restricted in that he may not fight with spears, take part in war or in any
dance other than one held for children. Before the *cong bul* he is not
allowed to wear certain kinds of ornaments.

The *cong bul* is attended by a boy when he is 14-16 years old, or
earlier if he has to take over the duties of family head through the death
of his father. A youth normally obtains his father's permission and another
man is appointed to act as his sponsor. The sponsor ceremonially adorns
the youth with ornaments before he enters the dance. At the beginning of
the dance the warriors salute the *jago*, advance in formation and fling themselves before him.

At the time of the *cong bul* the initiated is usually presented with two
spears by his father. Rich men give their sons an ox and they take their
ox-names from these animals. An ox so given is kept until it dies and then
a new one of the same colour is substituted. After the *cong bul* the
initiates visit relatives and travel round the countryside for a few months.

CLANS AND LINEAGES

There are about a hundred patrilineal clans in Shillukland. Each
clan has a name which is preceded by the word *kwar*, meaning 'descendants of'.
All clansmen trace their descent from a common ancestor. They are bound
by distinct rules of behaviour, by special observances and are exogamous.(2)

The Shilluk clans, like all Nilotic clans, are dispersed, each clan

---

(1) Howell, *S.N.R.* 1941, Vol.XXIV, p.57.   (2) *Ibid.*, p.47.

having a great number of local branches, or lineages, spread throughout Shillukland, and there are no periodic reunions.

Members of a lineage are bound not only by kinship ties but also by ties arising through occupation of the same territory. The lineage is an effective political and social unit. A person generally thinks in terms of his localised lineage and refers most often to the founder of his lineage in the district occupied. In relation to members of lineages of other clans, however, reference is most likely to be made to the founding ancestor of a person's clan. As previously mentioned, the occupants of a settlement belong to a collection of independent lineages which graft themselves onto the genealogical structure of the dominant lineage through marriage with its female members.

INHERITANCE

Only the smallest lineage unit is of any importance in the inheritance of property. Pumphrey states that there are no definite rules for the inheritance of chattels.[1] If distribution has not been made before death they are usually taken by the eldest son, or by the next of kin where there are no sons. Cattle are taken by the succeeding *gol* leader, either a married son or a married brother. He cannot do exactly as he likes with them for he inherits certain traditional obligations. He has the moral obligation to use his herds for providing bridewealth to enable the male members of the *gol* to marry, in order of seniority, and it is considered wrong for a *gol* leader to marry a second time himself while there are men of his *gol* still unmarried and requiring cattle. The *gol* leader is also responsible for paying compensation in cattle for any wrong which has been committed by one of his household. Finally, it is recognised that no cattle of the family herds should be sold except in times of famine and to purchase grain. Pumphrey states that a breach of these terms of trust would "be universally censured but would probably not be interfered with by the courts."[2]

Uncultivated land belongs to anyone who settles on it.

MARRIAGE

The Shilluk are polygynous; a wealthy and influential man has three or four wives, while members of the *kwareth* may have several more. Marriage is forbidden with any member of one's father's clan and between all persons in respect of whom relationship, either through the father or mother, could be traced directly. Apart from these obstacles it appears that freedom of choice is generally allowed to both sexes in matrimonial matters.

Bridewealth

Bridewealth consists of ten head of cattle and sheep and spears. In addition the suitor makes small gifts and performs services to win the favour of his future father- and mother-in-law. Bridewealth discussions and arguments proceed between representatives appointed by the suitor's *gol*

(1) Pumphrey, *S.N.R.* 1941, Vol.XXIV, p.24.
(2) *Ibid.*, p.23.

and by the girl's *gol*.   Payment of cattle may extend over many years and, until these payments are completed, the girl lives with her parents and her husband has to visit her there.

The bridewealth cattle go to the girl's *gol* leader, who is either her father, brother or paternal uncle.   Pumphrey states that the maternal uncle only receives cattle if there are any arrears outstanding from the marriage of his sister, the girl's mother.   Seligman quotes an instance in which 17 cattle were paid by a Dinka and of them 10 went directly to the girl's mother's family.

Marriage Ceremonies

If a girl receives a proposal of marriage from a suitor and accepts him, the first step is to obtain the consent of the girl's *gol*.   The acceptance of a sheep - the *dyel dhok* - by the girl's parents signifies that they consent to the engagement.   According to Pumphrey, the marriage is regarded as valid and binding as soon as this has taken place, and children born to the couple are legitimate even if the cattle payments have not been completed.[1]

A beer-brewing and wedding dance at the bride's village follow and serve to publicise the marriage and express public approval and recognition.   After the dance a long period may elapse during which the bridewealth is gradually paid off while the wife lives with her parents.   The final ceremony, the *mogho thiek*, marks the separation of the wife from her parents' home and only takes place when all the bridewealth has been paid, or at least the major part of it.   Sometimes a mock battle takes place in which the bride is symbolically seized by the groom's party.

There is no set order for the various stages in completing a marriage, for there are often complications, such as seduction or the inability of the man to pay the cattle and so forth.   In cases of seduction the seduction fine has to be paid first and then the full bridewealth.

Divorce

If a wife refuses to live with her husband her parents have to return the bridewealth.   Deductions are made for the children born of the union at the rate of two head of cattle for every son and five for each daughter. Similarly, if a woman marries another man, before the first suitor has paid all the bridewealth, the cattle which have been paid are given back, subject to the deductions for any children born, because, once the sheep has been accepted, any children of the union belong legally to their father.

If the wife dies her *gol* must either substitute an unmarried sister or give back the bridewealth, making deductions for children.

Sexual Offences

Fines for adultery are paid to the woman's husband.   The amount varies,

(1) Pumphrey, *S.N.R.* Vol.XXIV, 1941, p.26.

but the usual fine for making another man's wife pregnant consists of three
cows and one bull; if pregnancy does not result the fine is two head of
cattle.   Fines for seduction are paid to the girl's father and vary from
one to three head of cattle according to whether or not the girl is made
pregnant.   If a woman has committed adultery, she confesses it at the time
of childbirth; her husband then exacts the appropriate fines from the men
concerned.

If children have been born outside marriage the eventual husband may
take them over and will pay extra bridewealth cattle.   Failing this, they
are brought up in the *gol* of their maternal uncle and belong to his clan.
He will receive the bridewealth paid on the marriage of the girls.[1]

Widow Inheritance

According to Westermann widows are inherited by the brothers of the
dead husband or by his sons, who take the wives who are not their own
mothers.   He then adds that, if children are begotten from these wives,
they belong to the family of the dead man and "they are like his own children."[2]   This custom of raising up seed to the name of the dead man is
general among the Nilotic tribal groups.

KINSHIP   AND   KINSHIP   TERMINOLOGY

Ora

The in-law relationship of *ora* has been commented on by Seligman and
Pumphrey.   It appears to have two particular applications, being used in a
narrow and in a wider sense.

A man describes as *ora* all his wife's kinsmen and, strictly, all the
kinsmen of the wives of the men of his own generation belonging to his own
clan.   This extension may be because he is allowed, at any rate in theory,
to have access to the wives of such clansmen and temporarily takes over the
in-law relationship with their parents.   During the first years of marriage
the members of the husband's *gol* have to respect and to avoid the members of
the wife's *gol*.   Pumphrey suggests that the basic reason for this is that
the initial period of marriage is an unstable one and friction is gradually
resolved as the bridewealth is paid off and children are born.   To avoid
friction the husband does not speak to his *ora* and meets them as little as
possible.

In a wider sense the *ora* tie is connected with certain sex taboos.   The
breach of these taboos is believed to cause *dwalo* sickness, a form of illness believed to affect both mother and child who will die unless the man
who induced the mother to break the taboo will split a gourd in two and
sacrifice a sheep.[3]   There are certain *ora* relationships between lineages
and one lineage will be *ora* to another.   Thus, if men of lineage A have
married women of lineage B, C and D, there are *ora* relationships between A
and B; A and C; A and D.   In such a case no men of lineages B, C and D

(1)   Pumphrey, *S.N.R.* 1941, Vol.XXIV, pp.34-5.
(2)   Westermann, *The Shilluk People*, 1912, p.114.
(3)   Pumphrey, *S.N.R.* 1941, Vol.XXIV, p.29.

could marry women from lineage A as this would prevent the correct working
of the relationship of avoidance and would confuse the situation.   Each
lineage therefore develops a tendency to marry women of some other specific
lineage,[1] but this is a traditional convention only and not compulsory.

In addition to the ordinary *ora* relationship between two lineages it
is dangerous for a man to have sexual relations with a member of a lineage
which is *ora* in the second degree.   B, C and D may have an *ora* relationship, through customary intermarriage, with other lineages, E, F, G and H.
If a man of lineage A seduced a girl of lineage E then all the men of
lineage B would be offended, since they regard marriage with girls of E
as their prerogative, and there is an *ora* relationship between the two
lineages as there is through A and B.   *Dwalo* sickness would result from
the offence in the same way as if a man had relations with a woman who was
a blood relation.

Terminology

Pumphrey gives a list of Shilluk kinship terms,[2] among which may be
noted the absence of any single word for brother, such a kinsman being described as father's son or mother's son.   The Shilluk kinship terms used to
describe members of the immediate family are extended to others of the same
generation, and from this descriptive terminology a classificatory system
is formed.

RITUAL   AND   OTHER   CULTURAL
FEATURES

There are three major aspects of Shilluk belief and ritual;   the recognition and worship of Juok, the cult of Nyikang and the kings in whom
he has been reincarnated, and the cult of the ancestral spirits.   In addition there are less important beliefs such as the belief in the spirits of
the bush and river.

JUOK

The concept of Juok is found in many of the Nilotic tribal groups although beliefs concerning it vary.   Among the Shilluk Juok refers to a
spirit which is universal, formless and invisible like the air.   Juok is
above Nyikang and men though he is approached principally through Nyikang.
The Shilluk perform sacrifices to Nyikang which cause him to move Juok to
send rain, to prevent misfortune, remove sickness and so forth.   Juok is
so linked to Nyikang that he is seldom approached in prayer without mention
of the latter as intercessor.   Juok is vaguely associated with the firmament and is recognised as creator though he is believed to show little
interest in men owing to his greatness which is so far above them.

Hofmayr[3] states that the Shilluk put adjectives to the word Juok in
order to bring out one or other of his attributes:

(1) Pumphrey, *S.N.R.* 1941, Vol.XXIV, p.30.   (2) *Ibid.*, pp.37-9.
(3) Hofmayr, *Die Schilluk*, 1925, pp.186-7 and p.193.

Juok *Ficere*, means a whirlwind;
Juok *Nam*,   "   river spirit;
Juok *Acwaci*, "   creator;
Jame Juok,   "   things made by Juok such as food etc.;
Juok *Tim*,   "   wood spirit;
Juok *Ayim*,   "   protector.

Anything that cannot be understood is Juok.   Juok is thus a plurality but
he is also one spirit; he may be either good or bad, or neither, he is
potentially all three.   He may bring sickness, may protect people or he may
merely stand aloof from human affairs.   Certain diseases are specifically
associated with him.   The cult of Juok is not expressed in any external
action or ritual; it is found in a few songs and prayers, and Juok is invoked only when appeals to the ancestors and to Nyikang fail.

THE CULT OF NYIKANG

Nyikang is the hero of most of the Shilluk myths and traditions.   He
is the culture hero, founder of the nation, and the popular ideal, and
though probably an historical person in the first instance, his acts and
words have become sacralised in myths.   The Shilluk regard him as a divine
or semi-divine being.   They say he did not die but disappeared in a whirlwind during a festival held at Akurwa.   The spirit of Nyikang is supposed
to be present in certain places, men and animals.   Every *reth* at the moment
of his installation, when sitting on the royal stool, is possessed by the
spirit of Nyikang so that it is Nyikang who becomes king again (see above).
The spirit of Nyikang is regarded as closely associated with certain shrines,
which are regarded as his homesteads; in particular he is present, at certain times, in his effigy at Akurwa.

There are ten shrines of Nyikang in Shilluk country, the most important
being at Akurwa and Fenyikang.   Seligman describes them as a group of two
or more huts, of the same circular form as dwelling-huts but slightly larger,
enclosed in a fence of millet stalks.   The huts are particularly well
thatched and the apex of the roof terminates in an ostrich egg from which
projects the blade of a spear.(1)   The huts are taboo to all except the
priests of Nyikang and the old people who tend them.   The attendants and
priests of the royal grave shrines and the shrines to Nyikang are known as
bareth; they are the ex-wives of kings, people liable to epileptic fits
(which are held to indicate possession by Nyikang or a dead king), and certain old men who appear, according to Seligman, to have a hereditary connection with the shrine.   The *bareth* keep the shrine clean, receive the sacrifices and officiate at the ceremonies.   They eat the meat of the sacrifices
and drink the milk of the cattle belonging to the shrine.

The worship of Nyikang at his various shrines consists of sacrifices
and prayers.   The two most important annual ceremonies are the rain-making
ceremony, held just before the rains, and the harvest festival, when the
millet is cut and first-fruits are offered to Nyikang.   Each new *reth*
should send cattle to each shrine of Nyikang and also various other presents.
Offerings are given at the shrines when a person is sick so that Nyikang
should make him well.   Offerings and ceremonies invoking Nyikang's aid are

(1) Seligman, *Pagan Tribes of the Nilotic Sudan*, 1932, p.77.

made at all times of stress and misfortune. Everything round a shrine is sacred, especially trees - they are particularly rare in Shillukland in any case.

Certain Shilluk kings, particular incarnations of Nyikang, tend to be identified with particular species of animals. If such an animal approaches the shrine without signs of fear, it is assumed to be the form in which Nyikang appears, and a sacrifice is offered at the shrine. Almost any unusual behaviour on the part of an animal would lead the Shilluk to look on it as a temporary incarnation of Nyikang. Nyikang's mother, Nikaiva, is reputed to have been a crocodile and is believed to live in the river in that form. A sacrifice is made to her by throwing a live sheep into the river. The crocodile is generally spared even though these creatures are a danger in river crossings.

There is a limited cult of the Dinka spirit Dengsit, and also a belief in the spirits of the bush and river.

THE CULT OF THE ANCESTORS

Beliefs concerning the ancestral spirits are vague. Reference is made to *pan juok*, 'the country of the dead', which is reached by the spirit after long wandering through the bush, but it is also believed that the spirit persists in or around the grave. Offerings and sacrifices are made to the ancestral spirits by the head of a household or local lineage on behalf of the descendants. If there is sickness or misfortune or the possibility of danger, a person will pray to his ancestors and make an animal sacrifice to propitiate them.

The ancestral cult seems, however, to be overshadowed by the national cult of Nyikang and the royal ancestors.

TOTEMIC BELIEFS

Seligman suggests that Shilluk totemism may have been derived from the Dinka because it seems so slight and unimportant. According to Hofmayr and Westermann the clans appear to have totems and some clans derive themselves from an animal or fish which Nyikang took and turned into people in order to populate the country. Hofmayr states that totem animals are often killed but it is considered wrong to eat them.[1] Most totems are animals but a few are plants. Children inherit their totems from their fathers; a woman keeps hers even when she is married.[2]

MAGICAL PRACTICES

The Witchdoctor (Ajuago)

Ajuago means 'man of Juok'. Such people are regarded as possessing certain magical powers which they use for the good of the community. People go to them when they are in need of help and pay them for their assistance. The powers of the *ajuago* are believed to be due to their

(1) Hofmayr, *Die Schilluk*, 1925, p.235.
(2) *Ibid.*

periodic possession by the spirit of the early Shilluk kings.   The guard-
ians of the shrines of Nyikang may or may not be *ajuago*, for mere connection with a shrine does not automatically make a man an *ajuago*.

According to Seligman when a man becomes an *ajuago* he becomes ill and
has dreams.   On consulting one who is already in the profession, he is
told that he has in him a spirit of one of the early kings.   Special ceremonies are performed, the habits and skills marking an *ajuago* are acquired,
and the man begins to practise in his professional capacity.   The power
is frequently hereditary and a son or daughter or even a remote relative
may become possessed.   All witchdoctors live celibate lives whether they
are male or female.   According to Seligman an *ajuago* marries wives and
others beget children for him.[1]   Many witchdoctors are specialists in
some branch of magic but some have general powers.   Some of the main tasks
performed by them are: to give safety on a journey, to bring success in
hunting, to bring victory in war, and to detect those who will be killed
in a fight and forestall their deaths.   They are believed to have the
power of curing disease and also to kill by magic.   The witchdoctors are
essential to the community as diviners and they have the ability to ward
off evil spirits and bad magic.   Very often an *ajuago* possesses a 'gourd
of Juok', which is a gourd with a handle upon which is an iron band.   The
gourd is greased and some grain is put in it.   When it is shaken the grain
rattles and that is presumed to be Juok talking.   The gourd is kept in the
ajuago's house and is consulted for purposes of divination.[2]

Many of the witchdoctors exert a powerful influence over the people
and, in consequence of the fees they receive, are usually prosperous.

The Jalyat

The *jalyat*, 'the man of herbs', is a sorcerer dealing essentially in
bad magic, as opposed to the good magic of the *ajuago*.   The *jalyat* is
greatly feared.   He works in secret at night so that the Shilluk are never
sure who is a *jalyat*, though they will kill anyone whom they suspect of
practising sorcery.

The *jalyat* is thought of as being a monorchid and, as such, he should
be drowned at birth.   The father alone has the power to save his son.
When a sorcerer has reached maturity he cannot be killed openly unless the
people of his village determine to rid themselves of the evil they believe
him to be causing.   The power is not considered to be hereditary.   The
sorcerer, in practising his evil arts, uses parts of his victim's body or
things closely associated with him.   He makes mud effigies and pierces
them or puts them in a fire and is believed by these means to destroy the
persons they represent.   A sorcerer may cause sickness, bring misfortune
by ruining crops, by causing cattle to go barren and so forth.   Sorcerers
work against children in a large family and certain accidents and deaths
may be caused by their machinations.   The basis of the sorcerer's inten-
tions is considered to be envy of the successful and the prosperous, whom
he therefore endeavours to injure.

(1) Seligman, *Pagan Tribes of the Nilotic Sudan*, 1932, p.101.
(2) Oyler, *S.N.R.*, 1920, Vol.III, No.1, p.114.

If a man knows that he is being bewitched he can get the witchdoctor to counteract the bad magic and save him. When he gets old the sorcerer may hire out his powers to help people.[1]   It is a serious offence to accuse a man of being a sorcerer unless it can be proved, and an accuser may be heavily fined.   A sorcerer must be caught in the act if he is to be legitimately killed.

The Daiyat

Daiyat appear to be the feminine equivalents of the *jalyat*.   They are not regarded as being so evil and serious in intent as the *jalyat*.

The Evil Eye (Ywop)

The Shilluk believe firmly in the power of the evil eye and that it is inherited, passing from a parent (male or female) to the children.   It may also come suddenly upon a person.   Those who possess it try to conceal the power from others.[2]   Envy, jealousy or anger causes people with this power to bring illness or misfortune on others who are richer and more fortunate than themselves.   The *ajuago* can counteract the effects of the evil eye by prayer, sacrifice and countermagic.[3]

LIFE   CYCLE

BIRTH

About three months before her first child is born, a woman leaves her husband and returns to her parents' *gol* for the birth.[4]   Immediately after the birth the mother is exhorted to confess all her previous love affairs to the woman acting as midwife and it is believed that were she not to do so she and the baby would die.   The child is shown to the father and his friends who wish to see that it is not a monorchid or deformed in any way.   In the former case, the child would probably be killed, for it is believed that monorchids grow up to be sorcerers.[5]   Cleansing ceremonies are carried out a few days after birth.   It is considered wrong to have another child before the previous one has been weaned.

Twins are welcomed by the Shilluk.   They are called *nuole juok* children of god' and have special names.   Many ceremonies occur after the birth of twins.

Names are given soon after birth and usually refer to some incident which has occurred in the family.   The birth name is retained throughout life, although an ox-name and other names are taken later.

DEATH AND FUNERAL CEREMONIES

According to Seligman every living man has both a *wei* and a *tipo*. The *wei* is breath or life, the *tipo*, shadow or image.   In addition, the

(1) Oyler, *S.N.R.* Vol.II, 1919, No.2, p.123.   (2) *Ibid.*
(3) Hofmayr, *Die Schilluk*, 1925, p.221.   (4) *Ibid.*, p.271.
(5) Seligman, *Pagan Tribes of the Nilotic Sudan*, 1932, p.70.

Shilluk believe in *cen* which is thought to be the malevolent element that persists after the death of one who has died with a grievance and is angry at some wrong that has been done to him.[1] They also speak of *winyo*, meaning a bird, but Seligman was unable to discover what this meant.

A dead body is buried at full length, a few paces from the door of the house in which the deceased lived. The grave is usually dug by elderly male relatives. The body is wrapped in skins, and sacrifices of oxen, goats and fowls are made after the burial, according to the family wealth. The mourners bathe in the river; no food taboos are laid on them but they shave their heads and do not wear ornaments or go to dances during the period of mourning. After a month has passed the mortuary ceremonies are held, a number of sacrifices are made and beer is brewed for the mortuary feast. According to Westermann the horns of an ox are often placed on the grave.[2]

THE ANÙAK

Detailed information on the Anuak is derived almost entirely from two articles by Evans-Pritchard.

ECOLOGICAL CONDITIONS

The Anuak are, like the Shilluk, a riverain people and their villages are distributed along the banks of rivers in the Eastern Sudan and in Ethiopia. In the western regions of Anuakland the ecological conditions are somewhat different from those in the east. The western areas are true savannah, flat, almost treeless grassland, which is flooded in the wet season. In the east there is forest savannah which gradually turns into tropical rain forest. In the rainy season the western half of Anuakland is cut off from the eastern half by deep water-courses and swamps. These factors have had considerable repercussions on the political organisation of the country and largely determine the distribution of the villages and the economy.

In the savannah areas of the west, villages are built on rising ground at the edge of the flood plains and the occupants may have to move during the rainy season for fishing, fresh pastures and for drinking water. Villages built some miles back from the river (owing to flooding during the rains), also have to move. For such villages there is a wet-season village site and a dry-season village site. The regions in the west are thinly populated; small independent villages are strung out 5-20 miles apart and often with swamps and rivers in between so that in the wet season a village community may be completely cut off from the rest of the country for several months. In certain localities, as along the Gila river, villages are surrounded by dense beds of reeds and it is impossible to reach them except by the few paths available. Such villages are very difficult to attack. Where the villages of the savannah areas are not protected by these banks of reeds they are, or were in the past, protected by stockades and moats, the homesteads being closely wedged together owing to the lack of space on the mound occupied.

(1) Seligman, *Pagan Tribes of the Nilotic Sudan*, 1932, p.97.
(2) Westermann, *The Shilluk People*, 1912, p.113.

In the forest areas the villages are situated within a few hundred yards of the river. Trees and bushes grow all round and none of the forest villages are stockaded owing to the protection afforded by vegetation. They tend to straggle owing to the cultivations which divide one homestead from another and because there is plenty of suitable ground.

The sparse distribution of villages in the western part of Anuakland, the floods of the rainy season, together with the remains of stockades and defence works, make the villages autonomous political units with little co-operation between them and each ready to defend itself against both foreign raids and the assaults of neighbouring villages. In the forest regions, high ground, absence of flooding, and protection of thick vegetation enable the villages to be built nearer to each other, and to be more spread out themselves. For these reasons, according to Evans-Pritchard, we find in the east conditions favourable to a wider political organisation than is possible in the west.[1]

SOCIAL ORGANISATION AND POLITICAL STRUCTURE

CLANS AND LINEAGES

Anuak clans are patrilineal. The members trace descent from a common ancestor and share a common salutation. Each clan has a lineage structure similar to those in other Nilotic groups. The members of a lineage tend to live in tne same village but lineages of the same clan are dispersed in many different villages. There is little co-operation between dispersed lineages of one clan. Clans appear to be non-exogamous groups and this is certainly so in the case of the noble and *jowatong* lineages. Intermarriage is allowed between lineages of the same clan which are sufficiently distant from each other in the clan structure. When two distantly related persons marry, a winnowing tray is cut in two to prevent any evil consequences.[2]

Each clan has its own particular salutation *(math)*. A salutation is used by men and women in greeting members of other clans. All adults have ox-names but these are not used in greeting.

Each clan also has an honorific title, *paagha*. Girls take the honorific title of their father's clan, boys that of their mother's clan. Thus, all the women of a clan have the same title while the men have a variety of different titles. Although a man takes his mother's title he does not transmit it but hands on his own clan's title, which he does not use himself, to his daughter, and through her to her son where it ends.

The largest clans are the Jowatcuaa, the Jowatmaaro and the Jowatnaadhi. The Jowatcuaa trace their descent from Cuai and the clan centre is Pocala village on the Akobo river. The clan centre of the Jowatmaaro is Ukwac in the extreme east of Anuakland; the ancient home of the Jowatmaaro, however, was near Utalo from which they were driven out by the

(1) Evans-Pritchard, *The Political Systems of the Anuak*, 1940, pp.18-19.
(2) *Ibid.*, p.28.

nobles.   The Jowatcuaa and Jowatmaaro are said to be the two original clans but they were deprived of power by the coming of the noble clan. The commoner clans are listed and discussed by Evans-Pritchard and a distribution map is given. (See *The Political System of the Anuak*, pp.29-34.) The commoner clans include some which are of foreign origin as, for example, the Jowatjaango whose ancestor is said to have been captured by the first Anuak king, Giilo wa Koori.

Besides these clans there is the royal or noble clan, the *watnyiye*, and the *jowatong* lineages of royal stock who have lost royal rank. The *watnyiye* are restricted almost entirely to the east and south-east of Anuakland, while the *jowatong* are numerous and widespread.

THE VILLAGE

The Anuak village is the largest and most important political unit. Villages are grouped into a number of districts, but these appear to be little more than geographical divisions and are not distinct political segments.   According to Evans-Pritchard they are divisions in the sense that the villages of a district usually have more relations with one another than with villages of other districts because they live closer together and have the opportunity for a certain amount of intercourse.   Only in the case of Adongo, where the nobles are active, is the term sometimes used in a political sense.(1)   The Anuak districts along the Agwei, Oboth and Akobo rivers and tributaries of the Sudan are listed by Evans-Pritchard.(2)

Villages vary in size of population from several hundred to 2,000. Usually they number from 50 to 500 we are told.   The largest villages are found in the Ethiopian part of Anuakland and some, like Pinyghudu on the Gila, stretch for several miles along both river banks.   The largest villages are, in reality, a number of small villages and hamlets stretched out in a continuous line, but all the various segments acknowledge a single headman and they all unite to make war for defence or offence.   The structure of any village depends on its size.   If a village is small it consists merely of a number of homesteads; if it is large it will be divided into a number of hamlets.   Whatever the size, however, the basic structure and organisation of the Anuak village are the same.   The smallest unit is the compound owned by every married man.   It is circular in shape and each wife has a separate hut although there is a communal cooking hut.   There is a special hut for boys and unmarried men in the compound.(3)

The Anuak derive most of their food from cultivations.   Every village has its own land and, when this is exhausted, a move is made to another site nearby.   This horticultural economy which predominates over a pastoral economy makes every village self-subsistent and there is no inducement to co-operate with other villages.   Environmental conditions, particularly in the west, and the type of economy practised by the Anuak, both help to create and emphasise the isolation and independence of the village and its importance as a political unit.

(1) Evans-Pritchard, *The Political System of the Anuak*, 1940, p.23.
(2) See Evans-Pritchard, *S.N.R.*, 1947, Vol.XXVIII, pp.69-70 and also *The Political System of the Anuak*, pp.23-4.
(3) Bacon, *S.N.R.*, 1922, Vol.V No.3, p.116.

Adjacent villages may combine to defend themselves against attack but these combinations are only temporary expedients and no permanent authority is recognised by the villages which combine in this manner. Even when an Anuak noble combined a number of villages under his authority, which occasionally happened, the combination eventually fell apart and each segment became an independent autonomous unit again. The independence and autonomy of the villages was formerly asserted in frequent inter-village fights. According to Evans-Pritchard, the strongest sense of common interest between villages is found where a small number of contiguous villages are ruled by closely related nobles.

The Anuak village is a legal unit. No compensation can be obtained for homicide in inter-village feuds; the only remedy for the kin of the slain man is to kill one of the slayer's kin in a fight. On the other hand, payment of compensation is made when homicide occurs within a village. Compensation takes the form of handing over a girl to take the place of the dead person, for her bridewealth will be kept by the deceased person's family. Failing a girl, a boy is handed over or the slayer transfers himself. If compensation is withheld the kin of the dead man will intervene, with community backing, and force a settlement if necessary to prevent the village being disrupted by internal feuds.

THE VILLAGE AND THE LINEAGE SYSTEM

Every village is associated with the lineage of some clan, on which its cohesion and individuality is based.[1] The members of this dominant lineage (the *tung dwong*) are regarded as 'owners of the village site' and, where there is a village headman, he is selected from that lineage. Other lineages living in the village are generally related to the dominant lineage through intermarriage and are regarded as 'sister's sons'. In a very small village, or in a hamlet of a large village, the people nearly always belong to a single lineage, for lineages tend to settle in distinct territorial sections and preserve their solidarity. It is these kinship and structural differences which often lead to fights between rival sections within a village and the migration of the defeated party, so bringing about a further dispersion of the clans. The Anuak village has, besides the *kuaaro* (headman), the *kwai ngom*, the 'father of the land' who has certain ritual functions. The *kwai ngom*, as among the Shilluk, is the direct descendant of the first people who occupied the village site. He has a ritual connection with the earth, he obtains the rain and tells the people when to begin sowing. He has the power of blessing people by invoking the earth. If the lineage originally in possession is still powerful, then the offices of headman and father of the land are combined. When there are two officials it means that the original dominant clan has lost its position and a usurping lineage has taken over all but the ritual functions connected with the land.

In many respects the lineage structure of the Anuak village very closely resembles that of the Shilluk settlement. The headmanship is the focal point of the lineage although, like the Shilluk *jago*, if the headman is unpopular and weak the village will tend to break up. In spite of their self-sufficiency villages are occasionally forced to combine for defence;

(1) Evans-Pritchard, *The Political System of the Anuak*, 1940, p. 35.

moreover, intermarriage occurs and the clans are widely dispersed, so that
any one lineage will have related lineages of the same clan in other villages.   In addition there is the same cultural and social organisation
everywhere so that people can easily fit into other villages besides their
own.   Nevertheless, the village group is the only effective group in all
spheres of life.

THE VILLAGE HEADMAN

The Anuak have two types of political organisation: the nobles and
the kingship in the east and south east, and the village headmen in the
rest of the country.   These two organisations are described separately,
although they have much in common and one has enroached on and affected
the other.

The headman of a village, the *kuaari*, has certain prerogatives.   People.
pay him much ceremonial respect.   He possesses certain badges of office as,
for example, the village drums, which may only be held by him, special
strings of beads and sometimes certain sacred spears.   Special notched
poles are erected outside his homestead.   There are court officials
attached to his homestead: the *nyikurugu* and *nyiol* - whose functions are
not known - and the *kwai luak*, who appears to be the leader of the youths
of the village.   Headmen of different villages have special salutations
and their unique status is indicated also by the fact that there are
special words which may be used only in reference to them.   The villagers
owe allegiance to the headman, they hoe his cultivations and make him gifts
of game and fish, part of which are redistributed.   When compensation is
received for homicide, the headman takes a cow or its equivalent because
the man was killed on his land.

The headman's office, in spite of the outward respect attached to it,
is by no means stable.   If he loses the support of his village community
he will be turned out of office and expelled from the village by an *agem*, a
'village revolution'.

Candidates competing for the headmanship must have certain qualifications.   They must be male members of the dominant lineage of the village
and their fathers must have been headmen before them.   As the *agem* is a
frequent occurrence there are usually several candidates, sons of past headmen, who are competing.   It is said that a headman is usually expelled because of meanness.   To keep in office he has to kill his cattle for feasts,
help to provide young men with bridewealth and make gifts.   Even if he
has impoverished himself in fulfilling these duties he may still be expelled.   If he is unfair or has offended someone he increases the opposition against himself.   There are thus heavy obligations which counterbalance his privileges, while his authority depends entirely on the volun-
tary support of the village.   As a consequence, he has always to consider
the most influential people of the village and try to act in accordance with
the will of the majority.   In this sense he is a constitutional leader of
the people and far from being a despot.   The nature of his position is
indicated by the fact that he has not the power to hear disputes or to force
a settlement when he has given judgement.   People settle their torts among
themselves by self help and the backing of kinsmen.   The headman only
interferes if asked to assist one side against another.   In short, the

Anuak headman has as much power as the people care to invest him with on any occasion.[1]

A revolution (agem) is organised by the opposition to the ruling headman and discontented elements rally round one or more of the eligible candidates. The headman is not killed, normally, but he, and any close supporters, are expelled from the village, the amount of fighting first taking place depending on the relative strength of the parties in conflict. Sons of the same father compete and also paternal cousins, but a son would not try to replace his own father, nor would full brothers compete against each other. A dying headman's nominated successor may be accepted as he can always be turned out if not found congenial.

An expelled headman takes nothing with him but his wives; his successor has his herds, cultivations, huts and so forth because these belong to the office, being derived from gifts and services bestowed on the office and not on the individual occupying it. The kuaaro is not really an administering or governing official but a ritual figure deriving authority from the confidence which is placed in him and from the values and sentiments which centre round his office. The agem is general throughout the villages held by headmen but they are more likely to take place in certain structural situations. If most of the village population belongs to the tung dwong, the dominant lineage, the village will usually support its representatives wholeheartedly and not desire a change. If there are a number of stranger lineages they may support rival candidates in order to exert their power and so the many fissions in the society will lead to constant revolutions. Expelled headmen usually go to the village of their maternal relatives and stay there hoping that they may eventually be recalled.

THE NOBLES

In the villages of the south east of Anuakland there is a different system. In every village the great mass of the people are bang (commoners), but instead of a headman representing the village there is the nyiye, a noble. All nobles belong to the royal clan, which is restricted almost entirely to the villages of the east of Anuakland. Even if he is by birth a member of this clan, a man does not become a noble unless he is invested with the emblems of nobility. If he fails to be so invested his descendants also are excluded from the right and become watong, members of dispossessed noble lineages. In order to be invested with the emblems a number of nobles in every generation compete for their possession. The temporary holder of the emblems is merely the first among those who have already been invested and is distinguished from them only by actual possession for the time being. There is no word distinguishing him from the other nobles, according to Evans-Pritchard, and all nobles have the same status and display the same signs of rank. The holder of the emblems is only primus inter pares.[2] The royal emblems consist of five bead necklaces, four spears, two stools a spear-rest and a drum. It is investiture with the string of ucuok beads which confers nobility. The necklace is believed to have been worn by Ukiro, the founder of the royal clan, when

(1) Evans-Pritchard, The Political System of the Anuak, 1940, p. 44.
(2) Ibid., p. 52.

he came out of a pool or river as related in the Anuak myths.   The maternal uncle of a son of a noble places the necklace on his nephew and confers
nobility.   Like the village headman elsewhere, Anuak nobles have possession of the village drums and their homesteads are marked by forked poles.

Commoners treat all nobles with respect, have special greetings for
them, and spread skins for them to sit on, for a noble must not sit on
bare earth.   Nobles have a court and there is a small, special court
vocabulary.   There are court officials who look after various aspects of
the noble's household, such as the *Kwaikodo* who has charge of the court
drums and supervises the preparation of food and so on.   The *Kwai luak*
leads the noble's bodyguard and he is a particularly important official because a noble's authority finally rests on the armed band of youths.   A
noble will not eat food cooked by his wives, but has a special male cook.
A powerful noble who has influence over more than one village will place
his representatives in the villages where he does not reside himself.   A
noble's representative is called the *nyibur* and the descendants of such a
man may take over the headmanship when the power of the noble and his
successors has waned.   The *luak*, or the noble's bodyguard, is extremely
important as the basis of the noble's position in a village and is an
essential part of the political system prevailing in east Anuakland.   When
rifles were introduced from Ethiopia at the end of the 19th century the
luak became an effective armed force both within the village and against
neighbouring villages, so that the actual power of the nobles increased
tenfold.   The *luak* used to cultivate and build for the noble and form the
nucleus of the village army.   It was sent to punish a village or destroy
one which threatened the |noble's position.

The Transmission of the Royal Emblems

The *ucuok* beads, which play the predominant part in investiture,
derive their significance from their mythical association with Ukiro, the
founder of the line of nobles.   Ukiro is believed to have come out of a
lake or river wearing the *ucuok* beads.   Cuai, the ancestor of the Jowatcuaa
clan, gave him his daughter in marriage.   While Ukiro was in the village
he laid down the laws of the Anuak which have been observed to the present
day.   On disappearing into the water again he left behind a son, Giilo,
and he became the first noble of the Anuak holding the beads.   This myth,
with all its local variations, explains, justifies and sanctifies the important role played by the beads and the system of competition in the east
Anuak villages.   In addition, it provides a mystic justification for the
usurpation of the rights of the headmen by the members of the noble clan,
for, in the myth, the people forced nobility on Ukiro against his will and
Cuai, the headman of the village, voluntarily gave up his office to him and
his successors.   The myth upholds the traditional laws and customs of the
Anuak which Ukiro is believed to have made.[1]

The mode of transmitting the royal emblems has varied over the generations.   A brief outline of the historical changes is given below.

Period I.   (From Giilo to Goora, the ancestor of all living nobles)

In the earliest period a holder of the emblems kept them until he died

(1) Evans-Pritchard, *The Political System of the Anuak*, 1940, pp.76-9.

or was assassinated by one of his kinsmen.   In the very beginning it may
be that the emblems passed from father to son without violence and that
dynastic homicide started later.

Period II.   (From Goora to Gang)

After Goora's death the emblems were usually obtained by killing the
holder.   The nobles were restricted to a small area, as in the first
period, the district of Adongo (south of Oboth).   The holder of the emblems seems to have remained at Umar village which was the centre of the
nobility and there was no move made from village to village.   The holder
of the emblems would not allow his kinsmen to live in his village and they
resided in others, usually those of maternal relatives.   They came into
Umar to attack the holder, with the assistance of the maternal kin, to
kill him and take over the emblems.   The overwhelming and slaying of the
holder and the seizure of the emblems by his rival is called *agem* - the
same word which is used for the revolutions by which the headmen of the
commoner villages are expelled.   At this period, in fact, the two political systems of Anuakland are almost identical.

Period III.   (From the end of king-killing to the introduction of rifles)

In this period the emblems circulated rapidly and several nobles held
them more than once.   Killing became more rare and the emblems were often
passed on without a battle taking place.

Period IV.   (From the introduction of firearms to 1921)

In this period three nobles became so powerful that it was difficult
for other nobles to attack them and seize the emblems.   These men were
Akwei wa Cam of Nyindola lineage and two men of the Nyigoc lineage, Ulumi
war Agaanya and Udiel wa Kuat.   By obtaining guns these men dominated a
number of villages and kept the emblems for many years.   The majority of
the noble clan were thus threatened with loss of rank and the practice
arose whereby the dominant holder of the emblems kept them but allowed his
kinsmen, by payment, to visit him and be invested with the emblems.

Period V.   (From 1921 to 1935)

The heir of Awei wa Cam, Cam war Akwei, was recognised by the British
military administration and he held the emblems.   The other nobles did
not dare attack him because of government support.   Complaint was made to
the government that the emblems belonged to all the members of the noble
clan and not just to one person.   The government's decision that the emblems should be held for a year only and then passed on was not effective.
The payment of a fee has now replaced the *agem*.

THE AREA OF NOBILITY

In the early period, when a holder of the emblems was always slain by
his successor, there were few of noble rank who were eligible to compete
for them.   The area of nobility was restricted to Umar and a few surrounding villages and the status of the noble in actual possession of the emblems differed very little from that of a commoner headman of a village.

When the emblems were held for a short time only, as in period III, and the holders were not slain, the number of candidates eligible for the office increased and was distributed through a great number of villages. The emblems no longer remained in one village but travelled round a number of villages according to the residence of the holder. Thus, the kingship (possession of the emblems) became a common value for a large number of villages and a league of villages was formed, each member of which competed for the emblems on behalf of a resident noble. With the introduction of firearms the kingship became static for long periods and youths of the noble clan were invested with nobility but did not become kings, i.e. actual holders of the emblems. At the end of the 19th century the situation was that the king held the emblems and had one or two powerful rivals trying to wrest them from him. There was a large body of nobles who were invested at the king's pleasure and beyond them the great mass of commoners. The king's powers extended beyond one village and the league of separate villages competing individually changed into a number of loose federations of villages, each federation headed by a candidate, and ready to defend its possession of the emblems from the others.

The greater power given to the emblem holder by the possession of firearms enabled him to raid the 'headman villages' which before had been out of reach. He also led the Anuak on counter-raids against the Nuer and Beir and, had it not been for the intervention of the government, the king might have established a centralised government over the whole of Anuakland. In fact, the number of villages competing for kingship increased in the eastern areas but the far west remained untouched. The ritual aspects of the kingship and the emblems increased but the power of the holder did not. Even the most powerful holder with rifles at his command, Akwei wa Cam, was recognised in only four villages, at the height of his power, and had but a vague ritual authority in the rest of the area occupied by the nobles. They refused to co-operate with him against the Nuer and combined to raid his village of Utalo. Like the Shilluk *reth*-ship, the Anuak kingship and the competition for the emblems is essentially of ritual significance and comparatively little authority and power is accorded the holder of the office.

THE RELATIONSHIP BETWEEN THE AREA OF KINGSHIP AND THE AREA OF HEADMANSHIP

The expansion of the political system dominated by the nobles and their competition for the royal emblems has caused this system to come into conflict with the system of headmanship prevailing in the north west villages of Anuakland. The number of villages in which the *kuaari* have been replaced by the *nyiye* has increased since the earliest period.

Sons of nobles are generally brought up in the villages of their maternal uncles. The people of a village help their candidate to obtain the royal emblems while the maternal uncle performs the act of investiture by placing the *ucuok* beads round his nephew's neck. The headman belongs to a dominant clan but the noble is merely a sister's son in his relationship to it. A noble living in a village is not necessarily the headman also. A different procedure is followed when a village invites a noble to stay and be its *nyiye*. A village on the edge of the area in which the competition for the emblems is dominant may invite a noble to become its

headman, either because there is no other alternative to its present headman or because it wishes to have the prestige associated with a noble
headman. The headmanship is left in abeyance or perhaps the headman
exists in a subordinate position. Once a noble is installed he maintains
his position by encouraging the internal cleavages in the village structure. When installed the noble has the same position as the headman had
before him. He has the same symbols of office and the same privileges
and services. Likewise he has all the burden of distributing his wealth.
In reality nobles have little control and can do nothing unless the villages voluntarily support them. The one difference between the position
of the noble and that of the commoner headman is that a village cannot
turn out its noble by force. If he is not forced out by neglect he can
only be expelled by inviting another noble to replace him who will attack
him and perhaps kill him.

There are three stages in the full establishment of a noble in a
village. He is invested with the emblems through the support of his
maternal village. He may then be invited to become the noble of a village (usually other than that of his maternal kin) and is in this case
invested with the village emblems. Finally, the rights of the land (beel
ka ngom) may be given to him and he and his descendants are then permanently associated with the village site and become the dominant lineage.
The last stage has occurred only in the Adongo and Thim districts where
nobles have been fully established over a long period. The villages of
the south east are fully under the control of the nobles and recognise
the ritual value of the emblems of kingship. In the extreme north and
west the headmanship in the villages has not been affected at all by the
nobles and the system of competition. In the intermediate villages the
respective status of the nobles and the headmen vary owing to the interaction of the two political systems. Some nobles live without any
authority under the village headman, as guests or in virtue of property
ownership; others are virtually established in the place of headmen but
fear that they may be ousted by other nobles. Some nobles wander from
village to village. The villages of the eastern regions belong to one
system because of their common recognition of the emblems and the values
for which they stand. At the same time, the independence and autonomy
of each village is preserved by the competitive organisation in which each
village supports its noble or a noble residing in it. The whole process
has been an expansion of the sphere of nobility at the expense of the
sphere in which headmanship is dominant, and is clearly to be seen in the
villages lying on the periphery of the area in which there is competition
for the symbols of nobility.

The jowatong, or dispossessed lineages, consist of the descendants of
men who belonged to the noble clan but lost claim to nobility through
failure to be invested with the royal emblems. These lineages can trace
relationship to Ukiro, the founder of the noble clan, but are separate
owing to their disinheritance. The jowatong lineages have established
themselves in many of the villages which formerly had commoner headmen.
A record of the Gila river villages, given by Evans-Pritchard, shows that
in the vast majority the dominant lineage is jowatong, but only in two
cases were they the descendants of the original occupiers.(1) This shows

(1) See Evans-Pritchard, S.N.R., 1947, Vol.XXVIII, p.87.

how the *jowatong* lineages of the royal clan have spread at the expense of the commoner clans. Where *jowatong* lineages have been long established in their own right, the village organisation is similar to that outside the area of kingship and the *agem* functions. Where they have recently taken over, the organisation is more like that where nobles are established and there is no proper *kuaari* and no *agem*.

The headmanship of Anuak villages has had to contend against nobles who can still compete for the emblems as well as against those who cannot, and the area of headmanship has been lessened considerably by the increase of both.

*The Position of the
Holder of the Emblems*

The position of the emblem holder is not really different from that of the other nobles. He is in a more dangerous position and he has more prestige temporarily, but he has no more authority. People of other villages seek his help but he can only send his band of youths to assist them in taking action against wrongdoers, if the latter are not too strong to make this unprofitable.

No judicial decisions are made by the holder of the emblems; the office is not a legislative or administrative one and there is little secular authority attached to it. In the ritual field, the value and prestige attached to the emblems is great and, although the holder has no ritual duties like the Shilluk *reth*, the office itself is a ritual object. Elsewhere the headmanship has the dominant values and holds the interest of the people, though there is interest in and respect for the sacred emblems and their holder. In the area of kingship and its immediate neighbourhood the emblems and the competition for them dominate the scene and sentiments are concentrated on them. "The common values of the kingship in which all share and the parochialism of local communities, together explain the form of the polity and the position of the kingship in it."[1]

If we compare the two political systems of Anuakland it is found that, in spite of some obvious differences, they are alike in many basic features. The difference between them arises from the fact that the nobles established in villages all belong to one noble clan and, therefore, one can be substituted for another in any village recognising nobility. In addition, all villages recognise a common value in the possession of certain emblems by one dominant noble, or king, and that recognition is shown, not only in the prestige accorded to the holder, but also in the support given to various noble candidates who enter the competition for the emblems. Each village seeks the emblems for itself and backs a local candidate and so a competitive league of villages is formed. In this way the eastern villages are still politically independant, like the western villages, but they are not politically isolated.[2] It is this competition for the royal emblems which constitutes the whole difference between east and west Anuakland in political organisation.

(1) Evans-Pritchard, *The Political System of the Anuak*, 1940, pp.131-2.
(2) *Ibid.*, p.135.

AGE SETS

It is not certain whether the Anuak have an age-set system. Evans-Pritchard reports the existence of a band of youths, the *luak*, in the head-man villages. "In the Ciro area, and probably also along the Gila and Baro, every few years the youths of a village collect together in an enclo-sure near the headman's homestead and spend all day there for a period of several weeks. They sleep at their father's homestead. At the end of this time beer and an ox for slaughter are provided by the headman, who names the group at the feast."[1] Youths appear to be organised in this way every 7 or 8 years. Apart from hoeing the headman's cultivations the *luak* seem to have had no special functions.

In the nobles' villages each installed noble has a band of youths which serves as a bodyguard and is in the charge of a *kwailuak*, a leader of the bodyguard. The *luak* was an essential part of a noble's power, particularly after the introduction of rifles when it became an effective private army. In the same way as the village headman, the noble names his youths after they have lived at his court and served him and are due to be replaced by another younger set.

MARRIAGE

The Anuak are polygynous but most men have only one wife.[2]

Commoners and nobles pay bridewealth which, unlike the customs of most Nilotic peoples, goes to the bride's father alone. He need not give any to the bride's paternal uncles and her maternal uncle can only claim part of it if his sister was married with insufficient bridewealth. Bridewealth consists of an assortment of objects - strings of beads, bracelets, old spears, sheep and goats and cattle. According to Bacon *dumoy* beads (of opaque blue colour) always form part of the bridewealth and a single string about 30 ins. long was, at the time of his stay, worth one cow or 30 *okwen* spears.[3] The bridewealth is laid out on a skin in the homestead of the bridegroom and the bride's father takes it home with him.[4] Some days later, at a dance, the bridegroom seizes the bride and takes her to his home.

A noble sends an escort of young men to bring his bride home and when a daughter of a noble is married she is led in procession to her husband's home. Nobles do not observe the same rules of exogamy as commoners and tend to marry into lineages which are more closely related than would be considered desirable for the marriages of commoners.[5]

Bacon records four types of marriage arrangements. These include the marriage which is arranged for a daughter by her father, marriage which is preceeded by seduction, and the normal type of marriage in which the suitor proposes to a girl and then offers gifts of a spear-head and a white necklace to her father. Sometimes an early betrothal is arranged by a girl's father but on growing up the girl may refuse to marry her

(1) Evans-Pritchard, *op.cit.* p.42.
(2) Bacon, *S.N.R.*, 1912, Vol.V, No.3, p.120.   (3) *Ibid.*
(4) Evans-Pritchard, *The Political System of the Anuak*, 1940, p.112.
(5) *Ibid.*, p.113.

fiance. The man whom she eventually marries will then have to pay his bridewealth to the former fiancé.(1)

DIVORCE

If a man divorces his wife she returns to her parents' home and, if there are any children, the bridewealth is not repaid. If there are no children the father of the divorced woman must repay the bridewealth in full. Bacon's information is not clear, but it appears that the payment of bridewealth determines the sociological father of the child; physiologic fatherhood does not of itself count in determining legitimacy.(2)

RITUAL AND
OTHER CULTURAL FEATURES

Juok

The Anuak believe in an all-powerful and omnipresent spirit called Juok, who is regarded as the creator. In cases of illness an animal may be sacrificed to Juok and an individual sometimes sacrifices an animal when he wishes to bring down Juok's wrath on another person from whom he has suffered some wrong.(3) Juok plays much the same part among the Anuak as among the Shilluk, but prayers are made directly to him and not through an intercessor such as Nyikang.

Trees

According to Evans-Pritchard trees which spring up near the graves of dead nobles are sacred. Likewise conspicuous trees in a village are revered and are believed to have special powers. Trees have some connection with childbirth and the naming of children, according to Seligman; it is believed that anyone damaging these trees will die and their children also. Offerings of food and tobacco are made to certain trees.(4)

TOOMBS OF THE NOBLES

In former times people visited the tombs of the nobles to obtain assistance in their difficulties. It was believed that the spirits of the dead nobles appeared to them in the form of snakes and used to haunt the vicinity of the tombs. The most famous tombs are those near Othuon. These were said to be *juok* (sacred) and sacrifices used to be made at them. In times of drought or misfortune, or if a dead man appears in a dream and demands something, the assistance of a dead noble is sought. The local noble and the principal man of the village go to the tomb and offer prayers and sacrifices.(5)

The Ajwoa (Diviner)

The *ajwoa* divines the cause of illness and effects a cure by exercising

(1) Bacon, *S.N.R.*, 1922, Vol.V, No.3, p.122.   (2) *Ibid.*, pp.122-3.
(3) *Ibid.*, p.126.   (4) *Ibid.*
(5) Evans-Pritchard, *The Political System of the Anuak*, 1940, p.75.

his powers against the *cijor* who passes bones and such small objects into people's bodies causing their sickness or death.   The *ajwoa* does not claim to give victory in battle or to cure all disease as does the Shilluk *ajwago*.[1]   Bacon mentions a *kujur* who may be male or female (but more usually the latter) and is concerned with the treatment of illness by certain medicines rather than by magical performances.   The *kujur* also divines by throwing skin sandals into the air and seeing how they fall.[2]

The Cijor

The *cijor* is believed to exercise magical powers against persons whom he envies; his powers are passed on from father to son.   Monochids and deformed babies are drowned in the river as being potential *cijors* which would suggest that the *cijor* is the type of sorcerer found in many of the Nilotic tribal groups.

Acyeni (curse)

If a person has been seriously wronged he or she puts a curse on his oppressor, which operates only when the injured person has died.   Usually these curses are used by old people who are unable to avenge themselves by more direct means.   *Acyeni* visits a person in the form of illness, death, injury or any misfortune, apparently due to natural causes.   Bacon states that 'it would seem to have a distinctly restraining influence on injustice...'[3]   In many respects *acyeni* seems to be identical with the Shilluk *acyen*.

LIFE CYCLE

BIRTH

For thirty days after a birth the father is forbidden to enter the house where it has occurred, and a pregnant woman is similarly prohibited. If the latter prohibition is violated the baby will die and the offender must make compensation by handing over a child to take its place.[4]

Special names are given to twins, according to the sex of each child. The child born after twins is also given a special name.

BURIAL

According to Evans-Pritchard commoners are buried in shafts in the centre of their homesteads.   The face is covered with a skin and the graves are frequently enclosed by a fence.   According to Bacon the grave is dug a few paces from the door of the deceased's hut and the corpse is placed lying on its side with one hand under the head and the other stretched out along the body.[5]

(1) Seligman, *Pagan Tribes of the Nilotic Sudan*, 1932, p.112.
(2) Bacon, *S.N.R.*, 1922, Vol.V, No.3, p.127.
(3) *Ibid.*, p.128.
(4) *Ibid.*, pp.122-3.
(5) Evans-Pritchard, *The Political System of the Anuak*, 1940, pp.71-2.

Nobles are buried in a different manner.   A shaft is dug and a platform erected inside it on which the corpse, wrapped in skins, is placed;
the shaft is not filled in.   A second platform is erected above the first
and a hut is built round the grave, and surrounded with a fence of stakes.
A villager is appointed to look after the shrine and keep it clean.
Nevertheless, when the huts decay and fall down they are not rebuilt. The
Anuak respect the graves of nobles and remove their sandals and perform
certain acts of acknowledgement when they are in the vicinity of one of
these shrines.[1]

Sometimes a man may express a wish to have his body placed on a wooden
platform in the forest and left with only a covering of branches.   A
mortuary feast is held in memory of the deceased when the millet harvest
enables beer to be brewed.

THE ACHOLI

Available material is both inadequate and contradictory;   consequently
it is difficult to give a coherent outline of Acholi society.

The Acholi occupy about a thousand square miles of territory on the
borders of the Southern Sudan and Northern Uganda.   The majority of the
people live in Uganda, on the rolling plains, intersected by numerous water-
courses and swamps, which are typical of savannah country, though small
areas of forest and occasional hills and rocky outcrops add variety to the
landscape.   The northernmost Acholi occupy more hilly country.   Both
Driberg and Crazzolara consider these hill people to be ethnologically distinct from the people of the southern savannahs.   Unfortunately there is
no information available on the ecological differences between the two
regions.

SOCIAL   ORGANISATION
AND   POLITICAL   STRUCTURE

TERRITORIAL DIVISIONS

According to Crazzolara, the Acholi consist of a number of tribal
groups, some of them very small, each comprising several kingdoms or chiefdoms;   the chiefdoms are ruled by independent chiefs *(rwot)*.[2]   Girling[3]
states that a chiefdom usually consists of one or more villages, varying
greatly in size, and includes the surrounding territory.

KINSHIP UNITS

The relationship between territorial and kinship units is not known.

Clans are patrilineal and exogamous, though it is possible that intermarriage occurs between two distant maximal lineages of the same clan.

(1) Bacon, *S.N.R.*, 1922, Vol.V, No.3, p.126.
(2) Crazzolara, *A Study of the Acooli Language*, 1938, Introduction ix-x.
(3) Mr. Girling is engaged in Social Anthropological research among the Acholi and
     has kindly supplied information on some of the more doubtful points in the
     literature.

It is clear that there is a dispersion of lineages throughout a territory. Crazzolara writes: "One clan is never found wholly together in one
unit; it may be divided up and dispersed in various distant units. Such
dispersed groups never had a common headman; only the single clan group
within a unit has. Such a single clan group may consist of various collateral groups with their own headmen."[1] The single clan group, wherever
its parts may be, is characterised by exogamy, certain taboos and a common
war cry or *pak* (a form of words which may also be used as a symbol of
identity in situations such as at a hunt or dance).

It is probable that the Acholi have the same close association between
kinship groups and territorial units as the other Nilotes.

ROYAL LINEAGES

Crazzolara mentions the names of various royal clans found in a number
of Acholi tribes.[2] Royal clans he defines as those whose heads have the
traditional right to be *rwot* of independent political units (chiefdoms)
which are called after the royal clans. He states that such a unit consists of the royal clan (presumably a 'lineage', according to his own
statement concerning the dispersal of the branches of a clan) and up to 20
or more subject lineages. The royal lineage is called *lokaal* (or *lokeer*
or *lobito*) and the commoner clans are called *bon* or *lobon* or simply *lwak*,
meaning the mass or bulk.

It is probable that each chiefdom is associated with a dominant or
royal lineage from which is chosen the ruling chief. To this nucleus
numerous commoner lineages are attached, presumably by intermarriage and
therefore by female links. Since the *rwot* is chosen from the dominant
royal lineage this lineage must be the symbol of the cohesion of the unit,
the organising and leading force within, and the owner of, the territory
occupied.

COMMONER LINEAGES

Each of the commoner lineages has its own name and a headman, called
the *ladiit* for the smaller groups and *jago* for the larger ones. The *jago*,
a sub-chief, comes next to the *rwot* in authority. Girling states that
the larger village units in a chiefdom are represented by the *jago* while
the *ladiit* is an 'important man' and is head of a small kinship group.[3]
The *jago* is the head of the dominant lineage of his village as well as the
representative of the village as a whole. The dominant lineage to which
he belongs is not necessarily of the same clan as that of the *rwot* whom he
acknowledges. The exact relationship between the *jago* and his *rwot* is
not recorded. The system of dominant lineages with aggregated lineages
seems to be similar to that in other Nilotic tribal groups although further
information is required to confirm this.

THE VILLAGE

We are told that in former times villages were fairly large and were

(1) Crazzolara, *A Study of the Acooli Language*, 1938, Introduction x.
(2) *Ibid.*, vii-ix.   (3) Girling - personal communication

surrounded by stockades.   Many were built on hills or rising ground and
houses were packed closely together, the population being about 100-200.
Nowadays, stockades are no longer so important as in the past when there
was considerable inter-village raiding.   People have tended to split up
into very small groups of patrilineal kin now that they are safe from
attack.

The ō

Each village is divided into hamlets, consisting of a number of homesteads centering round an ō.[1]   Grove states that two or more ō are
found in every Acholi village according to its size, and each group of
people in the village builds its own club house for its ō, where members
sit, gossiping and smoking.   There is considerable rivalry between
neighbouring ō and "sham fights take place from time to time when a member of one ō has been insulted by a member of another.   The more serious
personal quarrels of the members are also taken up by the other members
and real fights often used to take place.   The ō also compete at *undilo*
(a kind of hockey)".[2]   From the account given by Grove it might be in-
ferred that the clubs consist of distinct patrilineal lineages belonging
to different clans, each living in its own section of the village with its
own social life and ritual procedure, its differentiation from the other ō
expressed in rivalry, in games, duels and fights.   This is supported by
Seligman's statement that a certain amount of ritual is connected with
the ō.   Information given by Lloyd suggests, on the other hand, that the
ō is an open courtyard in the middle of the village and is merely a meeting·
place for the men and that, unless it is very large, a village would not
have more than one ō.[3]   Girling states that few ō exist today owing to
the gradual dispersion of the village into smaller kinship groups.[4]

Information as a whole seems to suggest that in the past the Acholi
village was an important unit, economically self-sufficient and combining
for defence and offence under its own headman (or the *rwot*, if it was an
important village).   The village, however, is not the largest political
unit for it is one of a number of others in a chiefdom, all owing allegiance
to a *rwot* and co-operating in hunting and for defence and so forth.   That
these chiefdoms are recognised as co-operating units extending over a certain defined territory appears to be implicit in Grove's statement that it
is a *casus belli* if a chief trespasses on his neighbours' hunt.[5]

THE RWOT

The *rwot* is chosen from a reigning line of chiefs belonging to a royal
lineage of the district.   He is the head of a kingdom and, as such, a very
important factor in bringing about the cohesion of the various territorial
parts of it.   The *rwot* is sometimes the leader in war.

Acholi chiefs have sacred spears on which oaths may be taken.   The
rwot is very often an hereditary rain-maker and, when this is the case, his
authority is mainly derived from his rain-making powers and the ritual

(1) Grove, *S.N.R.*, 1919, Vol.II, No.3, p.162.   (2)   *Ibid.*
(3) Lloyd, *Uganda to Khartoum*, 1907, p.179.
(4) Girling, personal communication.
(5) Grove, *op.cit.*, pp.163-4.

nature of his office is predominant.   The skins of all lions and leopards killed are considered the property of the rain-maker and are brought to him.

It might be expected that the *rwot* would have certain judicial powers, together with the *jadongo*, who are his hereditary counsellors, but this is not definitely stated by any of the authorities.   Nothing is known of the customary law of the Acholi other than the fact that homicide is either avenged or is compensated by handing over a girl to the kin of the slain.

The *rwot* is given gifts of meat and fish.   Also, the village pays the bridewealth for the *rwot*'s chief wife, *dak ker*.   The heirs to the chiefship and to the rain-making function must be born from this union. The wife chosen must be the daughter of a rain-maker and may become a rain-maker herself.

It would seem that the *rwot* exercises ritual functions but has little administrative authority.

OTHER OFFICIAL POSITIONS

A number of other officials are mentioned in the literature.

The Won Ngom

The *won ngom* is 'the father of the land' or 'owner of the land', sometimes spoken of as *won tim*, the 'owner of the bush'.   This is an hereditary office.   The holder is responsible for burning the grass before hunting, for blessing the crops and performing ritual in connection with them and with the land.   He is probably the descendant of the people found living on the site by the incoming Acholi.[1]

The Wan Gang

The *wan gang* is 'the father of the village'.   He is said to be the village headman and is probably the senior and leading member of a small village or of the chief homestead of the village.   He is assisted by the elders with whom he settles the affairs of his unit.

The Otega

The *otega* is the war leader.   He is chosen by the warriors of his village but has no authority to engage in war without the permission of the *rwot* and his counsellors.   According to Nalder he commanded all the age classes.

The Won Kot

Nalder mentions the *won kot* (rain chief) and states that the *rwot* may exercise this function and also that of the land chief, *(won ngom)*.[2]

---

(1)   Grove, *S.N.R.*, 1919, Vol.II, No.3, p.172.
(2)   Nalder, *A Tribal Survey of Mongalla Province*, 1937, p.146.

MARRIAGE

There are several stages in the process from engagement to the completion of a marriage. A suitor proposes to a girl and, if he wins her consent, his first step is to offer a small instalment of the bridewealth to her father. If this is accepted the suitor begins to pay the bridewealth and also brings presents to his future in-laws and helps them in their cultivations. The girl meanwhile goes to visit him, only staying for short periods. She is not yet regarded as his wife and relations with other lovers are regarded not as adultery, but seduction, for which a fine is payable to her father. When most of the bridewealth has been paid the girl leaves her parents and goes to join her husband at his home. She sleeps with him in the *otogo* (the bachelor's hut), and during the day is under the direction of her mother-in-law. After a few months the husband's mother holds a feast for her and she is presented with the symbols of her new status, cooking pots etc. A special hut of her own is built for her by her husband and the marriage is complete.[1]

Bridewealth

Bridewealth may consist of sheep, spears, hoes, tobacco and lumps of iron, but rarely cows.[1] According to Seligman the usual bridewealth is about 50 sheep; 80 may be given by rain-makers and 100 for a *dak ker*, the daughter of a rain-maker, married by a rain-maker. Some of the bridewealth goes to the bride's maternal uncle, whose share is larger if the bridewealth for her mother[2] has not been paid in full.

In-law relationships

Avoidance is practised between a man and any woman whom he calls *mara* (wife's mother), but it is not complete, for a man may speak to his *mara* respectfully and may take drink, but not food, from her. There is, however, an absolute prohibition on an Acholi seeing his mother-in-law naked, and should this occur she must be given a sheep. A mother-in-law, on the other hand, must not see her son-in-law naked, and, as male Acholi are habitually naked, this, in reality, means total avoidance. If a mother-in-law is seen naked she must make beer for the whole of the local group.

A man must not eat with his father-in-law (*ora*) but the wife's brother, although he also is called *ora*, is not treated with any ceremony. The wife's maternal uncle is feared and respected and treated with much ceremony, while the *nera*'s wife is treated with the respect due to a mother-in-law.[3]

Divorce

Divorce is fairly common among the Acholi and women leave their husbands if they are ill-treated or tire of them. The new husband pays bridewealth to the woman's father who returns the former husband's bridewealth.

(1) Grove, *S.N.R.*, Vol.II, No.3, p.159.
(2) Seligman, *Pagan Tribes of the Nilotic Sudan*, 1932, p.117.
(3) *Ibid.*, p.118.

Sexual Offences

Fines are imposed for fornication and for adultery, amounting to 5 sheep for the former offence and 15 for the latter. It is believed that these offences would make the mother of the girl ill, or, in the case of a wife, adultery would make the husband ill. Generally, relations with an unmarried girl were ignored unless the mother happened to fall ill or pregnancy resulted.

AGE SETS

Nothing is known about Acholi age sets apart from information given by Nalder[1] who states that the Acholi have a well-defined system of age classes, initiated at intervals of about 10 years when boys are about 15 years old.

These classes, Nalder believed, formed the fighting organisation of the people and were organised on a village basis. Each class had its own name and uniform.[1]

INHERITANCE

Inheritance is in the male line and a man's goods go to his sons first, and failing them to his father and brothers. His widows are taken over by his sons or brothers.

RITUAL AND OTHER
CULTURAL FEATURES

There are three main aspects of Acholi beliefs and rituals, concerned with *Lubanga*, the *jok*, and the ancestral cult. There seem to be variations in these beliefs from tribe to tribe and there are also signs of influence from the neighbouring Bantu peoples. The available information is controversial and insufficient.

LUBANGA

There have been considerable arguments concerning the position of Lubanga in Acholi religion. According to both Wright and Crazzolara the word 'Lubanga' was brought into Acholiland from Bunyoro by the early missionaries and became the substitute for Juok, the real god of the old Acholi. Boccassino however, in his article "The Nature and Characteristics of the Supreme Being worshipped among the Acholi of Uganda",[2] attributes to Lubanga all the characteristics which Wright and Crazzolara claim for Juok. It is impossible at present to judge which view is more correct.

Lubanga, or Juok, who has many of the characteristics attributed to Juok among the Shilluk and Anuak, is believed to be the creator of the

(1) Nalder, *A Tribal Survey of Mongalla Province*, p.145.
(2) Boccassino, *Uganda Journal*, 1939, Vol.VI, No.4, p.196.

world and of all the things in it. He also taught men all the essential techniques of civilised living, such as cultivation, the making of beer, cooking and so forth. He is responsible for birth and death and for the social order of the Acholi, and anything unusual or unaccountable, such as twins and deformation, are attributed to him.[1]

He is regarded, generally, as inaccessible to men on whom his influence may be good or evil. Sacrifices are made to him and these may be rewarded, but in many cases Lubanga is believed to be inexorable. Certain sicknesses are believed to have been sent by the supreme spirit, as punishment for unpardonable actions, and in such cases the witchdoctors can do nothing. It is believed too, that Lubanga, or Juok, does not always punish a person directly but may leave the *jok* (lesser spirits) to do this. Certainly the *jok* seem to play a far greater part in everyday affairs.

THE JOK

According to Grove the *jok* are spirits - active forces for good and evil in men's lives.[2] Streams, rivers, hills and the bush often have *jok* of their own. All cases of epilepsy are due to the entry of a *jok* into the patient's head and curative measures consist solely in attempts to drive it out again. The *jok* spend their time in interfering in various ways in men's affairs and, when an Acholi is unlucky, he may say that his *jok* is a bad one. This may mean that his ancestor's spirits are annoyed with him or that some particular *jok* is working against him.

Seligman states that *jok* are usually connected with particular places or objects, especially with a certain type of tree, called the *kitoba* and *alua*, in or near which they live, often in snake form. A man breaking off the branch of such a tree would die unless the *ajwaka* performed a ceremony to save him. Small trees of this particular species have no *jok*. In addition to having the form of snakes, some *jok* are large-headed and hairy dwarfs.[3] In its least specialised sense *jok* may mean just 'good luck' or 'bad luck'. Although the word *jok* in general means 'a spirit', the *jok* may be manifested in anything unusual, in natural features of the landscape, such as jok *tino* (the *jok* of the bush), and they may also be seen in any forms of sickness and seizure which are unaccountable.

THE ANCESTRAL CULT

The spirits of the dead are held to be responsible for much of the good and evil which befalls the living and is not directly due to the *jok* spirits. The ritual of the ancestral cult is performed at certain shrines which are called *kac* or *abila* - according to the district. The Acholi believe that the spirits of the dead appear in the vicinity of the ancestral shrine at some indefinite time after death and indicate that they wish a shrine to be built for them. Once the shrine is built the spirits are propitiated and offerings are made to them in order to bring prosperity, good hunting and crops, fertility and general good fortune to the homestead. If they are forgotten or neglected they will cause all sorts of misfortunes to occur.

(1) Boccassino, *Uganda Journal*, 1939, Vol.VI, No.4, p.196.
(2) Grove, *S.N.R.*, 1919, Vol.II, No.3, p.174.
(3) Seligman, *Pagan Tribes of the Nilotic Sudan*, 1932, pp.126-7.

According to Seligman the ancestral shrines take various forms according to locality. A shrine is built usually near the grave of the deceased, in some places it is a very small hut with a roof made of grass supported by small forks fixed in the ground. The hut is normally small but where it is dedicated to a dead chief or someone of great importance it is made quite large. This is the *abila* of the southern Acholi.[1]

In northern Acholiland the ancestral shrine is the *kac*,[2] a small table of smooth stone supported by smaller pieces of the same stone. Offerings are inserted underneath it to appease the ancestral spirit associated with the shrine. In some instances the shrine is merely a single stone, perhaps placed at the foot of a tree. Occasionally two or more shrines, *abila* or *kac*, are erected, each representing a different ancestor. At the side of the shrine there is always a small tree, or some branches of a tree, used for hanging up hunting trophies, the remains of sacrifices and to provide shade for the ancestor. The souls of the ancestors are not thought to live in the shrine but to come there, on specific occasions, to eat the sacrifices. At such times the shrines are sacred and are repaired in readiness, but in the intervals between sacrifices they are often allowed to fall to pieces. Seligman mentions the 'four peg shrines' which consist of one or more groups of four wooden pegs. Sometimes two four peg shrines would be erected side by side, one to the householder's mother and the other to his mother's mother.[3]

According to Malandra a new shrine is built when a man abandons one village and goes to another, but a branch or two of the tree of the old one is planted by the new shrine.[4] A shrine may be dedicated to the ancestors in general, *abila pa kwaro* (the shrine of my ancestors) or it may be dedicated to a particular ancestor, such as the *abila pa wora* (the shrine of my father).[5]

The Building of an Ancestral Shrine

Usually the eldest married son erects the shrine. Circumstances connected with its erection vary. Sickness in the family, some disaster, bad luck in hunting, desire for help, thanksgiving for some avoidance of danger - any of these might provide the occasion for building a shrine. The shrine may also be built as the result of a dream. In any case the *ajwaka* (witchdoctor) is consulted, for it is his task to find out whether the ancestors are indicating the time for building. Sometimes many years pass before anything is done about building a shrine for a deceased person.

The time of building is during the first months of the dry season, in November and December. This is the time when people are beginning to hunt and need good fortune. It is also the time when there is plenty of food for the celebrations. The shrine is built in the central part of the courtyard of the homestead, according to Malandra, in front of the hut of the mother, if she is still alive, if not, in front of the hut of the

(1) Seligman, *Pagan Tribes of the Nilotic Sudan*, 1932, p.125.
(2) *Ibid*.
(3) Seligman, *op.cit.*, pp.123-4.
(4) Malandra, *Uganda Journal*, 1939, Vol.VII, No.1, p.30.
(5) *Ibid*.

chief wife.[1]   According to Seligman the shrine, like the grave, is built opposite the door of the hut so that the *tipo* (the spirit of the dead) may watch what is happening in the dwelling.[2]

The establishment of a shrine for a chief is carried out in the same way as are those of ordinary people, except that the shrine will be larger and a great dance will take place at the time as well as a feast and sacrifices.   The ceremony of the consecration of an ancestral shrine takes several days to complete.[3]

According to Wright the word *'kwer'* means a magical or religious cere- mony and refers to a particular class of ceremonies designed to bring the Acholi into contact with his ancestors.[4]   These ceremonies are performed before the *abila* or *kac* and not before the *ot jok* (the shrine of the spirits).   Their motive is to ward off evil and obtain strength: name- giving is a common feature of them.   Women have their own *kwer* which are similar to those of the men.[5]

Wright describes in detail several of these ceremonies, such as the' *kwer merok*, 'the ceremony for killing the enemy' and the *kwer lyech*, 'the ceremony for killing an elephant'.   In the same way there are ceremonies for the first pregnancy, for the newly-born child and for the harvest thanksgiving.   They all consist of sacrifices, prayers to the ancestors and various salutations and marks of respect displayed in front of the ancestral shrines.

The Cen

The *tipo* is the spirit of a person who has died, but if the man or woman dies embittered and with a grudge against anyone the spirit is refer- red to as *cen*.   The *cen* brings sickness, misfortune and often death to the person who is the object of his hatred.   Acholi particularly fear the spirit of a son whose father denied him bridewealth for marriage, the spirit of a slave killed for no reason, and the spirit of a man who was not avenged when killed in a feud.   It is believed that the souls of dogs and wild beasts may return in the same way.   No spirit can become *cen* unless it has been compelled to do so by evil; the *cen*, as opposed to the *tipo*, is always malignant.   The method of disposing of the *cen* consists primarily in digging up the bones of the deceased, burning them by the grave and killing a sheep and burying its intestines where the bones had previously been.   Further sacrifices might be required.   The *cen* is the avenging force in the conditional curse *kwun* discussed below.

RAIN-MAKING

The Acholi rain-maker, the *rwot*, is also known as the *'wun kot'*. Little is known about the methods by which the rain-makers are believed to procure rain, but the ritual seems to centre round the rain-stones which are owned by each rain-maker.   The rain-stones are certain crystals which

(1) Malandra, *Uganda Journal*, Vol.VII, No.1, p.33.
(2) Seligman, *Pagan Tribes of the Nilotic Sudan*, 1932, p.122.
(3) For description of a ceremony of consecration see Malandra, *loc.cit.*, pp.35-43.
(4) Wright, *Uganda Journal*, 1936, Vol.III, No.3, p.175.
(5) *Ibid.*

are only found in the beds of streams.[1]   Each rain-chief has two or
three special pots in which these rain-stones are kept and which are handed
down from generation to generation.   When rain is required the stones are
brought out and smeared with oil or part of a sacrificed animal;   an appeal
is made to the rain-maker's ancestors to send rain and the sacrifice is
offered at the ancestral shrine.[2]   When rain is to be driven away the
stones are put in a tree in the sun or in the fireplace.   According to
Crazzolara, the rain ceremony among the Acholi of Uganda is performed before a miniature hut called the *'ot pa juok'* (hut of god) which is situated under a tree near a stream.

A successful rain-maker must be born of parents who both come from
rain-making lineages.   A rain-maker may only beget a rain-making heir by
a wife who is the daughter of rain-making parents and who is married with
a special ceremony.   The *dak ker* is the chief wife even though she may
have been married later than the other wives.   She is ceremonially installed in her position and a sacrifice is made at the ancestral shrine of
the rain-maker.   As previously stated, the bridewealth for the *dak ker*
is provided by the lineage heads.   If the *dak ker* fails to give birth to
a male heir another wife is taken, also from rain-making parents.   In all
cases the chief wife must be taken from a different clan from that of the
husband.   In virtue of his powers the rain-maker is a very important
person among the Acholi.

The Ajwaka

The *ajwaka* is the Acholi witchdoctor.   Seligman states that although
Juok is believed to cause hysteria, such seizures were rare in *ajwaka* for
each is supposed to have within him an ancestral spirit from which he
derives his power.[3]   The Acholi goes to the witchdoctor when he suffers
misfortune or illness, for it is the *ajwaka*'s task to divine the cause of
the trouble and undertake its cure.   The *ajwaka* divines by means of a
collection of small stones which are shaken up and down in a pot.   In
addition, he advises on all matters concerning ceremonies and the building
of ancestral shrines and counteracts the bad magic used by sorcerers and
those of envious disposition.   The *ajwaka* manages ordeals which are used
to settle a dispute and organises both the water ordeal and the fire
ordeal.[4]

The Jatal

The *jatal* is the Acholi sorcerer.   Seligman states that he is supposed to be responsible for the introduction of foreign substances into a
person's body causing disease.[5]   Formerly people suspected of sorcery
were killed and burnt.   The *jatal* was believed to be a monorchid and,
according to Driberg, should normally be killed at birth.   Grove mentions
the *latal*, who is supposed by many to owe his powers to the root of a
plant treated in a secret way and eaten.   If he has a grudge against anyone and is jealous he is thought to dance in his enemy's doorway and spit

(1)   Grove, *S.N.R.*, 1919, Vol.II, No.3, p.172.
(2)   Seligman, *Pagan Tribes of the Nilotic Sudan*, 1932, p.130.
(3)   *Ibid.*, p.128.
(4)   Grove, *op.cit.*, p.176.
(5)   Seligman, *op.cit.*, p.128.

blood on the lintel three nights in succession.   On the fourth night the enemy will die.[1]

Grove also mentions the *lajok* who can blight a person by means of the evil eye, and the *jonu* who is believed to have the power of turning himself into a leopard and so killing his enemies.[2]

Kwun

The *kwun* is a conditional curse.   If a person performs some ill-natured or violent act, such as refusing food to a starving person or kill-ing a thief, he must in future always act in the same way towards people in a similar position.   Should he fail to do this, the favouritism will be resented by those who have suffered at his hands and he will be killed by the *cen* of the injured person.   A conditional curse thus imposed may be inherited by a man's descendants.[3]

LIFE   CYCLE

BIRTH

Certain prohibitions are imposed on the mother, lasting four days after birth for a boy and three for a girl.   The prohibitions vary in type from village to village.   After this time the child may be taken out of the hut in which it was born.

Twins are welcomed because they are a manifestation of Juok.   At the same time they are regarded as dangerous and if both live their near rela-tives may die.   Twins are given special names according to sex.   Their father builds a special shrine and sacrifices are made at it.[4]

DEATH

Burial takes place soon after death, outside the entrance of the hut. A man is buried on the right hand side of the door and a woman on the left hand side.   The body lies in a flexed position with hands placed under the cheek.   A tree is sometimes planted on the grave and there are sacri-fices of sheep and goats.   According to Grove, chiefs are buried in a special chiefs' burying ground and the body of a chief is wrapped in skins and placed on a platform.   Sand is thrown on the body and the grave is filled in when the body begins to decompose.   A tree is planted on the grave and a fence is built round it.[5]   Seligman states that a rain-maker is buried in a leopard-skin covering and a special type of tree is planted at the head of the grave.[6]

A ceremony called the *apuni* marks the end of the mourning period.

---

(1)   Grove, *S.N.R.*, 1919, Vol.II, No.3, pp.177-8.
(2)   *Ibid.*, pp.178-9.
(3)   *Ibid.*, pp.179-80.
(4)   Seligman, *The Pagan Tribes of the Nilotic Sudan*, 1932, p.120.
(5)   Grove, *op.cit.*, p.159.
(6)   Seligman, *op.cit.*, p.113.

THE LANGO

The Lango are situated in northern Uganda immediately north of Lake Kioga. There has been considerable controversy over whether they are a Nilotic or Nilo-Hamitic people for they exhibit traits which are character- istic of both ethnic groups.

The Lango follow a mixed economy of cattle herding and horticulture. According to Driberg cattle were fairly numerous in most parts of the country, but the 1890-91 rinderpest plague ravaged the country and there was such a dearth of cattle that, as a result, bridewealth dropped to a few goats and hoes.[1]   Because of these cattle diseases the Lango have been forced to rely more on cultivation and they are diligent gardeners. Their countryside is savannah relieved by occasional hills, stone outcrops and patches of bush and forest.   There are numerous water-courses and marshes with thick weedy vegetation, although in the north west, above Lira, the savannah gives way to more hilly and wooded country, the rivers flow more rapidly between more sharply defined banks, and there is less flooding and choking vegetation.

SOCIAL   ORGANISATION
AND   POLITICAL   STRUCTURE

TERRITORIAL UNITS

The Lango are divided into four geographical divisions.[2]

    1.   Jo Moita.
    2.   Jo Kidi.
    3.   Jo Aber.
    4.   Jo Burutok.

These divisions are distinguished from each other by variations in custom and material culture.   Except for the rain-making ceremonies, they appear to have no social significance.   We are told, however, that the whole tribe may unite for defence or offence and that all speak the same language and have the same traditions.   According to Hayley marriage usually occurs within the tribe.[3]

THE LANGO VILLAGE

The most important political and social unit among the Lango appears to be the village, which consists of from 10-150 huts; it is not, and probably never was, fortified.   During recent years, villages have tended to break up and straggle owing to the cessation of inter-village raiding. Previously all homesteads were built close together and the village was a compact group so that it could be better defended.   Within the village, each family occupies a homestead and the huts are built to form a segment of a circle.   Formerly there were bachelor huts and girls' dormitories in the village.

(1) Driberg, *The Lango*, 1923, p.91.
(2) Hayley, *The Anatomy of Lango Religion and Groups*, 1947, p.38.   (3) *Ibid.*, p.40.

The Lango village is an economic unit, having its own fishing, grazing and water, all of which are held in common by the inhabitants. There is the *wang tich,* the group for horticultural co-operation, and the *jo dwi dyang,* the group for co-operation in herding cattle. The people of a village are more highly organised for economic activities than is usual among the Nilotes.

The village combines for defence and offence, and this was particularly the case in the past when there was much inter-village fighting.

There are various ceremonies in which all inhabitants of the village participate, such as those held at the time of building a new cattle kraal.

The accounts of the internal structure of a village are not at all clear. The available information suggests that the greater number of people in a village belong to a single dominant lineage, the chief of which is the *jago.* The other lineages present have their own lineage heads and probably all are aggregated to the most powerful lineage through various kinship ties.

Law only operates with any certainty within the limits of the village. There is no administrative or judicial body apart from the informal gathering of the village elders, who have the task of settling, with the assistance of the *jago* or *rwot,* any disputes which may arise among the inhabitants themselves or with people of other villages.[1] The elders of a village seem to have no means of enforcing their decisions against an offender, other than the weight of public opinion. Hayley states that the *jago* or *rwot* could settle disputes within their spheres of influence as their verdicts would be supported by the man power of their lineages and linked lineages against a recalcitrant family group or lineage.[2] The *jago* or *rwot* could, provided he had the backing of the majority of the village, maintain the balance between group interests or force submission if necessary. In legal matters his position is thus comparable to the position of the Shilluk *reth* and the Anuak headman and noble.

In inter-village disputes much depended on the overall relations between the two villages involved. In a nearby friendly village a man might obtain some compensation for his grievance. In an unfriendly village or one under another *rwot* he would probably gain nothing without starting an inter-village feud. The meetings of the elders were courts of arbitration rather than of judicial decision, and there was no machinery for the legal enforcement of their pronouncements.

In the absence of a powerful, centralised authority the responsibility in legal matters rests with the lineage and perhaps, in extreme cases, with the village. A crime committed affects all the members of the clans of the wrong-doer and of the wronged. The kinsmen of a wronged person demand compensation for the wrong; kinsmen are also responsible for the payment of compensation due from one of their members. Ultimately the whole village may be involved, particularly if the dispute is between members of different villages.

(1) Driberg, *The Lango,* 1923, p.208.
(2) Hayley, *The Anatomy of Lango Religion and Groups,* 1947, p.58.

The chief public delicts are sorcery, incest and sexual aberrations. The chief private delict is homicide. In the case of homicide a feud might begin if the relatives of the deceased decided to retaliate in kind against the killer or someone of his clan. The usual procedure is, however, for the murderer to take refuge in the bush or in another village until arrangements for compensation have been made. Since 1890, it appears, 7 head of cattle has been the average price, although occasionally a marriageable sister or daughter has been handed over instead of cattle. Of the cattle two bulls are slaughtered as a sacrifice to the spirit of the deceased, one heifer is given to the deceased's maternal uncle and the remainder belong to the next of kin of the deceased.[1] If the murder occurs within the clan the act is regarded as a sin and two bulls are sacrificed to propitiate the ancestors and the spirit of the deceased. Various payments are made in compensation for injury, adultery, seduction and theft, defamation and other wrongs.

The Jago (Village headman)

So far as can be ascertained from the literature, every village has a chief or headman who is also head of the clan most powerfully represented in the village. The jago's office is not necessarily hereditary, though the selection often falls on the son of the deceased headman. Should he be unsuitable the most capable among the eligible candidates is chosen.[2] The duties of the jago in his village include:

1. Organising and leading the fighting men of the community, regardless of which lineage they belong to, and so protecting the village from the attacks of other jegdi.

2. Settling disputes within the village with the help of the elders. If necessary the jago backs one side against the other and throws his influence and the support of his lineage into the scales to settle the matter by superior force.

The village organisation is based on egalitarian principles and the jago has only such power as is freely accorded him by the majority of the villagers. The Lango village is thus an economic, ceremonial, military and legal unit with a structure based on the position of a powerful lineage. The entire village owes allegiance to a commoner headman who is the symbol of its solidarity and its independence.

In spite of the autonomy and independence of each self-contained village unit and its hostility towards others, there are certain factors which make for co-operation among groups of villages. This is most clearly expressed in the allegiance which may be freely accorded to the ruodi.

The Rwot

The jago may obtain a following in neighbouring villages if his lineage is particularly powerful and his ability in war especially remarkable. A jago who has thus extended his sphere of influence and is the

(1) Driberg, The Lango, 1923, pp.210-11.
(2) Ibid., p.206.

war leader for a district becomes a *rwot*. Driberg says of him, "The *rwot* was the nearest approach to a chief which the Lango knew, his sphere comprising a varying number of *jegdi* - possibly only three, but in exceptional cases as many as nine or ten. His functions were almost entirely military., and although often elected clan headman, he owed his position largely to military success, combining with other *rwodi* for larger operations under a *twon lwak* or war leader (lit. 'bull of the crowd')."[1] Hayley likewise maintains that a *jago* with outstanding military successes would exert an influence over a wider sphere than one village, and neighbouring *jegai* would acknowledge their subservience to him and style him their *rwot*.

Among the Lango the position of the *rwot* appears to be more precarious than the position of the *rwot* of the Acholi. He seems to have depended largely on the allegiance of his followers in other villages and this allegiance was only accorded to him if he was both able and fortunate in war as well as the representative of a powerful clan or lineage in the district.

The Twon Lwak

The *twon lwak*'s title depends entirely on his success in war, and the question of the power of his lineage does not arise. He is the war leader under whom several *rwodi* used to combine although Driberg states that liberality in beer was of considerable assistance to one who aspired to be a *twon lwak*.[2]

By its nature the office of *twon lwak* is a precarious one. The *rwodi* support him in hope of success and booty, and in time of failure they desert him for more successful war leaders. "Thus we find many cases of men winning a wide reputation and much renown, in fact becoming paramount chiefs of a large area, suddenly losing their position and following almost entirely."[3] Occasionally a *twon lwak* kept his position until he died in battle, and was then succeeded by a son or brother with the requisite ability. Such a succession depends entirely on ability and not on descent.

The result of this system of war leaders was that each *twon lwak* endeavoured to obtain the allegiance of the neighbouring *twon lwak*'s villages. This was perhaps one of the main causes of the period of internal strife among the Lango just before the coming of the British.[4]

During battle the various *rwodi* and *jegdi* are under the orders of the war leader they have accepted, but in other circumstances they have a much sounder position, for they have a certain degree of civil authority "being elected to their chiefdomships on the grounds of heredity or convenience."[5] The *twon lwak* in time of peace has no recognition or privilege.

INTER-VILLAGE WAR AND FEUD

According to Driberg, who is supported to some extent by Hayley, the Lango were almost continually at war among themselves during the period before the British administration. Driberg describes the organisation as

(1) Driberg, *The Lango*, 1923, p.206.
(2) *Ibid.*
(3) *Ibid.*
(4) *Ibid.*, p.207.
(5) *Ibid.*, p.208.

"essentially military".[1]

In wars against other tribes, clubs, spears and shields were used in fighting.   In feuds between Lango villages a different method was practised.   If feeling between villages over some dispute was such that there was no basis for mediation by the elders, a whipping duel was held.   A tree was cut down and the branches were lopped off.   The warriors of each village drew up in a line on each side of the tree, armed with lashes 8 feet long, and they would whip each other across the tree until an umpire, standing at one end, judged that enough punishment had been given and taken and that feelings on both sides were sufficiently relieved. Skill in wielding the whip was admired and no spears were allowed to be brought.[2]

Driberg maintains that it was largely as a result of participation in the wars of the Bunyoro with the Buganda that the Lango began to fight among themselves in a more violent manner than the duel described above.[3] According to him there was a perpetual state of war and no one was safe outside his village.   Although inter-village relations appear to have been particularly hostile about that time, it would seem that Driberg exaggerated.   Certain factors made for a degree of village co-operation and some of these factors are mentioned by Driberg himself in his accounts.

1.   Lineages of the same clan were spread over a number of villages and this must have mitigated feuds to a certain extent.

2.   The age-set system and rain-making ceremonies were on an inter-village basis in three of the four divisions of the Lango.

3.   Co-operation for hunting occurred, several villages taking part in a hunt in a large *arum*.

4.   There was the practice of placing cattle in the kraals of other villages to avoid a whole herd being destroyed by rinderpest and perhaps to express friendship or kinship.

5.   A number of neighbouring villages would recognise a *rwot* and the powerful lineage in the district which he represented.   A number of villages would unite under the *rwot* for war, and in times of particular hostility they would unite under a *twon lwak*.

It therefore seems that the villages, though structurally differentiated and opposed to each other to a certain extent, were loosely organised into associations for defensive and offensive purposes.   These associations were, no doubt, of the vaguest type, and perhaps only temporary, and they appear to have entailed few legal or political consequences.

AGE SETS

Information on the *ewor* ceremony and the age-set system is given by Driberg alone.   He records their existence during the period of his stay

(1) Driberg, *The Lango*, 1923, p.205.
(2) *Ibid.*, p.106.   (3) *Ibid.*, pp.106-7.

among the Lango.   Twenty years later, when Hayley went to study the Lango, he found that they were no longer observed and even the memory of these ceremonies was fast dying out.

The Ewor is a quinquennial festival held for the purpose of honouring the aged and instructing the young men in the mysteries of rain-making. At the end of every 16 years there was a gap of 9 years, instead of the usual 4, after which the cycle began again.   For rain-making purposes the initiates, consisting of those who had reached puberty and had been accepted into the *etogo* groups at the last *apuny* ceremony, were divided into one of four groups.   These groups were named after certain animals.(1)

1. *Lyech* (Elephant):   associated animals are wart-hog, giraffe, and zebra.

2. *Kwaich* (Leopard):   associated animals are serval and merekat.

3. *Amorung* (Rhinoceros): associated animal is hartebeeste.

4. *Jobi* (Buffalo):   associated animals are lion and waterbuck.

Each *ewor* is named after one of these animal groups and the rain festivities for the following 4 years are said to belong to that group.   The *jobi* call the *lyech* their fathers and the *kwaich* call the *amorung* theirs.   The *jobi* and *lyech* have certain features in common as have the *amorung* and *kwaich*.   Each group has its own specific songs.

The *ewor* festival occurs in November at three different localities, in three of the four divisions of Langoland.   The fourth division of the Lango, Jo Aber, does not hold one.   All the young men, who have reached puberty and have not yet been initiated, gather at the assembling place for their district and with them are the old men whose group year it may be. The old men spend three days teaching the initiates their social duties, the traditions of the Lango tribe and the mysteries of rain-making - together with the rain-dances and songs appertaining to their group.(2) The initiates are secluded from the rest of the people and during this period there is a suspension of all hostilities within Langoland.   Any breaker of the peace is killed, and his village is burned.   Sexual intercourse is forbidden during this period.   On the fourth day the initiates return to the village after certain cleansing rites.   The old men perform rituals and the *ewor* festival is completed.   All the initiates take as their group the one which is in charge of the rain-making for that year, irrespective of their father's group.

There is little information on the functions of the age-set system. It is certain that they were bound up with the important task of rain-making and that the initiation ceremonies provided an opportunity for teaching the young men of the tribe the traditions, ritual and cultural heritage of their people.   Connection with the political system is limited to the fact that the local communities of each district combine for the ceremonies and a tribal truce is called during the period of teaching.

(1) Driberg, *The Lango*, 1923, p.244.   (2) *Ibid.*, p.245.

The Lango age-set system is a cyclical system, unlike that of the other Nilotic groups which consists of a straight progression of non-recurring sets. It is very similar to that of the Kipsigis and other Nilo-Hamitic peoples, and it is generally recognised as deriving from Nilo-Hamitic origins.

CLANS AND LINEAGES

Information on Lango clans and lineages is very confusing because the authorities do not clearly distinguish between the two.

Hayley defines the Lango clan as being an exogamous patrilineal group of persons, all the members of which hold themselves to be related to one another and all of whom trace descent back to one common ancestor.[1]   A clan has a common name for its members, a special cry and certain ritual observances.

Driberg, Tarantino and Hayley all agree that the clans have a tendency to subdivide. Driberg states that this process of bifurcation was largely facilitated by the fact that the clans separated considerably owing to war and migrations and that the members of a clan were not settled together in one area.[2]   Most of the Lango clans are found scattered throughout the four divisions of Langoland, so that it is the local branch of a clan, the lineage, which is the effective unit.

Hayley gives information on the *adit*, whom he terms the clan chief.[3] He states that the ceremony of *chibo adit me atekere* is celebrated when a new clan chief is installed. This clan chief is elected by the people's judgment and the son's seniority is not important. Olyech states that he must be a war leader and must also settle disputes which arise in his village.[4]   The installation ceremony consists of anointing the new chief and admonishing him to be brave in war, to treat the people well and to consider the advice and welfare of the old men and women. A week or two later the new chief must call the warriors together and practise war drill. He would have to show his powers as being the best of them all with his spear and shield. He would kill a bull for his warriors and they would pick the meat from the fireplace with their teeth, not using their hands. This was usually done as a method fo swearing an oath before a chief.

As the Lango clans are dispersed it seems probable that the clan chief is really a lineage head or chief, whose function it would be to care for the members of the lineage, settle disputes within it and lead the men of the local lineage in war. Hayley states that a local leader, by his prowess in war, would dominate the clans of his neighbourhood. These clans would ally themselves under him for protection and style him their *jago*. He also writes, "The tribe was therefore divided up into ever-changing territorial spheres under the influence of the *jagi* and *rwodi*. These territorial leaders were at the same time the leaders of their respective clans."[5]   It would thus appear that, as among other Nilotic

(1) Hayley, *The Anatomy of Lango Religion and Groups*, 1947, p.41.
(2) Driberg, *The Lango*, 1923, p.191.
(3) Hayley, *op.cit.*, p.104.
(4) Olyech, *Uganda Journal*, 1937, Vol.IV, No.4, p.317.
(5) Hayley, *loc.cit.*, p.56.

groups, a dominant lineage tends to be associated with a specific area.

There is some confusion as to whether exogamy is the mark of a clan. According to Hayley, if a clan divides the exogamy rule does not hold between members of the seceding and the parent clans.[1] It might appear that the mark of a clan and its separation from a parent clan is the fact that the members of the two might intermarry, and very often it is an instance of sexual relations between a member of each which brings about the decision that two groups are separate and independent in every respect.[2]

Any woman marrying into a clan is taught the clan observances by her mother-in-law and she keeps them after the ceremony of tying on the leather tail. There are certain variations in ceremonies from clan to clan, and ceremonies at birth and during the bringing up of children are especially variable.

The Jo Doggola

The *jo doggola*, 'the people of the doorway', is a lineage group - a group of agnates comprising all those descended through the male line from a given individual. It is a relative term, for the group of individuals concerned depends on the particular person who is selected as the point of departure.[3] Hayley states that the clan was a more important group than the lineage; but it is difficult to see how this could be if the clans are dispersed as recorded. He also admits that "in the ceremonies as given for the clan it was actually the *jo doggola* who performed, though theoretically the whole clan took part." The *jo doggola* were those members of the clan from whom help was sought when difficulties arose, so that the lineage "may be considered as the practical unit whereby clan interests were maintained".[4] It is a matter for investigation as to whether the clan chief, the *adit*, is really a clan chief or whether he is the head of a large and powerful lineage of a district.

INHERITANCE

According to Driberg property in land is held by all the members of a village, as are all the grazing and water rights. Any village may build on unoccupied ground. Within a village each household has the sole use of its own portion of land for as long as it may be wanted. The *arum*, the hunting district, is personal property, but the owner cannot refuse the right to settle there if it is requested, for he owns the hunting rights rather than the land itself.[5]

Cattle are the most important property and are inherited from father to son. The head of the homestead cannot, however, do as he likes with the herds, because each member of the lineage has property rights in them and they are held in trust for succeeding generations. They must be preserved and allowed to multiply and are only alienated when bridewealth is required or when compensation has to be paid for some offence committed

(1) Hayley, *The Anatomy of Lango Religion and Groups*, 1947, p.45.
(2) *Ibid.*, p.41.
(3) *Ibid.*, p.52.   (4) *Ibid.*
(5) Driberg, *The Lango*, 1923, pp.170-71.

by a member of the lineage.   If the cattle-owner wants to kill any beasts he must explain his reasons to the rest of his kinsmen and obtain their permission.

Driberg states that a man's eldest son is usually his heir.   If there are no sons property goes to the deceased's brothers or brothers' sons.   In any case, younger sons or unmarried males of the lineage have the right to assistance in marriage and thus share in the inheritance if only indirectly.[1]

The wives of a dead man, if they are young, are inherited by his sons; aged wives live with their children and are not inherited.   Driberg states that a widow has the deciding voice as to which of several possible candidates she will accept as a husband.   If a woman refuses to live with any of the available relatives and returns to her own family, all the bridewealth which had been paid for her is restored by her family and goes to the heir to obtain another wife for the lineage.[2]

MARRIAGE

The Lango are polygynous although most men have only one wife.   It is the duty of a father to provide a wife for his son if he has the means, and the bridewealth obtained on the marriage of a daughter is reserved for this purpose.

Bridewealth

Bridewealth is paid in cattle to the bride's family.   Whatever the amount received, the principles of distribution remain the same, according to Driberg.[3]   The bride's maternal uncle obtains one heifer, as does her mother, while one bull is given for killing to the maternal grandmother.   The remaining beasts are given to various relatives on the father's side.

During the whole period of negotiations the bridegroom avoids his future mother-in-law, since it is thought that otherwise she might die. Avoidance does not extend to other members of the bride's family nor does she herself observe any special rules of behaviour towards members of the bridegroom's family.   These rules of avoidance apply also to a man making clandestine love to a woman's daughter.

Marriage Prohibitions

Marriage is forbidden within the father's and mother's clans.   Marriage with the wife's sister is, in certain cases, permitted.[4]   The only time the Lango intermarry with other tribes is when women are captured in raids.   Lango women very rarely marry out of the tribe and Lango men do so even less frequently.

Marriage Ceremonies

Generally, there is no formal betrothal apart from arrangements

(1) Driberg, *The Lango*, 1923, p.174.   (2) *Ibid.*
(3) *Ibid.*, p.158.   (4) *Ibid.*, p.157.

regarding bridewealth made by the two families concerned. The choice of a partner is left to the young people themselves and they generally agree first and ask their parents' permission afterwards. According to Driberg the marriage takes place as follows:-[1] Some of the bridewealth is taken to the bride's village and a few days later the remainder is brought. The groom and his friends and father are anointed with oil at the bride's village and the bride's father and mother lecture her on her duties as a wife. Some days later the bride is captured by her husband and a symbolic struggle takes place. She spends the night with her husband and the following day a wedding-feast is held at her parents' village.

The Tweyo Lau

The *tweyo lau* is the real marriage ceremony which signalises the completion of the marriage. Marriage is an alliance between two clans as well as a union between two people and this is not finally consolidated until the birth of a child. The *tweyo lau* ceremony is performed when the wife is pregnant and a leather tail, which extends from the small of the back to the ground, is tied on.

Divorce

If a divorce occurs the bridewealth is returned to the husband. In theory the offspring of the original animals should be handed over as well, but in fact only a number equivalent to what was formerly paid is given back. Ill-treatment and neglect may make a wife leave her husband, while a husband may leave his wife because of repeated infidelity, barrenness and neglect of duties. If the wife is barren, a younger sister may be given as a substitute and in this case the bridewealth is not returned.

Kinship

Driberg gives a long list of Lango kinship terms in *The Lango*, pages 176-9. He remarks that a classificatory terminology is used, but descriptive terms are reserved for occasions when it is necessary to define the degree of relationship more accurately. Certain modification occur when widow inheritance takes place. A man inheriting a widow ceases to call her children brothers and sisters; instead, he assumes the status of father in his father's place. Thus, the brother of the widow, formerly his *nero* - maternal uncle, becomes his *oro* - wife's brother; her sister, formerly *toto* - mother, becomes his *amu* - wife's sister.

According to Hayley the *wat* includes all those people who are connected with a person through his father, mother, brother, sister or wife. It refers, in fact, to the grouping of immediate cognatic and affinal relatives. Between the members of the *wat* group there is an incest barrier and, unless a connection is no longer recognised, a man's wife has to be from a different clan.[2]

The mother's brother's family is known collectively as the *neo*. There is a privileged relationship between an *okeo* - sister's son, and

(1) Driberg, *The Lango*, 1923, pp. 157-8.
(2) Hayley, *The Anatomy of Lango Religion and Groups*, 1947, p. 55.

nero - mother's brother.   This is a form of joking relationship for, theoretically, the *nero* has to grant all requests for small gifts made by the *okeo* and the *okeo* may seize some of his *nero*'s property and make off with it.   The *okeo* also has a joking relationship with the wives of the *neo* of his own generation and this takes the form of abuse, jokes of a sexual nature, lewd gestures etc.   According to Hayley all these actions reflect the fact that the *okeo* is likely to inherit his *nero*'s wife one day.[1]   The *neo* group provides a refuge in time of poverty and these relatives may help him to obtain a wife;   a man may send his children to live temporarily or even permanently with their *nero* in difficult times.

The opposite kin category to the *neo* is the *okeo*, the husband's sister's family.   The *okeo*'s mother demands a bull on the marriage of the *nero*'s daughter, just as the *nero* demands a heifer on the marriage of his sister's daughter *(akeo)*.   A great deal of co-operation takes place between the *neo* and *okeo* groups, especially if a lineage is growing weak and is dying out.

RITUAL AND OTHER CULTURAL FEATURES

THE ETOGO GROUPS[2]

The *etogo* is a grouping of certain lineages or clans within a village. The *etogo* groups come together for ceremonies of a ritual nature - primarily to eat a ritually killed animal;   they are thus an 'interlineage ceremonial organisation'.   The most important members of the *etogo* are the old men belonging to each associated lineage or clan.   The initiated men of the younger generations are also full *etogo* members and take the place of the older generation when they die.   Women and children attend the *etogo* meals but sit apart.   The members of the *etogo* are divided into three groups for the ritual eating of meat in circumstances in which it is dangerous for a non-member to join them.   Each of the three groups eats a certain part of the animal.[3]   The head is given to the owner of the animal so eaten.   Only small pieces of the meat are eaten ritually and most of it is taken home by the owner and eaten later.   Three pots of beer are also brewed for the ceremony.

A man belongs to the same *etogo* group as his father and if a lineage or clan splits up the offshoots remain members of the same *etogo* group as the parent body.   If a man goes to live in a place remote from his own *etogo* group, however, he attends the celebrations of a local *etogo* although he sits apart from the main group of eaters.   He cannot himself become a full member of this *etogo* group but his son may be initiated into it. Thus, a man can only eat ritually in his own *etogo* group or in one with the same name as his own.   Each *etogo* group has a name.   It is a religious group in that the old men taking part are believed to have control over the spirit of a dead man, and owing to the nature of Lango beliefs there is a considerable degree of dependence on them.

(1)   Hayley, *The Anatomy of Lango Religion and Groups*, 1947, p.55.
(2)   Information is derived almost entirely from Hayley;   see also Driberg, *op.cit.*, p.191, for slight reference.
(3)   Hayley, *op.cit.*, p.49.

Some of the main occasions on which an *etogo* group functions are:-[1]

1. At the feast marking the end of mourning.
2. At the *apuny* ceremony for a dead man.
3. At the ceremony of drawing out the evil *tipo* from a sick man.
4. At the killing of a bull for sickness caused by an ancestral spirit.
5. At the digging up of a dead man's bones.
6. At the mixing of the seed before sowing a dead man's field.
7. At the ritual feast of the rain-making ceremonies.
8. At the *abila* for potency caused by an ancestral spirit.

Hayley states that at the tribal ceremonies of *apuny*, rain-making and the various other ceremonies, the *etogo* groups of a locality perform together. The age sets also linked up with the *etogo* groups.   According to Hayley the *etogo* groups have two main functions;   that of maintaining relations with the dead so that an ill-disposed ancestral spirit is not able to affect an individual adversely, and that of killing and distributing meat with the least possible friction.[2]

Initiation into an *etogo* group occurs at the time of initiation into the age sets.   On reaching puberty a boy chooses one of his father's *etogo* group members to be his 'adopted father'.   This father may not belong to the same lineage or clan as the boy, but he has to belong to the same meat division as that intended for him.   The first son eats at a different meat division from that of his father, the second son eats at the remaining division while a third son eats at the same division as his father, and so on in rotation.   "As soon as the *etogo* members began to eat the initiates sat near their adopted fathers and the fathers handed them pieces of meat to eat, thus initiating them into the *etogo* group."[3] The men of the generation below these fathers eat in a group apart and at the following *etogo* ceremony the initiates would join this younger group for the ritual eating of meat.   Later an initiated boy digs in his adopted father's fields and receives presents from him.   The boy is not allowed to marry his adopted father's daughter for he is in the position of son to him.   Boys who have been initiated into the *etogo* at the *apuny* ceremony are initiated into the tribal age-set system at the following *ewor* ceremony.

The Apuny Ceremony

The *apuny* is the final burial rite for the dead and should be distinguished from the *achuban*, or funeral feast, which is held after the burial of the body and immediately on the arrival of the relations.

The *apuny* ensures a good rainfall which the dead might withhold if not

(1) Hayley, *The Anatomy of Lango Religion and Groups*, 1947, p.50.
(2) *Ibid.*   (3) *Ibid.*, p.64.

propitiated by the ceremony. It takes place after the harvest, about November or December. Hayley maintains that the *apuny* was held for the dead every two or three years. The rain-maker of Aduku used to give the order for the celebration and, as the news spread, every village celebrated its own *apuny*. The ceremony was performed as a final burial rite only for a grown man and not for a woman or immature boy. The Lango believe that if it were not held the rain would not fall and the crops would not grow.[1]

At the *apuny* the various *etogo* groups of a village assemble together. Each group kills a bull in memory of a dead *etogo* member and the meat is then eaten ritually by the three meat groups into which the *etogo* is divided. During the eating the new generation is initiated into the group. As only one bull is killed by each *etogo* group it may be many years before the *apuny* is performed for a dead man if a number of *etogo* members have died about the same time. During the *apuny* ceremony it is considered very unfortunate to quarrel over the sharing of meat.

THE LANGO CONCEPT OF JOK

Jok is described as being like moving air; he is omnipresent, like the wind or air, but is never seen, though his presence may be felt in whirlwinds or eddies of air, in rocks and hills, in springs and pools of water and he is especially connected with rain-making.[2] All hills are connected with Jok and for this reason Lango villages are never built on hills for such close association with Jok would be dangerous. Although he is regarded as an indivisible entity permeating the whole universe, Jok is known under a number of titles corresponding to his various manifestations and activities.

Jok is considered to be responsible for all births but particularly for abnormal ones. Twins are welcomed, but the presence of Jok which is manifested in twin births entails numerous ceremonies to protect those who are affected.

Any inexplicable or mystifying occurrences are attributed to the presence of Jok. The failure of the rains, destruction caused by hail, lightning and locusts, are believed to be manifestations of Jok's power. Appropriate magical ritual is performed to meet such disastrous events.

Hayley records two main categories of disease: the Jok Lango diseases - so called because they have always been with the Lango - and Jok Nam diseases, which have come from the 'peoples of the lakes' - the Bunyoro and others.[3] Not all diseases are caused by Jok. Most of the Jok afflictions are psychic disturbances or virulent diseases. As soon as a person becomes ill he is taken to the witchdoctor who announces which specific Jok has taken possession of him and what ceremony should be carried out in order to effect a cure. Jok Omarari is believed to bring bubonic plague, Jok Adongo, Jok Orongo, Jok Abong, Jok Orogo are diseases causing a man to behave as though mad. Incurable diseases are not necessarily attributed to Jok.

(1) Hayley, *The Anatomy of Lango Religion and Groups*, p.63.
(2) Driberg, *The Lango*, 1923, p.217.
(3) Hayley, *op.cit.*, p.7.

Jok is sometimes associated with trees and often a certain tree becomes his shrine and offerings are made there and oracles received. According to Driberg, Jok Adongo is that aspect of Jok associated with trees.[1]

Jok is believed to be associated with the hunt and with fierce animals; if a lion, elephant or some such dangerous animal is killed it may afflict a member of the slayer's family with Jok Orongo unless a purifying ceremony is held.

In addition to these manifestations, Jok is believed to be the creator of the world and of man, the dispenser of death and the decisive force in determining the period of a man's existence. He is benevolent in that rich harvests are believed to have been sent by him, as also the rain which ensures a good harvest and the dry season favourable to hunting. Jok is always accessible to the prayers of the people and will give advice on all matters and problems through the agency of the witchdoctor (ajoka). He punishes neglect and those who doubt him. Driberg points out that, in spite of his power, certain aspects of Jok can be circumvented by the use of magic, even though magic was originally derived from Jok. The Lango do not systematise their beliefs in any way and are conscious of no contradictions.

THE LANGO ANCESTRAL CULT

Human beings and certain animals have a spirit or soul which the Lango call *tipo*. The wandering of the *tipo* is believed to cause dreams. The *tipo* is intimately connected with a certain manifestation of Jok known as *orongo*, it might even be called *orongo*.[2]

The *tipo* becomes important at death when it can afflict members of its own family and lineage. A malevolent *tipo* is called *chyen* and is thought to be the spirit of a man who has died with a grievance and who will wreak his vengeance on his descendants unless certain precautions are taken to appease and render it harmless.

The *tipo* eventually becomes merged in Jok but it does not lose its personality until the individual is forgotten by his descendants. Contact with the ancestors is maintained by the building of a shrine (abila) where certain ceremonies are performed and offerings made. The shrine looks the same as that built for Jok. The *tipo* takes up residence therein and from time to time makes his requirements known, either by calling on his descendants at night or by causing minor misfortunes which drive them to the *ajoka* who interprets the *tipo*'s wishes. A *tipo* who takes up residence in a shrine is offended by neglect but, if looked after, it will give advice and help in the same way as Jok. It requires no intermediary, but is in direct communion with the descendant who has built the shrine and is known as *won abila*, the owner of the shrine. If the *tipo* shows no sign of wanting a shrine, it is thought to have reverted fully to Jok. On a man's death any shrine built by him to an ancestral spirit lapses, owing to the belief that the *tipo* gradually loses its separate potency and usually, after one generation, becomes indistinguishable from Jok.[3] Occasionally

(1) Driberg, *The Lango*, 1923, p.218.
(2) *Ibid.*, p.229.   (3) *Ibid.*, p.231.

the *tipo* will give advice to others through the agency of the *won abila*.

Normally, the funeral ceremonies are enough to pacify a *tipo*, but some malignant spirits *(chyen)* bring sickness and misfortune on the family. Since the *chyen* cannot hurt people of other clans than their own, it is the task of the *etogo* group to deal with them and render them harmless. There are several ways in which this may be done. The *etogo* group may perform the ritual eating of an animal into which the offending spirit has been attracted; the *etogo* members cannot be harmed by absorbing it into their bodies. Another course is for an *ajoka* to entice the *chyen* into a pot in which he imprisons it. The pot is then placed in a swamp and the *chyen* is merged in Jok. The final extremity to which the *etogo* resorts is to exhume and burn the dead man's bones and so destroy his spirit. In all cases the *ajoka* is consulted to find out which ceremony is appropriate.

The Ajoka

Men or women may be *ajoka* but the most competent and famous have always been women.[1] The task of the Lango witchdoctor is to interpret Jok's will and, by magical processes, to safeguard and cure the members of the community. They give advice and treatment for all ailments, but some have acquired special ability to cure a particular disease. The *ajoka* may lay a troublesome *chyen*, and may perform certain operations on the sick, such as sucking out the causes of pains from a person's body; he also has an intimate knowledge of the use of herbs for certain magical purposes.

A person will consult an *ajoka* who will question the sufferer and divine the cause of the misfortune. Divination is usually done by means of shaking his rattle *(aja)* and by communicating with Jok or a particular manifestation of Jok. Sometimes the cause is divined by throwing the sandals into the air and reading Jok's will from the position they assume when they fall.

When the cause of a misfortune is revealed some ritual performance, the observance of prohibitions, sacrifices and so forth will be suggested as remedy. The *ajoka* is paid for his services and also usually receives payment from apprentices who help him at public performances and to whom he hands on his knowledge.

The *ajoka*'s profession is not necessarily hereditary. On the other hand the rain-maker, the *won kot*, usually hands on his office to a direct descendant. Often the *ajoka* is one of twins or is the mother of twins or, perhaps, has some physical or mental abnormality, for it is believed that Jok is particularly immanent in the abnormal and the unusual.

There are also *ajoka* who serve the cult of Jok Omarari, their sole task being to entreat Omarari by song to avert a fatal result from a person suffering from plague.[2]

The Abanwa

Jok Nam is the manifestation of possession. The *abani* are men or

(1) See Driberg, *The Lango*, 1923, p.234.   (2) *Ibid.*, p.239.

women who have been exorcised and who, in turn, exorcise those who are
possessed by Jok Nam.   If Jok Nam wishes to communicate with a man he does
so through the medium of one of his *abani*.(1)

The Ajok

According to Driberg there are two types of *ajogi* (sorcerers):   the
ading and *achudany*.

The *ading* works only by day and relies on medicines for his evil work,
although he may use parts of the body (hair, nail-parings, etc.) to work
magic against their owners.

The *achudany* is more malignant and is much dreaded.   He practises bad
magic for its own sake and kills indiscriminately, whether or not he has any
grudge or enmity against his victim.   This type of *ajok* has powers which
are hereditary and the son of a known *ajok* is considered to be an *ajok* as
well.   An *ajok* dances at night and goes out to lie near a person's doorway
where his stomach swells up to a huge size.   Shortly after this the owner
of the house dies.(2)   The *achudany* is a ghoul and is believed to haunt
new graves and feast on the bodies of the dead.   He also has the evil eye.
The punishment for practising sorcery is death.   Jealousy is believed to
be the root cause of the sorcerer's activities and his evil powers may be
directed against the whole community, as when the rain is prevented from
falling;   more often they are directed against individuals.

No *ajoka* will openly admit that he practises this form of magic as
well as good magic.

Winyo, the concept of Luck and Chance

Literally, the word *winyo*, which is found in other Nilotic dialects,
means bird.   In many instances it is used to refer to some quality which
a person displays at a particular time.   Hayley translates *winyo* as 'luck'
and maintains that, as some people seem to have better luck than others,
the causeless nature of this luck is conceptualised by the Lango in the
form of *winyo*.(3)   *Winyo*, in the sense of good luck, can be invoked to a
certain extent by special rites, and a father will give his son *winyo* before the latter goes on a journey.   On the night before a hunt, the *won
arum*, the owner of the hunting ground, will, with the help of his *etogo*
group, invoke good luck.

LIFE   CYCLE

BIRTH

Jok is associated with births, particularly with abnormal births.
At birth the mother is secluded for a number of days and certain ritual
precautions are taken.   If, after a succession of infantile deaths, a

(1)   Driberg, *The Lango*, 1923, p.239.
(2)   Hayley, *The Anatomy of Lango Religion and Groups*, 1947, p.30.
(3)   *Ibid.*, p.5.

child is born, it is given a depreciatory name in order to deceive mali-
cious spirits.   A number of ceremonies are performed by the parents when
a child is ill, for example, the *yeyo lyeto* which is performed at the time
of its first illness.   It consists mainly of a display of good-will on
the part of the mother's kinsmen, for, according to Lango belief, the
wife's clan can bring misfortune on the children of a union, or can cause
barrenness if they are displeased with her husband's clan.

Male children are named after grandparents, grand uncles and other
paternal relatives;   the third child is often named after one of his
maternal uncles.   Apart from the name given at birth, the name of an ancestor is given by the old men of the clan while the child is still un-
weaned;   this is not the ancestor's birth name but his nickname.   A number
of other names may be acquired during the course of a man's life, such as
a war-name, a name of invocation and so forth.   Girls have four names.(1)
The birth of twins is regarded as bringing luck on the family, the clan
and the whole village, and it is celebrated with considerable ritual.
Throughout the ceremonies the symbolic number two is constantly introduced.
Twins are given special names according to sex and order of birth.(2)

BURIAL

Lango men are buried on the right-hand side of the door of their
houses, women on the left-hand side.   In both cases the head of the deceased should lie towards the sunrise.   The legs are bent and the knees
drawn up to the chest.(3)   The funeral feast *(achuban)* is held as soon as
all the relatives have arrived.   No further ceremonies take place until
the next harvest when all the relations assemble and celebrate the *apuny*.
Twins are buried with special ceremonies and are put in large jars for
burial.

THE LUO OF KENYA

GENERAL(4)

The Luo, or Nilotic Kavirondo, inhabit the territories bordering
Victoria Nyanza, north and south of the Kavirondo Gulf.   Kavirondo is in
the south, a flat plain relieved by a few rocky tors and ridges upon which
the people build their homesteads;   in the north the country is hilly.
The rolling, grassy savannahs, the swamps, numerous water-courses and
patches of thornwood forest make it comparable to the environments of the
other more northern Nilotic tribal groups.

The country is suitable for pastoral and agricultural activities, and
the lake is rich in fish.   The people are mainly agricultural and grain
foods form the chief part of their diet.   Cattle, sheep and goats are
kept.   Cattle are the chief criterion of wealth.   Women and girls are
strictly forbidden to have anything to do with them and there is every
indication that cattle enter into the social life of the people to the
same degree as among the Nuer and Dinka.   Fishing plays a large part in

(1) Driberg, *The Lango*, 1923, pp.148-52.
(2) *Ibid.*, p.152.   (3) *Ibid.*, pp.166-7.
(4) Except for three articles by Evans-Pritchard, there is practically no inform-
     ation on the Luo of Kenya.

economic activities and although, formerly, there were organised hunts, today hunting is not much practised.

LUO EXPANSION

Until the time of European intervention the Luo appear to have been gradually expanding towards the south. This resulted in their division into two parts (on the north and south of the Kavirondo Gulf) namely: the Luo of Central Kavirondo and the Luo of Southern Kavirondo. Evans-Pritchard writes, "The southwards migration seems to have been across the Gulf from Uyoma and Asembo to Karacuonyo, and not round it, and to have taken place over several generations, commencing, if genealogies are to be trusted, about seven generations ago. Across the Gulf the Luo came up against the Bantu (Mwa) and Nilo-Hamitic (Langu) tribes."[1] The assimilation and absorption of these tribes was incomplete at the time of European occupation of the country. During this process of expansion there was a considerable dispersal of lineages so that lineages of the same clan are found in both Central and South Kavirondo. The Luo tribes least influenced by the Bantu are the Uyoma, Seme and Asembo and such tribes as pushed the southernmost Luo into Bantu country.

SOCIAL ORGANISATION
AND POLITICAL STRUCTURE

At the present time Luoland is divided into a number of administrative locations which vary considerably in area and population. These locations, according to Evans-Pritchard, correspond approximately to the old tribal areas of the Luo. The expansion of the Luo has divided them into two main groups with Kisumu location forming a narrow territorial link between them:

1. The Luo of Central Kavirondo, known as *Joiye* (the inside people).

2. The Luo of Southern Kavirondo, known as *Jooko* (the outside people).[2]

THE TRIBE *(Piny)*

Among the Luo the tribe is an autonomous political unit. Like the Nuer tribes it may be defined in terms of the way in which homicide was formerly regarded and treated.

Compensation for homicide *(cut)* takes the form of handing over cattle, or a girl, to the kinsmen of a slain man so that heirs may be raised for him. Compensation is only paid for the killing of a tribesman, for men of other tribes, slain in war, raids or private conflict, are regarded as *wasigu*, enemies. On the other hand, compensation is not paid for killing a clansman, for such a deed is regarded as a sin, and propitiation and atonement have to be made by the sacrifice of an ox provided by the imme-

(1) Evans-Pritchard, *Rhodes-Livingstone Journal*, 1949, No.VII, p.2.
(2) *Ibid.*

diate kin of the slayer, and eaten by representatives of the entire clan.
It might, however, be insisted on that the slayer should marry a wife in
the name of the dead clansman and raise heirs to him.   Strangers having
close kinship links with a dominant clan, may refuse to pay compensation,
and they tend to regard killing as a sin, since the acceptance of compensation for homicide emphasised a distinction they are anxious to obliter-
ate.[1]   A Luo tribe can be defined as a unit in which compensation for
homicide is paid, or in which there is provision for payment and the
settlement of the feud.

The Tero Buru

Luo tribes were formerly separated from each other by the *thim* - a
stretch of bush country left unoccupied.   Between segments of the same
tribe there was no *thim*.   The ritual demonstration of *tero buru* took
place across these boundaries.   It was the custom of the Luo in the past
not to bury an important man, known for his wealth or for his military
ability, until the whole tribe, or a large part of it, had crossed the
thim and demonstrated in front of the homesteads of the neighbouring tribe.
The demonstration took the form of insults, challenges to fight and the
tempting parade of cattle.   It was a matter of honour for the challenging
party to stand their ground and defend their herds with their lives.   Such
demonstrations were also made against neighbouring Bantu who had a similar
structure to that of the Luo tribes.   The demonstrating party was not
usually attacked unless two *buru* parties of opposing tribes met.   Sometimes, however, the opportunity was taken to try and raid the cattle of
the neighbouring tribe.

Payment of compensation and the *tero buru* are the two main indications of tribal separation.   In addition there is the association of a
specific lineage unit with a tribe.

CLANS AND LINEAGES

Each Luo tribe has a dominant clan or lineage.   The clan *(dho-ot)*,
has a lineage structure and lineages are differentiated by adding to the
name of the clan or larger lineage *ma* and the individual name of the
smaller branch.   Formerly, the clans were exogamous but today the larger
clans are not always so.   Within the large clans maximal lineages can
intermarry when the distance between them has become great enough.

Where the separation between two lineages has not proceeded far
enough or where two clans are closely related there is a socially recognised form of love-making called *codo*, which takes place between the young
men and girls of both groups.   Marriage is not permitted until the
separation has proceeded further.   After some generations the less approved type of marriage *(por)* may be permitted.   This is marriage by abduction and it is eventually replaced by the ordinary form *(meko)* when
the complete separation and distinctiveness of the units is recognised.[2]

A man is forbidden to marry a women who is a *wat*, a cognatic relative.

(1) Evans-Pritchard, *Rhodes-Livingstone Journal*, 1949, No.VII, p.4.
(2) *Ibid.*, p.7.

Among the Luo a man is excluded from marrying into clans as distant as that of his maternal grandmother or into the maximal lineage of his maternal great-grandmother. Thus a Luo man may not marry his kin, but only *wasigu* (enemies) with whom no kinship is recognised. It is, therefore, difficult for a man to marry into a clan or lineage within his own tribe. The system of exogamy assists in the structural differentiation of a tribe but also it creates relations of a personal and kinship nature between individuals of two different tribes.

The relationship between kinship and territorial units seems to follow closely the pattern found in other Nilotic tribal groups. In the Alego tribe, for example, we are told that there is a dominant clan, the Jo Alego, and its maximal lineages, the Jo Sege and the Ka Denge. There are a number of other clans and large lineages living in the tribal territory as well as small stranger groups and individuals. The presence of these clans and lineages in Alego, and their relations with the Jo Alego, are accounted for by traditions or myths in which stranger lineages and the lineages in possession (which are personified) intermarry, and the stranger lineages assume the position of in-laws. Other tribal areas have a similar structure. Evans-Pritchard states that the relative values of lineages are the same as with the Nuer. In opposition to other maximal lineages a man will give the name of his own maximal lineage but when speaking of an opposed smaller lineage he will give his own immediate lineage, the particular branch of the maximal lineage to which it belongs.[1]

The Dominant Clan

The dominant clan is usually identified linguistically with the tribe. Thus, Alego means both the tribesmen of Alego tribal territory and the patrilineal descendants of Alego. Members of the dominant clan alone are *jopiny* or *jogweng* - the people of the land and the owners of it. The rest are *jodak* - the separated people, the strangers. Stranger lineages are grafted into the lineage structure of the dominant clan so that, through recognition of female links, the whole tribe may be regarded as a system of cognatic lineages. The Luo refer to the affiliated stranger lineages as *kaorce* - lineages of in-laws, or *kaner* - lineages of maternal uncles, since it is from them that they take their wives and the mothers of their children.[2]

For general purposes the *jopiny* and *jodak* are on equal terms and co-operate in matters of common interest. The differentiation only appears in matters of ritual, in marriage regulations and when homicide occurs. In recent times the differentiation has become plainer through land disputes. Formerly there was enough land for everyone and more could be obtained by war and migration. Now, there is considerable inter-lineage enmity about land. The *jopiny* claim the land in virtue of their ownership of the tribal territory and as proof of this they point to the ancestral graves. Stranger lineages which are numerous and powerful may also claim to be *jopiny* in the same area and, having dwelt there for some generations, can also point to their ancestral graves. It is the general rule that a lineage has the right to cultivate land where its forebears have lived for several genera-

---

(1) Evans-Pritchard, *Rhodes-Livingstone Journal*, 1949, No. VII, pp. 10-11.
(2) *Ibid.*, p. 14.

tions.   Sometimes several lineages can claim this right, and the structural differentiation and the type of connecting link between them is revealed in the resulting disputes.

IMPORTANT MEN AMONG THE LUO

There is no real political office in the Luo tribes, but there are a number of people who are of notable status.

The Ruoth

The *ruoth* is simply an influential man.   He is richer in wives and cattle than most people, and he may help a poor man to marry by giving him a cow.   Any man may become a *ruoth*, although he is usually a member of the dominant clan of the tribe.   No such political or ritual significance are attached to the Luo *ruoth* as are associated with the Lango and Acholi *rwodi*. [1]

Thuondi

The *thuondi* are warriors of reputation.   They lead all the raids against the tribal enemies.   Their position depends entirely on individual ability in war, and therefore they are not necessarily succeeded by their sons.

The Won Gweng

The *won gweng* is the father of the land and a man of influence in every district.   He is a senior member of a lineage of the dominant clan of the tribe, and settles land disputes within the tribe.   He also sacrifices to the sacred spear of the clan, and points it towards the enemy before a tribal war begins. [2]

RITUAL EXPERTS

The *jabilo* is the most important of the ritual experts and the chief tribal figure.   There may be more than one *jabilo* in each tribal segment, but usually one is more influential than the rest.   The *jabilo* inherits his position from his father.   His functions include divination of the fortunes of war, cursing the enemy and making magic to secure victory. Although he does not accompany the warriors, the *jabilo* receives part of the spoil in return for his services and is, therefore, usually a *ruoth* - a rich man.   A further investigation of the *jabilo*'s place in society would be particularly interesting.   It is said that he was also a peacemaker and could intervene in a fight by dragging his leopard-skin along the ground between the two opposing sides. [3]   The *jabilo* sometimes exercises the functions of rain-maker (*jakoth* or *won koth*).

Luo tribal structure appears to be, in all essentials, similar to that of the Nuer;   the typical segmentary lineage structure, associated

---

(1)   Evans-Pritchard, *Rhodes-Livingstone Journal*, 1949, No. VII, p. 5.
(2)   *Ibid.*, pp. 5-6.
(3)   *Ibid.*, p. 6.
        cf. Nuer leopard-skin chief.

with territorial unit, is not organised round a symbolic office such as the Shilluk *reth*ship, the Anuak nobility or the Acholi chiefship. The inter-action of the segmentary system is the basis of organisation and co-operation. The Lango organisation closely approaches that of the Luo but, until further information is forthcoming as to the exact position of the Lango *rwot* and the policican importance of the lineage system, the degree of similarity is difficult to determine. On the basis of present know-ledge it would seem that the Lango, with their hierarchy of village headman, *jago* and *rwoth* are more highly organised than the acephalous Luo, with their ritual experts, elders and lineage heads.

THE LUO HOMESTEAD

The homestead, the residence of an elementary, or sometimes a joint, family, is generally called a *dala* (Bantu) or *pacho* (Nilotic). It is sur-rounded with a thick hedge of euphorbia, in which is a narrow gap forming the entrance to the kraal round which are grouped the huts and granaries.

According to Evans-Pritchard, there is no real village group. The head of the homestead is the head of the family occupying it. Each married man has his own hut, with huts for his wives on either side. Unmarried women live in a hut looked after by an old woman, and single men occupy a bachelors' hut near the gate in order to guard against cattle thieves. Sons often go and found their own homesteads if they wish to be independent. The eldest son eventually builds his wife a hut of her own outside his father's homestead and the younger brothers will later do the same. The large polygynous family thus splits up gradually as the sons extend their own family units and form separate homesteads. This process is completed with the death of the original *won dala* and the inheritance of the widows. The first wife is the chief wife of the homestead, but a husband sets aside so many cattle for each of his wives for use by their families and these are inherited by the sons on the father's death.

INHERITANCE

Property is inherited by a man's sons or, failing sons, by his brother. A widow, on the death of her husband is inherited by one of his brothers, by a distant kinsman, or, if she is still young, by a son born of a different wife. The widow is *ci liend*, 'the wife of the grave',[1] and children born to her are called after the dead husband who is regarded as their *pater*.

MARRIAGE

Bridewealth

The number of bridewealth animals varies according to circumstances. Before the cattle plagues at the end of the 19th century 20 to 40 cattle were given; in 1932 the usual number was 15 to 20, and since that time the number has been further reduced. According to Evans-Pritchard the bride-wealth cattle fall into two parts:[2]

1. The *dho keny*: the animals first handed over by the husband and due to

(1) Evans-Pritchard, *Africa* XX, 1950, p.141.   (2) *Ibid.*, p.139.

certain relatives. According to Shaw these represent the conventional payment which is made without question or discussion.[1] They are the basic minimum required if the marriage is to be concluded. One or two at a time are transferred over a period of about two years.

2. The *dho i keny*: additional cattle, the number of which is determined after lengthy negotiations between the husband's people and the wife's people. They average about 5 to 7. A number of goats are also handed over. If the two families are very friendly the transfer of the last animal may be postponed until the marriage of a daughter of the union.[2]

The father of the bride gets the bulk of the animals, most of which will be used as bridewealth for the marriages of his sons. The bride's maternal uncle gets a heifer and, according to Shaw, her paternal uncle gets a bull and heifer.[3] Usually the bride's family make some return gifts to the bridegroom's people, amounting to at least three head of cattle.

If there is a divorce the husband can demand the return of the cattle with their progeny. Usually every effort is made to avoid repaying bridewealth and the wife is often replaced by a sister or cousin. If two children have been born no bridewealth cattle would be returned if the wife died or left her husband; if there were only one child the bridewealth would be returned but two or three beasts would be retained.

Marriage Ceremonies

According to Evans-Pritchard, there are two forms of marriage: *por* and *meko*.[4] *Por* is marriage by elopement, and is regarded as shameful. Usually the girl's parents accept the situation and the union is regularised by the acceptance of some cattle - but fewer than is normal. *Meko* is the correct and usual form of marriage; a long chain of events intervenes between the time of obtaining the parents' permission to marry, and the marriage itself. It takes several months to complete a marriage, sometimes several years, according to the individual family circumstances.[5]

When the parents on both sides agree to the proposal of marriage, there follows the ceremonial capture of the bride - the *mako nyako*. A mimic fight occurs between the bride's people and the bridegroom's party, and the bride resists to show that she is not eloping. She goes to the bridegroom's village and is deflowered in the presence of witnesses. She is given a girdle with a tail *(cieno)* which she wears as a sign of her new status.

The *diero* and *lupo* ceremonies take place within a few weeks and are followed by the *duoko* party, which consists of a visit to the bride's parents and the paying of respects to her mother. There is feasting, singing and drinking through the night, and a few days later the bride returns to her parents' home. The bride now spends part of her time with

(1) Shaw, *JEAUNHS*, 1932, Nos. 45-6, p.45.
(2) Evans-Pritchard, *Africa*, XX, 1950, p.139.
(3) Shaw, *op.cit.*
(4) Evans-Pritchard, *op.cit.*, p.132.
(5) Shaw, *op.cit.*

the bridegroom and part with her parents.   The bridewealth payments now
begin and the wife's parents try to hurry up the payments by luring her
home on frequent visits.   The bridegroom cannot prevent her departure or
demand her return.   To get her to return he hands over another animal and
she then stays with him for a short while.   This procedure is repeated
until the bride is definitely recognised as his wife and stays with him
except for brief visits to her old home.

The *riso* ceremony is the binding act of marriage.   After it the husband is entitled to redress if the wife has intercourse with other men.
As the husband is anxious to start a home and cannot do so while his wife
keeps running back to her parents, he presses for the *riso* ceremony to be
held as soon as he has paid 6 to 12 head of cattle.   It is rare for a
marriage to be broken off after this stage has been reached.   The *riso*
ceremony is held in the husband's homestead and is a day of celebration.
The wife is given a series of presents by her husband's people, each gift
being named as it is presented to her.   She herself keeps none of them
and they are taken by the girls of the *riso* party from her parents'
village.

The final ceremony takes place a few months later when the husband
tells his wife to cook for him instead of cooking in his mother's hut.
Usually after the birth of the first child be begins to built an *ot* - a
proper dwelling; up to this time the couple have lived in the bachelors'
hut *(simba)*.   Necessary household articles are collected by the wife from
her parents' home and so, after a great number of ceremonies and rituals,
the union is accomplished and the basis of a family is laid.

RESPECT *(LUR)*

The Luo practise extensive avoidance as a part of the general attitude of respect to a wife's family.   A man turns his back to his parents-
in-law when speaking to them and avoids them if he meets them on a path.
He never visits his mother-in-law naked.[1]   This attitude of respect is
extended to all the members of his wife's lineage, particularly the older
people, and including the lineage of her maternal uncle.   The husband's
brothers, on the other hand, respect only his parents-in-law and immediate
kin of their generation.

The avoidance rules are relaxed as the marriage gradually grows more
stable and children are born.   A ceremony is held at the birth of the
first child to enable the husband to enter his mother-in-law's hut and
eat there.   The husband and his brothers are invited to eat after a goat
has been presented to them.[2]

RITUAL   AND   OTHER
CULTURAL   FEATURES

RELIGIOUS BELIEFS

The Luo believe in a supreme being whom they call Nyasi.   He is

(1) Evans-Pritchard, *Africa*, XX, p.141.   (2) *Ibid.*

believed to be the creator and originator of all things but he is not worshipped. Birth and death are ascribed to his action. According to Roscoe, Nyasi is found in large trees, and in time of trouble or sickness offerings are made to him of an animal killed under a large tree; the meat is eaten at a little distance away.[1]

Johnston states that the Luo believe in a supreme god, Chieng, which is the name for the sun.[2] Stam, however, relegates the sun to an inferior position and writes that when a man comes out of his house in the morning he spits to the east and then to the north, south and west and implores the sun to give him good luck.[3] Northcote states that Luo worship the sun and, to a lesser degree, the moon. A similar spitting ritual is practised when the new moon appears.[4]

It is impossible at present to give a comprehensive account of Luo beliefs from the scanty information available.

ANCESTRAL SPIRITS

There is very little information on the ancestral cult. Evans-Pritchard describes a troublesome ghost *(jacien,* pl. *jociendi)* and the Luo methods of dealing with it. *Jacien* is the Luo equivalent of the Shilluk *cien,* the Acholi *lacen,* Lango *chyen* and the Anuak *acieni.* A spirit which has been forgotten by the living; the ghost of a man who died resentful or angry - or of a murdered man whose kin have not exacted revenge - any of these may become a *jacien,* and cause harm to those who wronged it. The Luo regard ghosts as one of the principal causes of sickness and other misfortunes, and, since it is held that almost any wrong done to a kinsman may be punished by him after death, this belief is a powerful sanction of conduct within the family and kinship group.[5]

The diviner *(ajuago)* discovers the cause of sickness and, if it is due to a particular spirit, sacrifices are offered at his grave with appropriate ritual. If the ghost is not appeased by this attention, another magician is called in, the *mugalu.* To protect the sick man's homestead the *mugalu* buries in or near it a pot containing medicines. In the last resort the *jadilo* is called in; an ox is sacrifices and the ghost warned that if he does not cease his activities his bones will be dug up, burned and the ashes thrown into the lake or marsh.

Normally, a ghost only haunts a kinsman, but a man who has been murdered may haunt his murderer. Purificatory rites are performed for someone who has killed a man in battle; these are conducted by a man called *jagut* who has himself slain a man in battle.

It is believed that some ghosts become nature spirits dwelling in water and air, while others occupy the gourds used by diviners and answer the questions put to them.

(1) Roscoe, *The Northern Bantu,* 1915, p.291.
(2) Johnston, *The Uganda Protectorate,* 1902, Vol.II, p.791.
(3) Stam, *Anthropos,* 1910, p.360.
(4) Northcote, *J.R.A.I.,* 1907, p.63
(5) Evans-Pritchard, *Man,* 1950 (July), No.133, p.86.

RAIN-MAKING

Little information is available on the processes of rain-making among the Luo. Roscoe states that it is an important ceremony and is performed by a *musoga* priests who lives among the people for this purpose.[1] According to Northcote, the rain-maker is greatly esteemed, and his homestead is usually found near a big tree which is considered sacred. When rain is wanted, he gathers some herbs, puts them in a large pot of water and boils them under the tree. He draws off a little into another pot and, sucking it up through a reed, squirts it into the air, after first blowing through the reed and making the pot bubble.[2] Evans-Pritchard mentions that the Luo rain-maker is called the *won koth* and that sometimes his functions are combined with those of the *jabilo*. Rain-makers among the neighbouring Bantu seem to have a higher reputation than Luo *jakoth* and are often consulted.

WITCHCRAFT

Sickness is thought to be due either to the malevolence of a ghost or, more frequently, to magic worked by some envious person who wishes to bring misfortune on his victim.[3] In either case the aid of a witchdoctor is sought and he, by means of various incantations, discovers the cause and the culprit. A sorcerer may cause death by spearing the shadow of his victim, by working spells, by hiding certain objects near the house which bring sickness to the inmates. If a ghost is causing trouble the witch-doctor prescribes offerings and sacrifices necessary for appeasement. He also discovers thieves, conducts ordeals and divines the causes of events. He makes counter-magic to defend people against the activities of sorcerers and is the general prescriber of all cures. Johnston mentions a 'deeper magic' *(jamkingo)* which, among the Gemi tribe is practised by the blacksmiths.[4]

LIFE CYCLE

BIRTH

After the birth of a boy the mother stays inside the house for four days; for a girl, she stays inside for three days. The father of the child does not eat or sleep in the hut until the child begins to cut its teeth.

Twins are considered lucky; their arrival is attended by many ceremonies and by propitiatory dances.

PUBERTY

Until marriage, girls help their mothers in the fields and assist them in cooking and carrying. Boys help in herding the animals. At puberty both boys and girls have their front lower teeth extracted and for four days they remain in their homes. After this period they go about visiting

(1) Roscoe, *The Northern Bantu*, 1915, p.292.
(2) Northcote, *J.R.A.I.*, 1907, p.64.   (3) *Ibid.*
(4) *The Uganda Protectorate*, Vol.II, 1902.

friends and receiving presents of fowls.   Girls, in addition, have their
bodies scarified on the sides and back.   From this time on until marriage
the boys live in the bachelors' hut and the girls in the unmarried women's
quarters.   There is no mention by any of the authorities of an age-set
system.

DEATH

The dead are buried close to their homes, a man on his right side with
the hand under the head and a woman on her left side, also with the hand
under the head.[1]

Friends and relatives gather shortly after death and, if the deceased
was a man of importance, the whole of his clan is represented.   Every man
brings his companion bull and rides it.   All dress up as if for war and
the *buru* party takes place.   If the dead man was not very important the
mourning is limited to shaving the head and painting the body with white
clay.   Offerings are put on the grave of the deceased.

THE DINKA

GENERAL

The Dinka country neighbours that of the Nuer, and is similar in
character.   The land is flat and low with extensive stretches of permanent swamp, choked with vegetation and dotted with small islands;   these
have provided refuge in times of invasion and raiding.   In the west of
Dinkaland the ground is higher and begins to merge into the countryside of
the ironstone plateau, changing from swamp savannah to thorn and forest
savannah;   the vegetation and the hydrological conditions are noticeably
different from those further east.

ECOLOGICAL CONDITIONS

The ecological cycle of the Dinka is similar to that of the Nuer.
They pursue a mixed economy but all their affections are centred on their
herds, and cattle play as important a part among them as they do among
their neighbours.

From an account given by Stubbs and Morison we can obtain the following outline of the Dinka annual cycle:[2]

May: Cattle are brought from the dry-season camp.   The animals are
tethered on the arable land at night and manure it.

May - June: the time for preparing the ground and sowing the land
lying nearest to the flood level.   By sowing there first a succession of
crops is obtained and the maximum amount of land used.

July: the cattle go to the high (*gok*) pastures on the uncultivated
rising ground near the village.   The young men and women go together to

(1) Johnston, *The Uganda Protectorate*, 1902, Vol.II, p.793.
(2) Stubbs & Morison, *S.N.R.*, 1938, Vol.XXI, Part II;   pp.251-65.

look after the herds and the old men and mature women remain in the village
to weed and tend the growing crops

August - September: the first harvest is gathered.

September - November: a succession of harvests are now gathered; the
cattle return from the *gok* pasture and are brought to the cultivations where
they consume *dura* stalks. At night the cattle are tethered in one large
cattle camp.

December: the country begins to dry up and nearby grazing and the
plains *(toich)* become available for pasture. Sometimes the cattle are
tethered on the cultivations after the harvest for manure, but when the dry
season is well advanced the pastures near the village become exhausted and,
as it is too far to drive the cattle out and back again, the whole population, except for the older people, moves into a dry-season camp. During
the dry season the sheep, goats and a few milking cows are kept in the
village in the care of the old people; these animals are allowed to find
what pasture they can and their manure is useful for the sowing of the early
crops.

December - May: the dry-season cattle camp is usually situated either
on the banks of a river or water-course which never completely dries up, or
at the edge of the permanent swamps. Here the cattle feed on creeping
water weed which is very fattening.

The dry-season camp consists of a circle of little huts, with smoulder-
ing dung fires, the circle having an outside fence of branches or thorns,
and a forest of tethering pegs.[1] Sometimes the people live in the open
with windscreens, and cattle and men sleep close to dung fires to keep off
mosquitoes.

The cattle of a sub-tribe are, during the latter part of the dry
season, herded together by clans in a sub-tribal cattle camp on the dry-
season grazing grounds.[2] A plan of a Cic dry season camp, given by
Seligman, shows that within the vast sub-tribal camp the village grouping
is followed, each village having its own section of the camping ground.[3]
The local wet-season divisions are maintained but, at the same time, are
merged in the larger tribal sub-division. This is similar to Nuer practice and, in the same way, the necessity of transhumance brings about an
annual structural transformation. The relationship of village to village
is replaced by more concentrated grouping, and the closer bonds of the
various segments of a sub-tribal camp.

The ecological cycle of the Dinka is determined by the necessity for a
mixed pastoral and horticultural economy. There seems to be the closest
similarity to that of the Nuer, except that their use of manure seems to
differentiate Dinka methods of cultivation from those of other Nilotes and
the Dinka have a short period in a wet-season cattle camp, the *gok* pastures.
As with the Nuer, the needs of the cattle are put first and the year is
similarly divided into two parts; the transhumant movement and the

(1) Tetherington, *S.N.R.*, 1927, Vol.X., p.176.
(2) Stubbs & Morison, *S.N.R.*, 1938, p.260.
(3) Seligman, *Pagan Tribes of the Nilotic Sudan*, 1932, opposite p.141.

ecological cycle in general, have similar political and social repercussions.

SOCIAL ORGANISATION
AND POLITICAL STRUCTURE

TERRITORIAL UNITS

The Dinka consist of a congeries of independent tribes spread over a vast area.   Although there are regional variations, all available information suggests that there is an essential similarity of social organisation, structure and belief.   Information is drawn from Tetherington on the Raik Dinka of the Bahr el Ghazal, Bedri on the Padang Dinka of the northern areas, Seligman on the White Nile Dinka, and Stubbs on the Malwal Dinka.

The Homestead

Members of the Dinka homestead consist of an enlarged family group with the huts of married males built together in a circle.   The group owns a number of cattle, each member having rights in the family herd.

The Village

The village group of each tribe often straggle over a large area, for the homesteads are separated by spacious cultivations, and these and the building sites have to be above flood level.

The Cattle Camp

The wet-season camp consists mainly of the youths and girls of one village or possibly of one or two closely connected neighbouring villages. The dry-season camp, on the other hand, consists of people from all the villages of the sub-tribal section, although within the camp the various village groups maintain a certain degree of separation.

THE TRIBE

There is at present, no information on the sub-tribal sections.   The tribe consists of a number of lesser segments and occupies a continuous territory.   Whether or not the tribe is a unit in which compensation is paid in case of disputes between members (as among the Nuer) is not yet known.   It is the largest unit combining habitually for defence and offence, and each contains a number of patrilineal clans which trace their descent from a mythical common ancestor.

The Dinka appear to use a general term 'wut' which is applied to several territorial units.   According to Bedri the wut is a collection of clans or lineages which originally combined for defensive purposes.   In the dry season when the Dinka move down to the river, all the cattle of one wut graze together.[1]   If the wut is a collection of clans or

(1) Bedri, *S.N.R.*, 1948, Vol.XXIX, Pt.I, p.42.

lineages, as thus asserted, it would seem that the term can be applied to
any territorial group larger than a homestead or hamlet, the members of
which belong to one lineage.   A *wut* may, therefore, refer to a cattle
camp, a village settlement and possibly to a district of a tribal section.[1]

KINSHIP UNITS

The word for clan varies from tribe to tribe.   Among the Bor, according to Seligman, it is *ut*;   among the Than, Aliab and Malwal it is *gol*;
among the Cic it is *deb*;   and among the Padang it is *din*.   Confusion en-
sues from the fact that the word for clan is also used to mean 'the cattle
camp round one hearth', the homestead and the local kinship groups.

Stubbs gives an account of the characteristics of the Malwal Dinka
gol.   He states that the members of a *gol* consider themselves blood relations and claim descent from a common forefather who is a legendary hero.
Intermarriage between members of the same *gol* is considered incestuous and
customary law renders the *gol* liable to contribute cattle as compensation
for certain offences committed by individual members.   Each *gol* has a
recognised leader who claims descent from its founder, and each has its
totems.

Information given by Stubbs[2] suggests that the clan is a dispersed
exogamous unit and also has a segmented structure, local lineages being
scattered over the tribal areas in the various villages and subsections,
and even in neighbouring tribal areas.   Each lineage is controlled by its
lineage heads and elders, and it seems that within a *wut* the members of a
lineage build their homesteads near each other and herd their cattle in
common.[3]

There appears to be a co-ordination of territorial and kinship units
which suggests the type of segmentary organisation typical of the neighbouring Nuer tribes.

The Mendyor and Kic of the Northern Dinka

According to Bedri the Dinka clans are divided into two classes:-[4]

1.   *The Kic*, comprising the majority, are clans whose members have
not the right to ritual offices in the community.

2.   *The Dindyor or Mendyor* are the descendants of a holy man or of
incarnate spirits.   *Yendyor* denotes the daughters of holy men.   These
holy men are believed to have been the descendants of the seven sons of the
legendary Aywil Dit, and the clans claiming descent from them are scattered
throughout Northern Dinkaland in the same way as the *kic* clans.

All members of the *mendyor* clans are credited with supernatural
powers, and from them are chosen the spear-chiefs of each section of the

(1)   Stubbs and Morison, *S.N.R.*, 1938, p.253.
(2)   Stubbs, *S.N.R.*, 1934, Vol.XVII, Pt.II, p.244.
(3)   Seligman, *Pagan Tribes of the Nilotic Sudan*, 1932, opposite p.141.
(4)   Bedri, *S.N.R.*, 1939, Vol.XXII, Pt.I, p.125.

tribe.   It appears, therefore, that, among the Northern Dinka at least,
each village settlement and territorial unit has not only a number of
lineages but also a branch of the *mendyor* clan which acts as the 'ritual
lineage' for the whole unit.   The *kic* lineages are subordinate in ritual
spheres but the relationships between the two types in political and legal
matters are unfortunately not known.   It is, however, possible that a
local lineage of the *kic* may have the chief say in more mundane affairs;
this is indicated in the myth concerning Awiel, in which the chief who
adopted him is said to have kept the ownership of the land for himself and
his people.[1]   It is recorded that when the spear-chief is installed two
elders become 'viziers' at the same time, and these may possibly be representatives of the *kic* lineages.

THE SPEAR-CHIEF

The Dinka spear-chiefs are ritual experts and are also important
politically but the literature on them is unfortunately confused and it is
difficult to assess their exact political role.   Seligman states that "in
each tribe the most important man, the undisputed religious head who also
wields much civil authority, is the rain-maker, commonly known as the *ban
bith* i.e. 'spear chief' or 'expert' ".[2]   According to Stubbs, on the
Malwal Dinka, "The spiritual head of each *gol* is called the *'bang a bith'*
which means chief of the (sacred) spear".[3]   Cummins takes the *beng* as
the equivalent of sheik and maintains that the *beng* of a village is invested with the power of enforcing the laws and in this is supported by the
force of public opinion.[4]   Finally, Bedri, in discussing the northern
Dinka of the Upper Nile, mentions that in former days the various sections
had a leader, known as *beny riem* (or *rem*), who was the spiritual head of
his tribe, ceremonially installed and ceremonially killed.   In another
article he mentions the *beny rem* as being the chief of blood or chief of
warriors and says that he was the real power and authority of his country.[5]

It would appear that one or more spear-chiefs are associated with each
of the Dinka tribes.   Cummins states that there is a spear-chief in each
village, while Stubbs, who takes the *gol* to refer to a cattle-camp group
and to indicate a lineage group, states that the *bang a bith* is a chief in
such a unit.[6]   It follows, therefore, from the close association of the
kinship system with the territorial units of a Dinka tribe, that the spear-
chief is the symbol of the unity of his own lineage and also of the entire
unit of which his lineage is a part.   In ritual matters at least, his
lineage - a *mendyor* lineage with sacred associations - acts as the core
of the community, while the head of the ritual lineage, the spear-chief,
acts as the ritual leader.

There are also indications that the spear-chief plays an important
role in political organisation, since his lineage is in a powerful position
in the community and he is head of it.   The spear-chief is the most important man in a village and is also the head of a dry-season cattle camp,

(1) Bedri, *S.N.R.*, 1939, Vol.XXII, Pt.I, pp.125-9.
(2) Seligman, *Pagan Tribes of the Nilotic Sudan*, 1932, p.142.
(3) Stubbs, *S.N.R.*, 1934, Vol.XVII, Pt.II, p.247.
(4) Cummins, *J.R.A.I.*, 1904, Vol.XXXIV, p.156.
(5) Bedri, *op.cit.*, p.130.
(6) Stubbs, *S.N.R.*, 1934, pp.243-4 and p.247.

a tribal sub-section; there is no information about his status in larger tribal segments. It might well be that there is a *mendyor* clan associated with each Dinka tribe and a lineage of the clan associated with each tribal segment; if this is so the recognition of the spear-chief as the head of each lineage would be an important aspect of the cohesion of each unit and an organising force in structural relationships.

All authorities agree that the office of spear-chief is hereditary, but that the eldest son does not necessarily succeed his father. A young men would not assume the position until he reached middle age, although he might have been initiated into the rites by his father before his death. Bedri says that the *beny rem* must possess certain characteristics and qualifications; "he should be of very good character, and temperate, and ..... against bloodshed and any ferocious deeds, prone to forgiveness rather than punishment." If an heir is deficient in these qualities, then a brother or cousin, or any male member of the lineage may be installed.[1]

Spear-chiefs are so called because they have a particular form of spear *(bith)* or spears which are sacred and play an important part in cere-monies. Some of them are extremely old and have been handed down from father to son for generations. New spears are, nevertheless, accorded great respect, and on certain occasions may be made and consecrated. The Cic believe that at death the spirit of the spear-chief goes into his spear until it takes up residence in the new holder of the *bith*.

Every spear-chief has immanent in him the spirit of a great ancestor who has come to him down the generations, just as every Shilluk *reth* incarnates Nyikang,[2] and it is this which gives him his special powers and wisdom.

The spear-chief is ceremonially installed. A big feast is held fol-lowed by a religious ceremony, and the elders of both the *kic* and *mendyor* clans attend. All the young men parade in their dance apparel. Two bulls are sacrificed and are eaten by the elders, while the fire used for roasting them is taken to the spear-chief's house and becomes his fire. It is sacred and must not be extinguished until the day of his death, when it is put out together with all the fires of the tribal section.

At the actual ceremony of installation the *kic* elders place the spear-chief elect on an *ambach* bed and wash him in water; the *kic* and *mendyor* elders place two or more strings of ostrich egg-shells round his neck, crown him with a ring made from the mane of a roan antelope, and anoint his body. He then sits on the hide of a bull which has been sacrificed, and all who had any claim to the office of spear-chief cut off a portion of one of the legs of the hide and thus renounce their rights and swear loyalty to the new chief. The ostrich eggs are said to represent the lives of all the members of the tribal section of the spear-chief; one of the necklaces should be buried in a secret place and the other should be worn. It is said that the spear-chief could kill anyone instantaneously if he crushed a bead while pronouncing the victim's name.[3]

(1) Bedri, *S.N.R.*, 1939, Vol.XXII, Pt.I, p.130.
(2) Seligman, *Pagan Tribes of the Nilotic Sudan*, 1932, pp.195-6.
(3) Bedri, *op.cit.*

Bedri states that, among the northern Dinka, if a *mendyor* clan member who is very highly esteemed and of exceptional character becomes a spear-chief, he is known as *beny nial*, 'chief of heaven', and is held in greater honour and considered to have more power than the ordinary spear-chief. He is installed as the *beny rem*, but in addition is carried on an *ambach* bed on the shoulders of the elders. He imitates a dead man and the elders run with him towards each of the four points of the compass singing. The people then lower the ambach bed and, before it reaches the ground, the spear-chief jumps from it 'as if returning to life again'. He wears a leopard-skin which has been obtained by the warriors.[1]

The Dinka spear-chiefs are divine rulers but their period of existence is longer than that traditionally assigned to the Shilluk divine ruler. Spear-chiefs are not ceremonially killed until they themselves decide that they are too old to continue in office. According to Bedri, speaking of the Northern Denka, the practice of killing the spear-chief was not common at the time of government intervention but, if a *beny rem* has been raised on the shoulders of the elders on the day of his installation and is a *beny nial*, then he is more powerful and must be killed.[2] If he is killed, his spirit will look after the tribe and rule it until someone is chosen in his place; then his spirit enters into the new *beny nial*. If the spear-chief is left to die a natural death, his spirit will also die; the divine grace and virtue vested in him on behalf of his tribe will be lost and evil will befall the country.

There are several methods by which the spear-chief may be ceremonially killed. Bedri records that the elders enter his hut and suffocate him. His joints are broken and his limbs are stretched; he is buried secretly at night, usually in the bed of a water-course. All the fires of the village are extinguished and a fast is observed from the time of death till the burial. At the first harvest after his death, a big sacrificial ceremony is held. It is also recorded that a famous rain-maker and spear-chief was shut up in his barn with his first wife and favourite bull, and left to die of starvation. Seligman describes the procedure of burying alive the spear-chiefs of the Bahr el Ghazal Province.[3] If a *beny rem* dies by illness or accident a sheep is suffocated and the usual rites are performed. It is not always necessary to kill an ordinary spear-chief, and it is generally sufficient if a sheep is killed and buried with him at his death.

Duties of the Spear-chief

(a) According to Bedri, the spear-chief of the Northern Dinka is responsible for the initiation of all boys of the tribe when they attain the age of puberty. They parade in front of him in their age classes wearing war costume. The spear-chief does not teach the youths anything of religion, only the rules and moral precepts of the community.

(b) The spear-chief also has the task of carrying out the various rituals and offering appropriate sacrifices to ensure the spiritual well-being of the people. He conducts ritual procedures to drive away illness or to

(1) Bedri, *S.N.R.*, 1948, p.50. (2) *Ibid.*, p.51.
(3) Seligman, *Pagan Tribes of the Nilotic Sudan*, 1932, p.197.

give the people resistance against the ravages of the disease.

The spear-chief also officiates at the sacrifices to the totem *(yat)*.

(c) The spear-chief takes a leading part in peace ceremonies and helps to compose feuds. In cases of homicide, he is responsible for handing over the blood cattle and arranging the necessary sacrifices; in this his activities are reminiscent of those of the Nuer leopard-skin chief. When cattle are being gathered for compensation and both parties are ready to settle their differences and end a feud, the elders of each section are led by their spear-chief. Relatives of the deceased and of the killer are present and they sit separately while independent elders act as mediators. The preliminaries very often take several days to arrange and, when every-thing is ready, an independent spear-chief hands over the cattle by touch-ing each animal with a mallet made of the *suffar* tree. He kindles a fire and a bull from the cattle of compensation is sacrificed and divided into two halves, each to be roasted by one party. Then, each section brings a part of the roasted meat; they mix the two parts and eat together. Pipes and tobacco are exchanged between them, and so the feud is settled. The *beny rem* who kindled the fire and handed over the cattle, receives a cow calf from the blood money cattle for the part he has played in resolving the dispute. The settlement of feuds is one of the major functions of the spear-chief.

(d) The spear-chief is not allowed to join in or witness a fight person-ally. He leads the people who are to fight outside the village, he blesses them and then retires to his hut to cause harm to the enemy by his prayers and the use of his power. Prayers are offered to Nyalich, to the totem or to his *wa dit* (great ancestor). The prayers on such serious occasions are accompanied by sacrifices.

According to Bedri, a spear-chief of the Northern Dinka is said to have power to kill anyone outside his tribal section. To do this he will build a clay image of a person and then pierce it with a spear. Apart from his functions as a rain-maker, described below (p.132), the spear-chief has other, miscellaneous activities, such as blessing the seed at the beginning of the agricultural year. He offers prayers to cure the sick and to harm enemies, and he will do this by pointing his spear at the person concerned or at the animal to be sacrifices. He also supervises the swearing of oaths by the parties to a dispute.

Various sacred objects are associated with the office of spear-chief. These include strings of beads made of ostrich egg-shells, a sacred stool and rope, and the sacred hide of the bull sacrificed at his installation. The spear-chief also has a sacred cow, a sacred fishing spear (the *bith yat*) and a bundle of small axes which are found in front of any *mendyor* elder's hut. The most important object of all is the *tong de yat*, the sacred spear which is believed among the Northern Dinka to have originated in the time of the mythological figure Aywil Longar. An ordinary spear may be turned into a *tong de yat* if all the *mendyor* elders of the tribal section agree to do so. When an attack from an enemy is feared the *beny rem* cere-monially takes the spear and polishes it, then aims it in the direction from which the enemy is expected. The *tong mendyor* is a replica of the *tong de yat*. It is the badge of office which the spear-chief carries with him, and is used for curing sick people and for everyday purposes.

OTHER DINKA OFFICIALS

1. The *ban wut* is the cattle chief and war leader who is responsible for good order, and the safety of the village cattle.

2. The *ban de rap* practises magic against small birds which attack the crops.

3. The *ban de rec* is the fishing expert.

LEGAL PROCEDURE

Each village in Dinkaland is, to a large degree, autonomous. Legal disputes are settled by the elders of the village and the local spear-chief.

Compensation, in the form of cattle, is exacted for injuries, including homicide, seduction, rape and adultery. In cases of homicide the compensation amounts to 20-30 head of cattle;[1] the withholding of compensation results in a blood feud between the kin of the slain man and the kin of the slayer.

AGE SETS

At the age of about 8 to 10 years both boys and girls have the lower incisor teeth removed. This has, apparently, nothing to do with initiation into an age set which occurs at about 14 years.[2] Initiation does not appear to be an elaborate procedure. According to Seligman there is a period of seclusion, when the youths go out into the marshes and fend for themselves. At the end of the month heads are shaved, and every father is supposed to give his son an ox, a canoe, a spear, a fishing spear, a harpoon for hunting hippopotami, fishing lines and arm ornaments. If a father is prosperous he gives cows also. A feast is prepared for the youths on their return to the village; one of their members is selected for leader and they follow him in single file when visiting neighbouring villages to dance.[3]

The names of the age sets appear to commemorate incidents occurring at the time of formation. According to Bedri the spear-chief among the Northern Dinka is responsible for the initiation of all the boys of a tribe when they attain the age of puberty.

Among the Kiro, in the neighbourhood of the Bor Dinka, to enter an age class is to give up milking.[4] At the initiation ceremonies, Dinka boys have a number of deep cuts made on their foreheads. This is referred to as the *gornum* but it is not known how widespread this practice is throughout Dinkaland.

(1) O'Sullivan, *J.R.A.I.*, 1910, Vol.XI, p.177.
(2) Titherington, *S.N.R.*, 1927, Vol.X, p.205.
(3) Seligman, *Pagan Tribes of the Nilotic Sudan*, 1932, p.171.
(4) *Ibid.*, p.170.

Seligman regards the age sets and the age organisation in general as essentially military.   Whether this is so is not clear at present. Socially, men of the same age class regard themselves as brothers and they hunt, dance and ceremonially eat together.   The organisation therefore has a certain social significance, as well as being useful as a basis for the military organisation of a community.

MARRIAGE

A man may not marry a woman of his own clan or any woman to whom he may be related through his mother.

Bridewealth consists mainly of cattle and the number transferred varies.   According to Titherington, 20 head form an average bridewealth but as many as 100 might be paid if a man's family were rich.[1]   (This is probably only a conventional number.)   Seligman records that the bridewealth handed over by a Than Dinka consisted of 5 head of cattle, several sheep, some goats and various miscellaneous articles.   The Than, however, have few cattle.   According to his account the bridewealth is distributed to the bride's near paternal relatives; a cow is given to the bride's mother and a calf to the maternal grandfather, while the mother's brothers receive a goat each.[2]   The iron-working clans do not own cattle and pay their bridewealth in pieces of iron.   A woman's reputation is enhanced by the payment of a large bridewealth.

When a man wishes to marry a girl, he obtains the permission of her parents, and a long series of visits and ceremonies takes place between the two families and villages concerned.   Payment of the instalments of bridewealth proceeds in conjunction with the ceremonies.   The marriage is consummated after a symbolic show of reluctance by the bride, but the couple do not live continuously together until most of the bridewealth has been paid.   A dance is held and a bullock sacrificed when a final settlement has been reached.   A woman returns to her parents' home for the birth of her first child, and possibly for the birth of her second.

SEXUAL OFFENCES

If incest has been committed the offender must supply the cattle for the sacrifice of atonement.   For seduction a fine is paid to the father of the girl by the man at fault.   If a child is born, a heavier fine is imposed and, if the girl dies in childbed, the offender has to pay full compensation as for homicide.   If marriage follows seduction the payment of bridewealth covers the fine.   Fines for adultery are paid to the aggrieved husband and may consist of 5 to 8 cattle.[3]   All children resulting from sexual offences belong to the man who paid the bridewealth.

DIVORCE

When divorce occurs the cattle of bridewealth are returned together with their offspring.   If the husband wishes to retain any of the children

(1)   Titherington, *S.N.R.*, Vol.X, 1927, p.206.
(2)   Seligman, *Pagan Tribes of the Nilotic Sudan*, 1932, p.161.
(3)   O'Sullivan, *J.R.A.I.*, 1910, p.188.

of the marriage he leaves a certain number of cattle with the woman's
father, the number varying according to the number of children he retains.
Reasons for divorce may be barrenness, the girl's running away, or
quarrelling between the two families.   If the wife dies within two years
of marriage or fails to give birth to a child, her father will either return most of the bridewealth or give a sister of the girl in her place.
If a child is alive at the time of the wife's death no claim for the return of bridewealth can be made.[1]

INHERITANCE OF WIDOWS AND
GHOST MARRIAGE

Like the Nuer, the Dinka consider it essential for a mature man to
leave offspring behind when he dies.   Thus, when an unmarried man dies,
or a married man dies without children, a male kinsman must marry a woman
to his name in order to beget children for him.   If this is not done it
is believed that the spirit of the dead man will haunt his near relatives
and cause their children to die.   If a man has several unmarried
brothers who have died he must take a wife for each before he may take
one for himself.[2]

It is the duty of a widow to bear children to her deceased husband
by the man who inherits her.   A widow is inherited either by her husband's brother or, if she is still young, by one of his sons by another
wife.   No remarriage takes place and the widow is always regarded as
the wife of the deceased;   any children she may bear are counted as his
children and he is their pater, although he may have died several years
before their birth.   If a widow insists on marrying again the bridewealth
received from her new husband is used by the relations of the deceased
husband to obtain a wife who will live with a male kinsman and raise
heirs to the name of the dead man.[3]   A widow who is beyond childbearing
age and who has charge of her deceased husband's herds will marry a girl
in his name, using the cattle for bridewealth.   She arranges for a relative to cohabit with the girl and the children are in name and inheritance
the children of the dead man.

INHERITANCE

During a man's lifetime his herds are commonly parcelled out among
his wives for the use of their separate households, so that there is milk
available for the children of each.   According to Seligman, the youngest
son of the chief wife, the kun, receives no cattle on his father's death
but inherits all the cattle attached to his mother's household on her
death and has the management of them while she is alive.   The children
of the other wives share the cattle specifically allocated for the use of
their mother's household.   Family herds are not in the absolute ownership of any one man, although the senior member of the family will inherit
and nominally hold and control everything.   Each male member has rights
in the family herds and can claim assistance in paying bridewealth or
compensation.[4]

(1)   O'Sullivan, *J.R.A.I.*, 1910, p. 184.
(2)   Seligman, *The Pagan Tribes of the Nilotic Sudan*, 1932, p. 164.
(3)   O'Sullivan, *op.cit.*, p.185.
(4)   *Ibid.*, p.187.

KINSHIP TERMINOLOGY

Seligman gives a list of the kinship terminology used by the Bor and Cic Dinka.[1] He notes that the Dinka use the terms for mother and father as a polite form for addressing elders, while the term for brother (father's son) is used for clan brother. There is, therefore, some classificatory usage of descriptive terms. Men of the same age sets address each other as *wenawa* (father's son). A woman generally addresses her husband's relatives by the same terms as she uses for her own, but there are some descriptive terms expressing affinity.

Members of a woman's family display respect towards members of her husband's family, but do not avoid them. A man however, practises ceremonial avoidance towards his wife's immediate family: he must not encounter his mother-in-law face to face or accept food from her. A man must avoid his son's mother-in-law and should make a detour if he meets her on a path. There is also respect between a man and his wife's father, at least until a male child has been born to the couple. When the father-in-law presents his son-in-law with a calf he may eat and drink in the father-in-law's house. There is considerable familiarity between a man and his wife's sister but respect between him and his wife's brother's wife. A man cannot marry any of his female cousins but there is no avoidance between them.

Seligman notes that the mother's brother is shown the respect due to a father and it is believed that if he is treated disrespectfully death will follow.[2]

RITUAL AND OTHER
CULTURAL FEATURES

TOTEMISM

A Dinka tribe is divided into a number of totemic clans which are exogamous and trace descent in the male line. The stories which, in the course of generations, have been woven round the founding ancestor of each clan, usually contain references to some animate or inanimate object which, during the founder's lifetime, rendered him some conspicuous service. This animal or object becomes the totem of the clan and its adoption as such is justified in the myth. As a rule each clan has one or two totems.

They are known as *yat* by the Malwal Dinka, and *kwar* by the Than tribes. Dinka totems are usually animals, sometimes plants and, more rarely, a natural object or phenomenon. The clans speak of certain animals as their ancestors. A Than informant told Seligman that the *kwar* is the animal which is the spirit (*jok*) of the clan (*gol*). *Ruai*, meaning 'related', is used when speaking of the bond between a man and his *kwar*. A man will never injure his totem animal but respects it in various ways, as also with plants and totem objects.[3]

(1) Seligman, *Pagan Tribes of the Nilotic Sudan*, 1932, pp.152-3.
(2) *Ibid.*, p.175.
(3) *Ibid.*, pp.142-3.

Many of the Dinka clans whose *kwar* is an animal, derive their origin
from a man born as one of twins, his fellow twin being an animal of the
species that is the totem of the clan.   Sometimes the totem animal is believed to have put certain commands upon one of the members of the clan,
offering in return certain benefits.

Among the Malwal Dinka a girl, when given in marriage, renounces her
own totem and takes that of her husband.[1]   The marriage payments will
include at least one calf of the husband's totem cow (each family dedi-
cates a bull or cow to the principal totem) which the wife's people will
dedicate to the girl's former totem in order to conciliate it.   Although
children take their father's totem they respect that of their mother's
people and for this reason an animal may be avoided for generations.   In
certain rare cases a man may assume the totem of his mother's people and
he must then renounce all the rights and privileges to which he is entitled
as a member of his father's clan.[2]

In some clans the observances of the totem are more strictly adhered
to than in others.   In many cases a clan member will not kill or eat the
totem animal, in others he may eat it if killed by another clan member.
Fire as a totem may not be extinguished with water;   water as a totem is
respected and its use is regulated by rules.   When a river is a totem,
sacrifices are made to it before the beginning of the fishing season.
Should a person be killed by his totem, or struck by lightning, it is considered to be a well-merited punishment sent by Nyalich.   In certain *gol*
names the totem is perpetuated by prefixing *fa* or *pa* (an abbreviation
meaning 'related',) to the word denoting the totem.   Thus Gol Fakor is
the clan which has *kor*, a stone, for its totem.[3]

ANCESTRAL SPIRITS - THE JOK

The Dinka believe that every human being has a spirit and this they
call *atiep* or *tiep*.   The wandering of a person's *tiep* during sleep is believed to account for dreams;   moreover the *tiep* of a dead person may also
appear in dreams and make certain demands on the living, such as requests
for food and sacrifices.   When a man or woman dies, every effort is made
at the funeral ceremonies to propitiate the *tiep* and prevent a disgruntled
ghost from sending sickness and misfortune.   The spirit of a person recently dead is usually referred to as *tiep* but occasionally as *jok*.   The
term *jok* is normally reserved for the spirits of people who have long been
dead and who may be reckoned as powerful ancestors.   The spirit of the
founder of a clan or of a lineage, and the spirit of the animal ancestor,
are considered to be *jok*.   Both the *jok* and the *atiep* make their habit-
ations near the villages in which their descendants live.   *Jok* are more
powerful and energetic than *atiep*, and sometimes special shrines are built
for them.   *Atiep* are strongest immediately after death and funeral feasts
are held to placate them lest they should bring sickness or death.   They
gradually grow weaker as they are forgotten but if they are important
from the structural and social point of view, then they are remembered in
legends and traditions and become *jok*.[4]

(1)   Stubbs, *S.N.R.*, 1934, Vol.XVII, Pt.II, p.246.
(2)   *Ibid.*
(3)   *Ibid.*
(4)   Seligman, *Pagan Tribes of the Nilotic Sudan*, 1932, p.186.

Sickness and misfortune and death are believed to be caused by ancestral spirits when they are angered by neglect or displeased by the behaviour of their descendants. Childlessness may be attributed to the displeasure of the *jok* who then have to be appeased. Incest angers the *jok* and is believed to cause barrenness. In times of danger a man may invoke the *jok* of his ancestors to give him strength, calling on the spirits of both mother and father without discrimination.[1]

There is a close relationship between the *jok* and Nyalich, and among the Padang Dinka, according to Bedri, sickness is said to be sent by Nyalich, the *jok* being only the instruments of his will. Others believe that *Acek* and *Jok* are one: when he creates he is known as *Acek* and when he destroys as *Jok*.[2]

According to Stubbs, when a spirit haunts its descendants it may be propitiated by sacrifices, or the corpse of the deceased may be disinterred and the incisor teeth extracted and worn round the neck of the persecuted person.[3] This is reminiscent of the various practices of other Nilotic groups in their efforts to deal with an evil ancestral spirit or *chyen*. Like these other groups the Dinka believe that sickness and death come, in the main, from ancestral spirits rather than from witchcraft and sorcery.

Besides the offerings which are continually being made, annual sacrifices are offered to the *jok* at certain specified seasons.

NYALICH

Nyalich is associated with the firmament and his name means literally 'in the above'. He is believed to have created the world and the established order of things; it is he who sends rain from the sky.[4] Bedri records that the Padang Dinka believe in the existence of a supreme being, known as Nialic, creator of everything, and also as Acek, although Acek may possibly be the female counterpart of Nialic. "Apart from sickness and death all earthly occurrences such as barrenness, pregnancy, the care of the embryo child, and giving it life, sowing seeds, are referred to as being done by Acek. When they talk of the sky, rain and the sun they refer to Nialic." [5]

DENG

Deng (lit. rain) is closely linked with Nyalich and there is some confusion in the beliefs concerning the relationship of the two. In some regions Deng is regarded as the supreme being and Nyalich is not mentioned, while in others (as among the Malwal Dinka) Nyalich and Deng are believed to be the same spirit.[6] Seligman states that among the White Nile Dinka, Nyalich and Deng are definitely regarded as two separate spirits.[7] Dengdit may perhaps be regarded as an emanation or offspring of Nyalich.

(1) Seligman, *Pagan Tribes of the Nilotic Sudan*, 1932, p.190.
(2) Bedri, *S.N.R.*, 1948, Vol.XXIX, Pt.I, p.43.
(3) Stubbs, *S.N.R.*, 1934, Vol.XVII, Pt.II, p.246.
(4) Seligman, *op.cit.*, p.179.
(5) Bedri, *op.cit.*, p.42.
(6) Stubbs, *op.cit.*, p.243.
(7) Seligman, *loc.cit.*, p.179.

There appear to be few legends concerning Deng.   Among the Niel Dinka
he appears as a culture hero rather than as a supreme spirit.   Offerings
are made to Dengdit at shrines scattered all over Dinka territory.   Most
Dinka tribes appear to have at least one shrine.   The great central rain-
making ceremony of each tribe takes place at one of these shrines, and
also the harvest ceremony after the cutting of the millet.   The shrine at
Luang Deng, formerly held by the Dinka and now in Nuer territory owing to
the advance of the latter, is still served by Dinka and is their principal
shrine.   A man wishing for offspring will go and make offerings at such a
shrine.   The shrines are called *lwek* (sing. *lwak*), the word for cattle
byres.   These shrines contain sacred objects, including spears, some of
which are associated with rain-making.   Oaths may be sworn on the shrine
of Dengdit.

RITUAL OFFICES

Rain-making

The spear-chief is the most important rain-maker among the Dinka.
There is little information on the methods of rain-making.   According to
Seligman the rain-maker is asked by the people, at the height of the dry
season, to seek rain from the particular spirit - locally regarded as being
connected with rain.   A sacrifice is made, and the spirit is induced to
intercede with Dengdit.   The rain-maker prays for rain and goes through
the various rituals in which the sacred spear is used.[1]   In general the
spear-chief appears to rely on the ancestral spirit immanent in him, on his
sacred spears and on prayers and sacrifices to Deng, Nyalich and lesser
spirits.

There are other lesser rain-makers, such as the *ban de deng* who is not
a spear-chief.   He has certain types of rain magic and collaborates with
the spear-chief in rain-making.   He also blesses agricultural implements
and the seed of his *gol* before sowing time.

Among the Malwal Dinka, a minor official, the *bang raich*, sacrifices
a goat to the fishing-pools before fishing can begin.[2]   When, however,
the river is the totem of a clan this ceremony becomes important and is
performed by the spear-chief.

THE WITCHDOCTOR

According to Seligman magic *(theth)* plays a comparatively small part
in Dinka life.[3]   The Dinka witch-doctor has the task of divining the
cause of illness and misfortunes, of suggesting a remedy and using herbs
and certain surgical techniques to effect a cure.   The office is not
necessarily hereditary.   Titherington lists a number of people among the
Raik Dinka whom he classes as magicians.[4]

1.   *The Alueng*:   a witch-doctor who cures cattle sickness, presides at

---

(1)   Seligman, *Pagan Tribes of the Nilotic Sudan*, 1932, p.198.
(2)   Stubbs, *S.N.R.*, 1934, Vol.XVII, Pt.II, p.249.
(3)   Seligman, *op.cit.*, p.194.
(4)   G.W.T., *S.N.R.*, 1925, Vol.VIII. p.195.

weddings and arranges for the first child to be a son. Sometimes he is called *ashom* or *awudweng* and his office is hereditary.

2. *The Atit*: a bone-setter who may also be a straightener of spear hafts.

3. *Doll*: a man or woman who cures sickness in children.

4. *Keitt*: a leader in war but, owing to the people's independence and hatred of discipline, the office only exists on the Nuer border.

All these specialists are beneficient and are known as *tiet*, that is, men and women who are able to see and communicate with the spirits, *atiep* and *jok*.[1] Their power is attributed to the indwelling of a spirit, generally an ancestral spirit. As the spirit, on the death of a *tiet*, will generally take up its abode in the body of a near relative, the office tends to become hereditary. Often a *tiet* will tell a relative that he or she will return after death and possess this person. Fits and periods of unconsciousness are signs that a person is possessed by a spirit. Sometimes a person is possessed by Deng or by lesser spirits and by the *jok*. Divination, methods of propitiation, cures and counter-magic to meet sorcery are the chief duties of a *tiet*. The skill and reputation of the *tiet* vary enormously.

SORCERY

Bad magic is often credited to foreign tribes and defeated enemies, such as the Jo Luo people. Nevertheless, certain Dinka are believed to practise sorcery and produce various illnesses and troubles. Bad magic is regarded as criminal and may be punished by death. Iron-workers are supposed to possess these evil powers. Titherington mentions the *ashen*, who uses a gourd to cast spells on the enemies of those who pay him.[2] According to Seligman, a powerful man may make people ill merely by desiring it. There is no cure for such sickness. A man who hates another may take a ring of iron from his finger, place on it a tuft of grass and address the ring, expressing the hope that his enemy will die. After breaking the ring in two he places one piece on top of a tuft of grass and buries the other half under its roots.[3]

CURSES

The Dinka firmly believe in the efficacy of curses and blessings when uttered by relatives. The force behind them is the *atiep*. The curses of a father, son or brother, are terrible in their supposed effects. Thus, a brother may cause his sister to be barren and a son may cause his father to be severely ill.

LIFE   CYCLE

BIRTH

During the period just before and after the birth of a child the

(1) Seligman, *Pagan Tribes of the Nilotic Sudan*, 1932, p. 187.
(2) G.W.T., *S.N.R.*, 1925, Vol. VIII, p. 195.   (3) Seligman, *op.cit.*, p. 194.

mother observes certain taboos.   Usually the first-born child is delivered
in the home of the maternal grandparents and, when strong enough, is taken
to its father's home.

Twins are believed to be a manifestation of Nyalich.   If they are
both boys, it is said that they will desire their mother's death; if girls
they will desire their father's death; but if one is a girl and the other
a boy, each will defend one parent and so both mother and father are safe
from their ill-will.   After the birth of twins, prayers are made to
Nyalich and a bull calf is sacrificed.

BURIAL

Death is followed by immediate burial.   The body is placed in the
position of sleep, being curled up on its side facing westwards.   Skins
are placed above and below it.   The place of burial is on the right-hand
side of the doorway of the house inhabited in life.   The head of a household may, however, be buried near his father's burial place or in his own
cattle byre.[1]   The *ban wut* is buried in the cattle enclosure.   Except
for 'bull tombs', graves are not marked.

For four days the brothers and the father of the deceased sit around
the grave and sleep there; during this time they are not allowed to drink
milk or to go near the cows.   At the end of this period they wash, and
food taboos are over.   After the death of an important man, the head of
a lineage, the warriors make mock raids upon their neighbours 'to find
the man who killed him' and to raid any cattle.

The Buor

The *buor* is a particular kind of shrine which resembles the front
half of a bull; it is made of mud and has real horn inserted.   Some of
these shrines are surrounded by a fence and all have pegs near them to
which cattle may be tied, to delight the ancestors when the shrine is repaired each year after the rains, and sacrifice is made.   Bull tombs are
not common.   They are built a few days after death in the compound near
the grave.   Offerings of milk, beer and food are made there, rather than
at the grave itself.   If the lineage moves, the descendants may built a
buor in the new settlement.   It is not at all clear who is entitled to
build these shrines but among the Dinka of the Bahr el Ghazal they are made
for departed spear-chiefs.

THE NUER[2]

ECOLOGICAL CONDITIONS

The Nuer inhabit the marshes and savannahs which stretch from either
side of the Nile south of the point where it is joined by the Sobat and
Bahr el Ghazal tributaries.   These regions have all the most extreme

(1) Seligman, *Pagan Tribes of the Nilotic Sudan*, 1932, p.201.
(2) Professor Evans-Pritchard has published a number of full length studies of
     different aspects of Nuer society, particulars of these are given in the
     bibliography.   The present volume attempts only a summary outline of the
     essential material.

features characteristic of the areas occupied by the majority of the Nilotes - flatness, heavy clay soil, thick, tall grasses, swamp in the wet season and parched, brown stubble in the dry season. It is an area of true savannah.

The influence of environment on Nuer economy is profound. Although cattle form the great interest of the Nuer people, and are important socially as well as economically, horticulture is a necessary part of their economy owing to the prevalence of cattle diseases and the difficulties of obtaining adequate pastures in the dry season. Horticulture and cattle herding are, therefore, the two main economic activities, and together they determine the ecological cycle, as well as the distribution of population, village sites, and also the relationships between the various segments into which the Nuer are divided.

Nuer villages are situated on elevated ground out of reach of the wet season floods. In the early rains the cattle feed on young shoots near the village but, as the vegetation becomes too rank and the waters rise, the herds have to graze off the short grasses of the village ridges. During the wet season millet and other grains, vegetables and tobacco are grown in the gardens situated behind the homesteads. At the end of the rains, in November, the floods begin to recede. When the tall, tough grasses, which are unsuitable for the cattle to eat, are sufficiently dry they are burned. Since some varieties send up shoots a few days later, the cattle have fresh pasture until the height of the dry season when the water supplies fail in many regions. The Nuer then seek the permanent water-courses and dry-season pastures. When the harvests are finished they move from the villages to the dry-season camps; a period of wandering divides the two periods of stable residence. The dry-season camps are situated on the banks of rivers which do not completely dry up or on the edge of permanent swamps.

When the rains begin again in April and May, water and pasture become plentiful and a move is made back to the villages above flood level, in order to prepare the ground for cultivation.

The annual cycle is approximately set out below. It has considerable repercussions on social life and, although local conditions may cause some variation, the principles underlying the annual cycle are the same everywhere in Nuerland.

November - December. Youths and girls take cattle to camps while the old people remain in the village to harvest the second millet crop. Fishing camps may be formed on the banks of rivers. When the second harvest is finished the cattle are brought back to eat the millet stalks but as the pasturage becomes exhausted all eventually go to occupy new cattle camps. A period of wandering precedes the final settlement in the camp.

January - February. The married people join the youths when they settle in the final camping grounds. Camps get larger and larger as pastures become scarcer and more people join existing camps. Different villages and tribal sections tend to move at about the same time and to visit the same pools so that the sites of the main dry-season camps do not change from year to year.

March - April. When the rains begin the old people return to the village for sowing.

June. The rest of the people follow with the cattle. The move from camp to village is direct, whereas in the move from village to camp there is an intervening period of wandering.

The Nuer year is therefore divided into two parts, consisting of a period in the villages and a period in the camp. This annual transhumance is necessary for the very existence of the Nuer. Rinderpest prevents complete dependence on cattle, so that they must have villages on highlands, with gardens, in order to grow the necessary supplies of grain. Climatic conditions prevent complete reliance on cultivation and the need of fresh pastures and water for the cattle forces them into dry-season camps near permanent supplies.

Homesteads may be strung out along sandy ridges with gardens at the back and grazing in front and the location and size of the villages depend on the distribution and extent of the higher ground suitable for cultivation. The direction of the dry-season movements are determined by ecological conditions. Transhumance enhances the importance of units larger than the villages which, for economic reasons, cannot easily maintain a self-sufficient isolation as do the Shilluk, Anuak, Acholi and Lango villages where the emphasis is on cultivation.

ECONOMY

The economic importance of
cattle to the Nuer

Economically, cattle are chiefly important for milk and milk products, such as whey and liquid cheese. We are told that the Nuer value their cows according to the amount of milk they give.

Nuer eat meat boiled and roasted but, although they are particularly fond of it, they do not raise cattle for slaughter. It is considered that people ought not to kill cattle solely for food and, except on sacrificial and special occasions with a ritual aspect, the Nuer refrain from doing so. It is even thought that animals killed specifically for food might curse their owners:

Like other pastoral peoples in East Africa, the Nuer extract blood from the necks of their cattle and use it as a supplementary article of diet in dry season camps. The blood is boiled and taken with porridge as flavouring or is allowed to coagulate into a block which is roasted and then cut in slices.

Milk, meat and blood are the food products derived from cattle but the herds also furnish the materials for implements and other necessary articles. Skins are used for sleeping on, for trays, for carrying fuel, making cord for tethering, leather collars for oxen and in making pipes, spears and shields. Tail hairs are used for ornamentation, bones and horns are used for instruments, scrapers and beaters. Cattle dung is used for plastering walls and floors of huts; dried dung is used for fuel and ashes from it are smeared over the body. Cattle urine is used in churning and cheese-making and also for washing. Evans-Pritchard rightly calls the Nuer 'parasites of the cow'.[1]

The social importance of cattle among the Nuer

The fact that cattle have more than an economic value may be amply illustrated from the part they play in social life.

Relationships with neighbouring tribal groups are partly dependent on the value attached to cattle. The Nuer are contemptuous of those who have no cattle, while they raid those who have in order that they may augment their own herds. A man will defend his cattle to the last and will die for the sake of the herds. Disputes within the Nuer tribe are often about cattle and about the ownership of pastures and water supplies necessary for their well-being. Cattle are paid in compensation for homicide and injury. It is the needs of the cattle which compel the yearly dry-season migration to fresh pastures.

Cattle form the bridewealth of the Nuer, that is, the successive transfers of cattle from the bridegroom's family to that of the bride marking the fact of marriage. Cattle are farmed out among friends as a precaution against the total destruction of a herd by disease; thus they tend to consolidate friendships and to maintain the network of relationships between people within a village and between the inhabitants of separate villages.

Family relationships are expressed in terms of cattle, as are the rules of incest and the status of an individual. Men take 'ox-names' - names which refer to the colour or other peculiarities of their favourite animals. In ritual cattle play an important part; they are sacrificed to the spirits and, when he desires to establish contact with ghosts and spirits, a man rubs ashes along the back of an animal, invoking the ancestral spirits as he does so. Cows are dedicated to the totemic spirits and the sky spirits. Daily life revolves round the needs of cattle; Nuer think cattle and talk cattle. Oxen are valued for display and prestige, and the merits of their favourite beasts are boasted of by their owners. Nuer language is rich in terms describing the various attributes of cattle. Tassels, decorations and carved tethering pegs are made by the owners, while the favourites in the herd will be played with, sung to and have poems made up about them. Young men will get boys to lead their favourite ox round the village for all to admire and will themselves leap behind it. Among the Nuer there is scarcely any aspect of life into which cattle do not enter and play an important part. Evans-Pritchard writes that the Nuer define all social processes and relationships in terms of cattle and that their social idiom is a bovine idiom.

(1) Evans-Pritchard, *The Nuer*, 1940, p.30.

SOCIAL ORGANISATION AND POLITICAL STRUCTURE

SOCIAL UNITS

1.   A single living hut occupied by a wife, her children and, at times, her husband if the family is a polygynous one.

2.   The homestead *(gol)* consisting of a byre and huts, and containing a simple family group or polygynous family, sometimes with other relatives attached.

3.   The hamlet *(dhor)* consisting of a cluster of homesteads surrounded by their pastures and cultivations.   Each hamlet has its own name and is generally inhabited by close agnatic kinsmen, often brothers and their families.

4.   The village, a very distinct unit, usually referred to as *cieng* (home).   The population may be anything from fifty to several hundred. If the village is built on a ridge, homesteads and hamlets may be strung out for a considerable distance.   Villages are usually distinct from each other, there being several miles of bush, swamp and grass between them. Well-marked paths, made by the constant visits exchanged by the inhabit-ants, join the villages to each other.

   A village consists of a community linked by common residence and by a network of kinship and affinal ties.   The inhabitants co-operate in many activities - social, economic and military - and form dry-season camps together.   The village is the political unit of Nuerland and is the small-est group which is not specifically of a kinship order.[1]   People of one village have a strong feeling of solidarity vis à vis people of other villages.

5.   The cattle camp *(wec)*;   early cattle camps may be found wherever there are depressions, pools, and patches of fresh pasture.   The location of the larger camps is largely predetermined, as only a few places provide adequate pasture and water at the height of the dry season.   The size of the camp depends on these resources and, whereas early camps consist only of a few households, later camps vary from 100 to 1,000 souls.   Such con-centrations comprise larger or smaller tribal sections and each group has its own separate section of the camping ground.   Neighbouring villages participate in a cattle camp, and relatives from distant villages may join their kinsmen.   There is more co-operation within a camp than within a village, as the cattle are herded together and milked at the same time, whereas in a village each homestead, in the main, herds its own cattle. A large camp is called after the dominant lineage in it or after the main village community occupying it.

6.   The district, "an aggregate of villages and camps which have easy intercommunication".[2]   It corresponds to a small tribal segment, al-though it may include a whole tribe or more in the case of very small

(1)   Evans-Pritchard, *The Nuer*, 1940, p. 115.
(2)   *Ibid.*, p. 116.

tribes. The people in a district intermarry, conduct feuds, go raiding together, and so forth.

Nowhere in Nuerland do environmental conditions permit complete autonomy and exclusiveness of small village units. Pastoral pursuits and the needs determining transhumance cause concentrations of people and co-operation for half the year in dry-season camps, thus creating a wide inter-dependence which is lacking among the Anuak and many other tribal groups.

TRIBAL CHARACTERISTICS

Each tribe has a name, occupies a particular territory and owns and defends its own building sites, pastures and water supplies. Large rivers, or wide stretches of uninhabited country, generally divide adjacent sections of contiguous tribes, and these sections tend to move in different directions in the drought. Members of the same tribe have feelings of cohesion and fellowship with each other which do not extend to members of other tribes.[1] The age sets are organised tribally.

The tribe is the largest group of which the members habitually combine for raiding and for defensive measures. During the period of military unity, there is a truce to internal disputes. Inter-tribal fighting is fierce but is subject to certain conventions concerning women and children which do not extend to fighting between Nuer and Dinka or other neighbours.

Within a tribe compensation *(cut)* is paid for homicide. This is the invariable definition of tribal allegiance in every part of Nuerland.[2] Between tribesmen there is also *ruok* - compensation for torts other than homicide. If a man kills or injures a man of another tribe no breach of law is recognised; no obligation is felt to settle the dispute and there is no machinery to do so.

A tribe is a segmented structure in that it consists of a number of small divisions, each occupying a particular part of the tribal territory. There is opposition between these segments as well as a certain co-operation and cohesion.

Within each tribe there is a dominant clan and there is a close relationship between the lineage structure of this clan and the various territorial segments of the tribe. This is of the greatest importance for understanding Nuer structure and organisation.

Nuer tribes have no common organisation or central administration making for political unity in the generally accepted sense of the word. Yet adjacent tribes do form a political system and, in spite of inter-tribal opposition, will display a united opposition to different neighbouring groups.

(1) Evans-Pritchard, *The Nuer*, 1940, p.121.
(2) *Ibid.*

TERRITORIAL SEGMENTS

Nuer tribes are split into a number of segments.   For example, the
Lou tribe is segmented into Gun and Mor primary sections; Gun primary
section is segmented into Rumjok and Gaatbal secondary sections and the
Gaatbal secondary section into Leng and Nyarkwac tertiary sections.   A
tertiary section consists of a number of village communities.   The diagram
given by Evans-Pritchard to illustrate this tribal segmention is reproduced
below.[1]

LOU TRIBE

Mor prim. sect.	*Gun prim. sect.*	
Gaaliek sec. sect.	Rumjok sec. sect.	
Jimac sec. sect.		
Jaajoah sec. sect.	Leng tert. sect.	Gaatbal sec. sect.
	Nyarkwac tert. sect.	

All other Nuer tribes follow this pattern, although the degree of segmention may vary according to the size of the tribal unit.   The segments of
a tribe have the same characteristics as a tribe, but the smaller the segment
the stronger the sentiments of unity.   Each segment of a tribe tends to
have its own special dry-season pastures.   Each segment in its turn has a
segmented structure and there is opposition between its parts.   Members of
any segment unite for war against adjacent segments of the same order and
unite with these adjacent segments against larger sections.   For example,
if there is a fight between Mor and Gun primary sections Rumjok and Gaatbal
(the secondary segments of Gun primary segment), will unite against the
combined Mor secondary sections.   Both primary sections (each comprising
all their smaller segments) will unite against another tribe.   This
principle of segmentation and the opposition between segments is the same
in every section of a tribe and even extends beyond the tribe.[2]

The Nuer distinguish between various types of hostility:

1. *Dwac*.   Individual duelling.
2. *Ter*.   A feud within a tribe where compensation can be made.
3. *Kur*.   A fight between tribes where no compensation can be made.
4. *Pec*.   Raiding Dinka.

When a man conceives himself to have been wronged there is no court of
law to which an appeal may be made.   The only method of settlement is by a
duel.   Boys fight with spiked bracelets;   men of the same village or camp

(1) Evans-Pritchard, *The Nuer*, 1940, p.139.
(2) *Ibid.*, p.143.

with clubs.   Spears are not used between neighbours lest someone be killed
and a blood feud started which will disrupt the community.   No third person may intervene in these duels.

In fights between persons of different villages spears are used and
every adult male takes part.   Fighting occurs mainly between small tribal
segments;   only occasionally between primary segments or tribes.   Feuds
cannot occur except within a tribe for it is only in the tribal unit that
a breach of law is recognised and the machinery for settlement exists.   Between tribes settlement can only be effected by war.

THE SETTLEMENT OF A BLOOD FEUD

The slaver seeks sanctuary with the leopard-skin chief who will
ritually cleanse him and make a sacrifice to protect him from the vengeance
of the spirit of the slaughtered man and his kinsmen.   Vengeance is the
most binding obligation of paternal kinship.   After an interval, negotiations for compensation are begun.   In theory 40 to 50 cattle are paid;
in practice ceremonies of atonement are performed when about 20 have been
handed over.   The cattle are distributed among the kin of the dead man and
a certain number of them are used to secure a wife who will be married in
the dead man's name.   The leopard-skin chief receives two beasts, and the
meat of the sacrifices, but in fact he often gets nothing and may have to
help in paying the compensation.   He also has the expense of keeping the
slayer during the period before settlement.

Feuds occurring between small groups are settled quickly, especially
those within a village, where ties are so close that ordinary life would
be completely disrupted if a blood feud were to continue for any length of
time.   It is much more difficult to settle a feud between persons of different tribal segments than between persons in the same tribal segment.[1]

Theoretically, all feuds in a tribe can be settled by compensation but
this does not always occur in feuds involving primary tribal sections.   If
people are killed in a large-scale fight, compensation is not always paid
nor revenge taken;   kinsmen merely wait until the next fight occurs.

A feud arises only between two agnatic kin groups but, owing to the
extent of kinship ties and local sentiment, a whole tribal section may support the lineage within it which is at feud with a lineage in another tribal
section.   The close association between territorial units and kinship
units makes the feud an important aspect of inter-segment relationships.

HOSTILITY BETWEEN THE NUER AND DINKA

The Nuer and Central Dinka are very similar in culture and organisation, but they are ancient enemies and constantly raided each other in the
past.   The attack was usually made after the rains by the Nuer, who would
establish a base in Dinka country and spend several weeks there raiding in
all directions.   The Dinka did not offer much resistance, merely attempt-
ing to flee to safety with their cattle.   This constant raiding was partly
due to lack of resistance, and the advantages of obtaining extra cattle,

(1) Evans-Pritchard, *The Nuer*, 1940, p.159.

142

grain supplies, women and so forth, but it has been suggested that war between the two groups is a structural relationship.[1]   The Nuer have
incorporated a considerable area of Dinkaland into their own territories
and have also absorbed the Dinka population: the result has been fusion
and not a class structure.[2]

THE NATURE OF LAW AMONG THE NUER

The settlement of feuds is effected only when both parties to a dispute are willing to come to an agreement and apply to the leopard-skin
chief as mediator.   He hears the matter discussed by both sides, and then
gives his opinion, which is accepted as a verdict if both parties agree to
it.   He cannot order a discussion or compel either party to accept a
decision.   Compensation in cattle, according to a recognised scale, is
paid for homicide, adultery, fornication and physical injury.

Sorcerers are killed by individuals or groups;   it does not appear
that any actions are regarded as injurious to the whole community.

Law is relative to the positions of the parties in the social structure, and to the distance between them in the kinship, lineage, age-set
and political systems.   The more widely separated are the two parties to
a dispute the weaker is the obligation to settle it and the more difficult
the task of enforcing settlement.   Unless a man resorts to self-help and
is backed by powerful kinsmen and by public opinion, he has little chance
of redress.   Traditional modes of settling disputes, a recognition of a
notion of right *(cuong)* and the acknowledgment of certain scales of compensation, form the basis of Nuer law.

RECOGNISED SOCIAL FIGURES AMONG THE NUER

The Leopard-Skin Chief   (kuaar muon)

He is a sacred person and is believed to have a mystical association
with the earth which gives him certain ritual powers to bless or curse it.
His acts are mainly of a ritual nature and he has no great political
authority, though some importance attaches to him since relations between
groups are regulated through him;[3]   his powers do not, however, normally
extend beyond a tribal section.   He functions are as follows:-

(a) His intervention is necessary in settling feuds and disputes.
Leopard-skin chiefs sometimes prevent fights between two communities
by running between the two opposing forces, hoeing up earth here and
there.   Probably this can only be done when the majority on both
sides is unwilling to come to blows.

(b) He performs ritual to cleanse those who have broken incest
rules.

(c) He has slight rain-making powers.

(1) Evans-Pritchard, *The Nuer,* 1940, p.131.
(2) *Ibid.,* p.125.   (3) *Ibid.,* p.176.

Leopard-skin chiefs are usually men from certain lineages and, although they are not all members of the same clan, they are believed to have a kind of kinship through their office. The leopard-skin chief, unlike similar ritual officials in other Nilotic groups, does not represent or symbolise the unity and exclusiveness of any political group.

The Elders

The elders of a local community provide leadership and advice when required. Prestige and influence do not come with age alone, however; a man of outstanding reputation is called *tut* (bull), a term used to refer to men of high social standing who belong to lineages other than those of the dominant clan. A *tut* is head of a family and in charge of a homestead and a herd of cattle; he has the support of a large number of relatives and, in addition, he must be an able man with personality.

The *gat twot* is 'the bull of the camp'. He has no defined status or authority but enjoys considerable prestige through a combination of factors - ownership of cattle, age, ritual powers, many children and relatives, personal ability and tact, and so forth. His prestige makes his personal actions and decisions influential so that, when he decides to move his homestead, others will naturally follow suit.

Districts and villages have no headmen or councils. There is not even a war leader except that, in a fight, the warriors automatically follow their most notable and brave fighters. There is thus an absence of legal institutions, official leadership and organised political activity. Evans-Pritchard writes: "their state is an acephalous kinship state...." and it is the kinship structure, in conjunction with territorial segmentation, which forms the basis of Nuer political organisation.[1]

RELATIONSHIP BETWEEN NUER TRIBAL SEGMENTS AND THE LINEAGE SYSTEM

There are at least 20 clans in Nuerland, together with a number of small lineages of Dinka origin. A Nuer clan is an exogamous group of agnates who trace their descent from a common ancestor. The clans are segmented into lineages and each lineage is further segmented. Thus, a clan is segmented into maximal lineages, the maximal lineages are segmented into major lineages, the major lineages into minor lineages and minor lineages into minimal lineages. A minimal lineage, in the case of the Nuer, consists of a descent group deriving from a great-grandfather or great-great-grandfather. Clans and lineages are distinguished by separate names, ritual symbols and honorific titles.

The political and lineage groups are not identical but there is a certain correspondence. Often they bear the same name; for example, Gaawar is the name of a tribal area, of the tribesmen inhabiting it and also of the most powerful clan in it. Like the tribe, the Nuer clan has many of the characteristics accompanying segmentation. Lineages are distinct groups only in relation to one another and there is fusion of collateral

(1) Evans-Pritchard, *The Nuer*, 1940, p.181.

lineages of the same branch in relation to a collateral branch.(1)

Although Nuer lineages are not corporate, localised communities, they are frequently associated with territorial units.(2)   Every Nuer village is associated with a lineage, though the members of it may form only a small part of the population.   The village community is identified with, and called by the name of, the lineage which forms the agnatic core to which the other families and lineages are aggregated.   For everyday purposes the position of this dominant lineage does not appear to be very different from that of the other lineages in the community.   It is only in connection with certain ritual matters and in reference to rules of exogamy, that lineages are completely autonomous groups and become clearly differentiated from each other.   Lineages function within, and as part of, local communities of all sizes, from the village to the tribe.

THE DOMINANT LINEAGES AND STRANGER LINEAGES

When a tribal section is called after a lineage it does not follow that all the members of the lineage live there, though the majority may do so.   It merely means that the lineage is a dominant one, the nucleus of the community, although large stranger lineages are often included in the area.

Migration, quarrels, intermarriage and so forth, have caused a dispersion of lineages.   If, for some reason, a man or a group of brothers leave their village, they may go and live at the village of a married sister.   Here they are respected as *jiciengthu* (in-laws) and their children are accepted as *gaat nar* (children of the mother's brother).   The people they join are to them *cieng conymar* - 'the people of my sister's husband', and *gaat nyal* - children of a female agnate.   Except for ceremonial purposes, they will enter into close relationships with the dominant lineage of the community.   However closely associated lineages may become, a lineage never merges into a different clan, for there are always certain ritual observances which cannot be shared;   and only a certain amount of inter-marriage may occur, for otherwise the incest rules would be violated.   A lineage can only merge with a collateral lineage of the same clan.

The close association between lineages and territorial segments, which constitutes the political importance of the clan system, is seen in the correspondence between the segments of a dominant clan and the tribal or territorial segments.(3)   A certain tribe has a dominant clan associated with it.   The maximal lineage of the clan corresponds to the primary sections of the clan;   the major lineages correspond to the secondary sections, the minor lineages to the tertiary sections and the minimal lineages are associated with the villages comprising the tertiary sections (see above p.140).   The dominant clan is therefore a framework on which the political system of the tribe is built up through a complex series of kinship links.(4)

(1)   See Evans-Pritchard, *The Nuer*, 1940, pp.192-3, for full discussion of the segmentation of lineages and underlying structural principles.
(2)   Evans-Pritchard, *The Nuer*, 1940, p.205.
(3)   *Ibid.*, pp.211-12.   (4)   *Ibid.*, pp.205-12 for further details.

DIFFERENTIATION OF STATUS AMONG THE NUER

There are three categories in a Nuer tribe: *diel, rul* and *jaang*.

The dominant clan is *diel* and members of other clans settling after the establishment of the dominant lineage are *rul* (strangers). Not every member of a clan lives in a tribe where his clan has a superior status; a man is a *dil* (an aristocrat) only in the tribe in which his clan is dominant, for the status of *diel* derives from residence on land owned by the clan. Prestige, not authority or any particular power, is attached to the *diel*; they are owners of the land, the village sites and pastures. Strangers live on the land through some link with, and the recognition of, the true owners.

A *rul* (stranger) is a Nuer who is not a *dil* in the tribe in which he lives. He may be influential, highly respected and even a *tut* (bull), though not belonging to the aristocratic clan. He may, indeed, group round him an entire village community in spite of the presence of several tribal aristocrats in the same village; in this respect personality and influence may count for more in everyday local affairs than a particular lineage affiliation.(1)   In fact, in the everyday life of a village community, the only socially significant difference between aristocrats and strangers is in the assessment of blood cattle, and this is only found among the Jikany tribes.

'Tribal bulls', on the other hand, belonging to a lineage of the dominant clan of a tribe, are far more important in the political system than the *rul* bulls, for they are centres of clusters of kin and are also agnates, each having in relation to the others a structural position in the lineage system of the dominant clan.(2)

A Dinka adopted into a joint family is a *jaang* to the people of the family. To people outside the family he is a member of it and his status is not differentiated; he has all the rights and obligations of other members. Only the assessment of his value in blood cattle differentiates him from the Nuer.

Strangers may be attached to the dominant clan by adoption or by marriage.

Kinship-values are the strongest sentiments and norms in Nuer society, and all social interrelations tend to be expressed in kinship idioms. Since there are no headmen or councils or any of the usual forms of government, it seems that kinship values, combined with the position of the dominant lineage and its linked stranger lineages, are the originising agencies and the means of unity in each community.

The political system of the Nuer is constituted by the relations between territorial segments in the tribal system; cohesion and organisation are achieved through the association of the lineage system with the territorial units. The lines of cleavage tend to coincide, for lineages are

(1) Evans-Pritchard, *Kinship and Local Community among the Nuer*, 1950, p.370.
(2) *Ibid.*, p.390.

not corporate groups but are embodied in local communities through which they function structurally.[1]   The tendency towards the co-ordination of territorial and lineage segmentation can be seen in various stages of territorial expansion between the household and the tribe.[2]

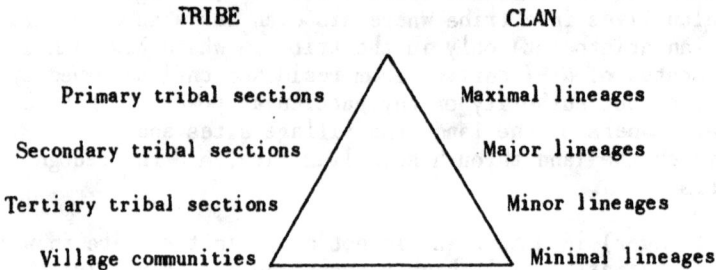

```
            TRIBE                           CLAN

   Primary tribal sections      /\       Maximal lineages
                               /  \
  Secondary tribal sections   /    \     Major lineages
                             /      \
  Tertiary tribal sections  /        \   Minor lineages
                           /          \
  Village communities     /_____\ Minimal lineages
```

The action and interaction of the various tribal segments and the under-lying principles of opposition and fusion are seen in operation when disputes and cases of homicide are dealt with, and in times of feud and war. This acephalous kinship system has a determining influence on the nature of the age sets, on the rules of exogamy, on the character of kinship, on the people, and indeed on every aspect of Nuer life.

NUER NAMES

Every Nuer has a personal or birth name *(cot pany)* which is given without ceremony by the parents shortly after birth; he may have a second personal name given by his maternal grand-parents.   In later life, he is addressed as *gwa* (father) by the younger generation.   In addition, every-one inherits a *cot paak*, an honorific or praise name of the clan of his father, which is used mostly on ceremonial occasions.   A man's maternal kin will tend to use the honorific name of the mother's clan.

At initiation a man acquires an ox name derived from the colour or characteristics of the ox given him on this occasion by his father. A man is given his ox name by his age mates in particular.   Maidens take ox names from the bulls calved by the cows they milk, but these are seldom used except at dances.

A dance name, nickname, or traditional name may be used in conjunction with ox names at dances.   In addition a man is often addressed as 'son of --' followed by the name of his father.   Among maternal relatives the matronymic is used instead of the patronymic used among paternal kinsmen. A man is called after his elder son by his in-laws, while a woman who has status in her husband's home in virtue of having borne him a child is addressed by the name of her eldest child.   A Nuer, therefore, may be addressed by a number of different names or titles.   The one actually used on any occasion depends on the age, relationship, and clan of the speaker, and also on the response and mode of behaviour which it is intended to evoke.[3]

(1) Evans-Pritchard, *The Nuer*, 1940, p.240.   (2) *Ibid.*, p.248.
(3) Evans-Pritchard, *Uganda Journal*, 1948, Vol.12, No.2, p.166.

AGE-SET ORGANISATION

INITIATION

Formerly boys were initiated at the age of 16 to 18, each village making its arrangements independently. The ceremony usually takes place after the rains. The officer in charge of initiation into age sets is the wut *ghok* (the man of the cattle). He opens the period when initiation may take place, 'when the knife is brought out' *(ngom kam rar)* and closes it 'when the knife is hung up' *(ba ngom ngah)*. At the beginning of an initiation period the cattle expert kills a bullock, a big dance is held and he makes a speech opening a new period of initiation. In each tribe there is a cattle expert whose authority is acknowledged in matters concerning age-set organisation.

At the initiation ceremony 6 deep cuts are made across the forehead of the boy, extending from ear to ear. After the cutting *(gar)* the boys, who suffer great pain, are shut up in a hut for two days. There is a period of confinement (lasting one to two weeks) which is followed by one of mild licence. During the whole of this time the initiates must strictly avoid any contact with cattle. Finally, cleansing ceremonies are carried out and a concluding ceremony and dance. After this the youths are recognised as adults and enter into normal adult life and affairs, and into lifelong contact with the herds.

AGE SETS

All boys initiated during a number of successive years belong to a single age set *(ric)*. Until recently there was a four years' interval between the end of one set and the beginning of the next, and this was the period when the man of the cattle hung up his knife and no more initiations were held.

The age sets are organised independently in each tribe, but it often happens that, when a new set has been started in one tribe, an adjacent tribe will follow suit.[1] A set usually lasts for ten years before being cut and there are generally members of six sets alive at any one time. The names of the sets are not uniform for the whole of Nuerland, and they are not repeated. Each age set has two or three subdivisions, each with a separate name. Subdivisions are made up of those initiated together in one year or possibly the combined initiates of two years. All the members of a set are known by the name of the first division. At initiation the individual enters the set in which he will remain for the rest of his life. The members of a set have a common name, equal status, and observe certain patterns of behaviour towards one another and towards members of senior and junior sets (see below p.148).

The sets are not specifically graded as boys, warriors, and elders, as in some forms of age-set organisation, nor have they any political, juridical or military functions. Their importance is of a social nature in that a person's position in the age-set structure determines his social behaviour. Milking and other women's work is forbidden to a youth after

(1) Evans-Pritchard, *The Nuer*, 1940, p.250.

initiation.   He is a *wut*, a man, whereas before he was one of the *dholi*
(boys).   He is now treated by his elders as a man and he has close contacts with the cattle;   he herds them, has his own ox and takes an ox name.
He goes to dances and indulges in love-making and flirting as the preliminaries to marriage.

Certain ritual observances are practised between members of the same
age set, and between members of different sets: sets are segregated at
sacrificial feasts;   members of a set cannot bury an age mate or participate in the mortuary ceremonies;   a man may not marry or have sexual relations with the daughter of an age mate, for he is as a father to her;   a
man should not marry a daughter of one of his father's age mates unless
his or her father is dead, because the strained relations between the two
fathers-in-law would be incompatible with the free and easy relations of
equality which should exist between age mates.

Members of a junior set are expected to show respect to members of
senior sets.   Since every Nuer has an age relationship to every other
Nuer, the attitudes and types of behaviour between two men are determined
in advance of meeting, unless there is any particularly strong and over-
ruling tie of kinship.

Relations between sets are defined in ordinary kinship terms.   Members of a father's age set are fathers, their wives are mothers;   members
of one's own age set are brothers, their wives are sisters, and so forth.
When speaking of a set immediately senior to his own, but not his father's,
a man will call the men fathers-in-law and the women mothers-in-law, because he is usually courting the daughters of this age set in preparation
for marriage.

MARRIAGE

Marriage is not permitted between clansfolk, close cognates, close
kinsfolk by adoption, close affines or persons who stand to one another
as father and daughter in the age-set system.   If it is uncertain whether
the genealogical distance between a couple is wide enough to permit
marriage, a sacrifice (generally a beast) will be offered to cut the bonds
of kinship if any exist.[1]

There are several types of marriage among the Nuer.

1.   *Ghost Marriage*.   If a man dies before he has married or if his wife
does not bear him male children, one of his close kinsmen has the obligation of marrying a wife to his name, for it is held that no initiated male
should be allowed to lie in his grave unremembered in his children.   A
vicarious marriage is contracted, and the vicarious husband acts as though
he were the true husband in the marriage ritual.   Evans-Pritchard states
that "in physiological and in domestic roles he is husband, in all but
the legal sense..... The legal husband is the ghost in whose name the
bride cattle are paid and the marriage ritual performed."[2]   The ghost
family is a legal family and such families are almost as numerous as simple

(1)   Evans-Pritchard, "Nuer rules of exogamy and incest", 1949, p.90.
(2)   Evans-Pritchard, "Some aspects of marriage and the family among the Nuer",
      1938, pp.308-9.

families; it is only in question of descent and inheritance that the difference is seen. It is the dead pater's name which will survive in genealogies.

Ghost marriages are arranged on behalf of brother, paternal uncles, maternal uncles and fathers (i.e. physiological fathers who are not also paters). A man of a senior generation is not allowed to marry a wife to the name of a kinsman of a junior generation because the man would be both vicarious husband to the woman and her father-in-law. A man never marries a woman to the name of his father's father or his mother's father since that was the duty of their sons. Only a kinsman takes a wife to the name of a dead man. Occasionally a woman marries someone to the name of a dead kinsman, and the wife so married would cohabit with a stranger to raise up children for the ghost.[1]

2. *The Levirate*. When a husband dies, the children his wife may subsequently bear are still counted as the children of the dead man. It is held that the woman should live with one of the dead man's brothers for she was married with the cattle of their kraal. Whoever inherits the widow does not marry her; she is still the wife of the dead man, and the man with whom she lives merely acts as genitor. Children born of the union regard themselves as their pater's family and inherit from him and not from their genitor. Leviratic marriage is different from ghost marriage. In ghost marriage bridewealth is paid and the marriage rites are performed by the vicarious husband; in leviratic marriage the husband has already performed these actions and the brother or other male kinsman inheriting the widow merely enters, as pro-husband, a family already in being.[2]

Tradition, threat of divorce and social pressure, all persuade a young widow to live with her husband's brother or with a son by a co-wife. She has a certain amount of choice among the relatives available. If she prefers to go and live with lovers and to 'give birth in the bush', all children born are counted as those of her dead husband, and his lineage has legal rights over them. Some widows return to their parents' village and live with a man there.

3. *Widow Concubinage*. A widow living with a stranger after the death of her husband, is called a *cek ma lak* (widow concubine).[3] Her lover has no legal rights over her and cannot compel her to stay with him, nor has he any legal control over children born of the union. A man, a widow concubine and their children form a natural, as opposed to a legal, family, and the position of the genitor, though precarious, is acknowledged socially in several ways.

4. *Unmarried Concubinage*. A child of an unmarried woman has no pater but his genitor may become his pater on payment of a fee of 4 to 6 cattle to legitimise him. If the fee is not paid, the child belongs to the mother's lineage, and any man whom the mother cares to live with for the time being is regarded as his foster father. In certain respects the status

(1) Evans-Pritchard, "Some aspects of marriage and the family among the Nuer", 1938, p.318.
(2) Evans-Pritchard, *op.cit.*, 1938, p.320.
(3) *Ibid.*, p.325.

of an unmarried mother is inferior to that of the mother for whom bridewealth has been paid,[1] but her position may be regularised at any time by payment of cattle to her lineage.

The rules of exogamy apply to simple legal marriages and to all other unions. Physiological paternity does not appear to be stressed by the Nuer, but what is important to them is that the legal parentage of a child should be well established. The various types of union practised give rise to various difficulties owing to the clash of interests which may occur when the legal pater of a child is not his genitor, or his foster father. These difficulties are least likely to arise in the simple legal family where sentiment and interests go together and inheritance is plain.

Adultery is not uncommon and, if it can be proved, the adulterer has to pay a fine of 6 cattle to the husband, except when a child has been born, for it seems that the adulterer has a claim on the child. If a man is caught in the act, he may be speared or clubbed.

BRIDEWEALTH

Instalments of the bridewealth are handed over by the bridegroom's family to that of the bride, *pari passu* with a series of ceremonial acts, until the union is completed by the birth of a child.

The ideal amount of bridewealth consists of 40 head of cattle, and of these 20 go to the father's side of the bride's family and 20 to the mother's side. The actual distribution in any particular marriage approximates as nearly as possible to the ideal distribution.[2]

The number of animals actually handed over is usually less than 40, but in all cases there is a minimum number without which marriage could not take place. Essential claims are settled at the first bridewealth discussion; those due to the maternal relatives have priority, as they represent a deferred payment standing over from the marriage of the bride's mother. Lengthy arguments take place over the remainder of the animals. Paternal and other kinsmen, whose relationship is not close enough to carry a title to a defined share of the bridewealth, may claim a small gift; the genitor of the bride has a right to a cow if he is not also her legal father.

Bridewealth has two main functions: in the first place it creates new social ties between persons and regulates their relations until these have become assimilated to kinship patterns; secondly, it determines the lineage affiliations of the children of the union.[3]

MARRIAGE CEREMONIES

A number of rites are necessary for the conclusion of a marriage, and the sequence of rites is linked with the transfer of cattle; thus, the performance of a given ritual is a recognition that the required number of

(1) Evans-Pritchard, "Some aspects of marriage and the family among the Nuer", 1938, p.329.
(2) Evans-Pritchard, *Africa*, XVI, 1946, p.249.
(3) Evans-Pritchard, *African Studies*, XI.4, 1947, p.185.

cattle has been handed over.[1]   A marriage which has reached the final
rites may be regarded as a stable union.

The first step occurs when a youth reaches an understanding with a
girl and, having some of the necessary cattle, asks her consent to marriage.
Both families are consulted and arrangements are made for the betrothal
(larcieng).

When a definite agreement has been reached about bridewealth cattle,
the wedding ceremony (ngut) is held at the bride's homestead.   The main
features of a wedding are: discussions about cattle, which are held in
the morning;   the invocation over the cattle of the bridewealth, followed
by the wedding dance and the wedding sacrifice in the afternoon and even-
ing.   Though this ceremony does not conclude the marriage there is every
chance, once this point is reached, that the union will be completed.

The third of the public ceremonies is the one which, at least among
the Eastern Nuer, makes the union legally binding.   This is the mut
(consummation).   After it the husband can claim compensation for adultery
and the cattle are regarded as marriage cattle and not as a pledge.

Marriage is completed by the birth of a child.   Until then the wife
sleeps in a hut at her parents' homestead and she remains with her parents
until the child is weaned.   The first-born child belongs to the home of
his maternal grandparents and even if he is weaned in his father's home he
returns to live with them.   A boy stays with his maternal grandparents
until he is initiated, a girl until she is betrothed.   The baby is always
brought to the father's home for the ceremony of laying him on the ashes
of the hearth in the centre of his grandfather's byre, which takes place
shortly after birth.

After the weaning, the husband builds his wife a hut in his father's
homestead.   She goes to live with him as a true wife in that she will now
milk his cows and hoe his gardens and not those of her father.   She makes
a buor, a mud fire screen, and the spirit of his lineage comes to dwell
there.   Later his father tells him to build a byre and gives him a few
cows to start a herd.[2]

In-Law Relationships

In-law relationships are marked by certain avoidances and displays of
respect.   Until his first child is born a husband does not openly visit
his parents-in-law's village except in some formal capacity.   After the
birth he makes public visits, but he treats his parents-in-law with great
respect and must not eat with them or appear naked before them.   When two
of three children have been born, a ceremony takes place after which he no
longer has to observe these rules and prohibitions.   When the father-in-
law visits the husband's home and is entertained and given a bull, calf or
sheep, his son-in-law may regard him as a father.   The only in-law whom
a man need not treat with formal respect is his wife's sister.

---

(1)   Evans-Pritchard, *Africa*, XVIII, 1948, p.29.
(2)   Evans-Pritchard, *Africa*, XVIII, 1948, p.40.

For a man's wife, avoidance is impracticable, but she treats her parents-in-law with great respect; and, in the early days of marriage, keeps herself apart from them as much as possible. She is on joking terms with her husband's brothers since, among brothers, the wife of one is, in the social sense, the wife of all.[1]

DIVORCE

If a wife dies childless or if her husband divorces her the bride-wealth cattle have to be returned. If a child has been born and is left with the husband then the cattle are returned, minus six. If two children have been born, no cattle are returned. Divorce is recognised as having taken place only if cattle are returned; if a wife leaves her husband to live with another man, and her husband does not claim return of the bridewealth, any children she may bear are his. Divorce after the birth of a child is very unusual, and after the birth of a second child, almost unknown.

RITUAL AND OTHER
CULTURAL FEATURES

TOTEMISM

The various Nuer lineages have specific ritual attitudes towards certain natural objects and living creatures. They respect the lion, reptiles, birds and plants; some lineages respect rivers and streams but, for all Nuer, rivers are specially associated with the mother spirit, Buk Mandeang, who is held in reverence by all the people. Some lineages respect cattle with certain markings and therefore do not keep them. The largest clan in Nuerland - the Gaatgankiir of the Jikany tribes - respect gourds, since, it is said, the ancestor of the clan was found in a gourd. In general, however, totems are associated with lineages rather than with clans.

Nuer totems (kwoth) are neither peculiar nor particularly important, and the Nuer themselves state that the majority of the totems come from the Dinka; they further maintain that the kuth of Nuer lineages are sky spirits, or spirits of persons who have been killed by lightning and have become sky spirits. The totemic relationship is explained in the myths which tell how ancestors of the lineages and the members of the species related to the lineages, were born twins. A man respects his wife's totems and a woman her husband's, while children respect their mother's totem generally. A totemic relationship of the same type does not prevent marriage.

Respect for a totem consists in refraining from hurting it or eating it; in paying it some recognition and consideration, and in making an expression of regret should it be found dead. In turn the totemic species is expected not to cause any harm to those who respect it. Sacrifices and prayers are made to the totem and cattle are dedicated to it. The species itself is not worshipped although the representatives are

(1) Evans-Pritchard, Man, 1948, No.2, p.5.

respected; it is the spiritual being, the *kwoth*, which the totem stands for, which is revered. The totems are symbols or manifestations of a spirit which can be in communion with men and beasts.[1]

Totem spirits are called *kuth piny* (earth spirits) a category which includes fetishes; this is in contrast to the much more important *kuth nhial*, sky spirits. Yet, although the two categories are thus distinguished, the Nuer maintain that they worship totemic spirits and that these spirits are with god in the sky. The totem seems to be the symbol of the spirit and the spirit to be an aspect of the spirit of the sky which is connected with the various lineages and is symbolised differently in each.

Kwoth

In addition to totemic spirits, *kwoth* also refers to 'god in the sky' and can mean any one of the sons of the sky god - the *kwoth dwanga*. Each sky spirit is associated with a certain aspect of nature; for example, Deng refers to the rain spirit. Another group of spirits are the *col wic* - the spirits of persons who have been killed by lightning and taken up to heaven. Persons supposed to have been taken into heaven by a whirlwind and those found dead in the bush without any apparent cause are also *col wic*. A *col wic* is considered to be a sacred spirit of his lineage - a *kwoth goal* - and most lineages have at least one of these spirits to whom cows are dedicated. Sometimes a *col wic* spirit enters into a member of his family or lineage and, when this happens, the man whom he possesses falls sick; on recovery, he makes a shrine in his homestead and becomes a prophet of Col *(guk cuol)*, and the spirit of lightning contacts the people through him.[2]

SACRIFICES

Sacrifices play an important part in all ritual practices, and are usually all of a similar nature. An animal is selected and is dedicated to a spirit by rubbing ashes along its back. An invocation is then made and the animal is killed by spearing it through the heart. It is cut in two halves when there is a cutting of social ties, and also at mortuary ceremonies when there is one half for the living and another for the dead. Sickness is the most frequent occasion for sacrifices.

THE CONCEPTS OF THEK AND NUEER

Thek means 'to respect', and is used in various social contexts; for example, it denotes the behaviour expected of a man towards his parents-in-law; in blood feuds the kin of the slayer and of the slain may not eat from the utensils which the other party has used, and these are respected. In mortuary ceremonies a man's age-mates *thek* the meat which has been sacrificed in his honour. A man also pays respect to his totem. Failure to show respect where there is a *thek* relationship is thought to bring about misfortune.[3] Any serious sickness following the breach of a *thek* taboo is called *nueer*.

(1) Evans-Pritchard, *Annali Lateranensi*, 1949, Vol.XIII, p.247.
(2) Evans-Pritchard, *Man*, 1949, No.2, p.9.
(3) *Ibid.*, 1949, No.96, p.75.

Cien

Cien is the vengeance wrought by a ghost which produces sickness and misfortune; like the other Nilotic tribal groups, the Nuer hold the concept of *cien*, and believe that ghostly vengeance will fall on those who have wronged a man and allowed him to die with a grudge. Fear of *cien* tends to make a Nuer more careful to treat others with justice.

To stop the effects of *cien* it is necessary to make a sacrifice to god in the sky and, when possible, to make reparation.

NUER CURSES AND GHOSTLY VENGEANCE

Curses are uttered by someone who has been wronged. The efficacy of a curse is largely conditioned by the relationship of the curser to the cursed. The Nuer regard the curse of a mother or father as serious; it may result in death. The curse of a mother's brother is feared because, being of a different lineage, he may curse cattle, which is the worst of all curses in the eyes of the Nuer. The curse of an eldest child is feared by the mother and maternal uncle.

There are other curses imposed by those of the *ric* (age-set), by the leopard-skin chief, the man of the cattle and *guk*, the prophet.[1] The Nuer also believe in conditional curses which may be laid on a man and become operative if he, or any of his descendants, should do a certain thing.

RITUAL PERSONS

There are several ritual figures among the Nuer who are important in the village community.

1. *The Leopard-Skin Chiefs.* They have a special relationship with the earth and can affect the welfare of the crops. They also have a limited role in rain-making and in the general regulation of the weather. They conduct the rituals concerned with homicide, with cleansing the parties to incestuous relations, with preventing feuds, and protecting warriors on raiding expeditions.

2. *The Wut Ghok.* Members of certain lineages have hereditary ritual powers in relation to cattle; they are asked to cure cows of various diseases and to ensure the fertility of barren animals. Their role is, however, a more restricted one than that of the leopard-skin chief, who has functions relating to social as well as to natural processes. Usually the *wut ghok* is a member of a stranger lineage, as is the leopard-skin chief, and this is presumably an advantage when they have to mediate between powerful and antagonistic lineages.

3. *Totemic Experts.* There are a number of totemic experts whose ritual connections with lions, crocodiles, and other dangerous creatures, enable them to influence the beasts' behaviour to the advantage of the community. A totemic specialist is the possessor of the spirit of his totem; he has no political significance.

(1) Evans-Pritchard, *Africa*, 1949, IXX, p.289.

4. *War Specialist.* It is the duty of the war specialist to shake a spear in the face of the enemy and to make an invocation against them. The war specialist is known as the *gwan muot*, the possessor of the spear. He is often a member of a senior lineage of the dominant clan.

5. *Magicians.* The Nuer have a number of leeches, diviners, owners of medicine and fetishes. Only the owners of fetishes obtain any consider-able status, and this is because the people are afraid of fetish spirits and believe them to be so powerful that they will even give cattle to purchase them. A fetish owner may become the most influential man in the village, but he holds no special office and does not represent the village in inter-village relationships.

6. *The Gwan Buthni.* Each small lineage has its *gwan buthni* - an offi-cial who performs certain ritual services for the family members. He functions at marriages, at mortuary ceremonies, and also performs the task of severing kinship bonds when a marriage is arranged between two very distantly related people; this he does by splitting a gourd in two or cutting a sheep in half.

7. *Prophets.* A prophet is a man possessed by one of the sky spirits or gods whom the Nuer regard as sons of the sky god.[1] Since the Nuer greatly respect and reverence these spirits they fear those possessed by them. Prophets exert a wider influence than any other category of persons in the entire society. Ngundeng was the first prophet *(guk)* to gain great influence by means of his healing powers, prophecies, and prolonged fasts. He led expeditions against the Dinka and, according to his followers, was possessed by the sky god Deng. He built a vast pyramid of earth and ashes with a palisade of ivory tusks. Originally each prophet's influence was confined to a small locality, but at the end of the nineteenth century they began to have a tribal significance and organised the opposition against the Arabs and Europeans. Eventually the power of the more import-ant prophets spread beyond tribal boundaries and they came to represent the unity of a tribe or a number of tribes. This development of the political powers of individuals brought about a structural change;[2] since the sky gods passed into the sons of a prophet after his death it would appear that the hereditary principle was beginning to assert itself. The prophets were eventually suppressed by the Administration. It seems probable that, if this action had not been taken, they would have become divine kings of some sort, perhaps similar to the Shilluk *reth*. In general, the predomin-ant interests of the Nuer in ritual matters are expressed in beliefs of a spiritual rather than a magical nature. Unlike the other Nilotes the Nuer have comparatively few magical practices; even magic coming from the west through Dinkaland tends to be spiritualised by them.

RAIN-MAKING

The Nuer attach little importance to rain-making. Any member of the Gaawar clan can act as rain-maker, since the ancestor of the clan came down from heaven holding a sprig of the *nyot* tree and a small round stone. He has no special political status or any extra prestige.

---

(1) Evans-Pritchard, *The Nuer*, 1940, p.185.
(2) *Ibid.*, p.189.

In certain parts of Nuerland, land experts and prophets claim to be able to produce rain. In certain areas, the leopard-skin chief acts as rain-maker. The title *gwan pini* (owner of water) is given to any ritual specialist who has powers in connection with rain and floods.

The Tiet

The Nuer distinguish clearly between the prophet *(guk)* and the specialist in magic *(tiet)*. The former relies on the sky spirit which possesses and indwells him; the latter relies on various magical substances and actions. The *tiet* has a minor earth spirit, such as a totem spirit. A *tiet* is always a local specialist practising in his own community only, though a magician who possesses powerful magic *(gwan wal)* may become well known and be recognised by a whole district. All these spirits come under the general category of *kwoth* but[1] three main classes may be distinguished:

1. *Guk.* The prophet in whom a sky spirit dwells.

2. *Tiet.* A specialist in magic, acting as leech and diviner.

3. *Gwan Wal.* These are of two types: one using ordinary medicines *(wal)*; another using 'talking medicines'; the latter are owners of fetishes, since their medicines are inhabited by earth spirits known as *kulangni*.

The *tiet gweeni* (mussel shell diviner) answers questions put to him by throwing mussel shells on the convex surface of a gourd and divining from the positions into which they fall on the ground. Every mussel shell diviner has his *kwoth*, the spirit which assists him in his practice.

The *Tiet Dala* cures headaches, recovers lost property, and performs magic to lessen the watchfulness of those who have stolen cattle so that the true owner may get them back again undetected. He also performs magic to ensure safe journeys and to protect warriors from danger. He possesses love magic. *Tiet me Ngwet (or Tiet Coli)* removes objects placed by a witch in a sick man's body.

There are also various other specialists[2] who treat barren women, important men and so forth.

NUER MEDICINES *(WAL)*

Most of the Nuer medicines have been borrowed from neighbouring peoples, especially from the Dinka; the Nuer, however, endow them with spirits.[3] The most powerful medicines are *kulangni* (talking medicines). Although the earth spirits in the medicines cannot compete in power with the sky spirits, the people fear the owners of fetishes and respect them. In the past a fetish owner was in great danger of being killed by avengers. He was safe among his fellow villagers, for it was believed that a man would not harm a member of his own kin and community; but if a fetish

(1) Evans-Pritchard, *S.N.R.*, 1935, Vol.XVIII, pt.1, p.67.
(2) *Ibid.*, p.70, for fuller details on Nuer magical experts.
(3) *Ibid.*

owner killed a man of another district, he began a feud and was liable to be killed by the kin of his victim. It seems that fetish owners were treated differently in different areas. Many people possess medicines which protect them from fetishes.

Death may be due to one of three causes: *olia kwoth* (a sickness of god), sorcery and the evil eye, or sickness due to fetishes. This last is sudden and may kill a man quickly, whereas a sickness sent by god is usually prolonged.[1] A man believing himself to be ill on account of a fetish summons a fetish owner to discover whose fetish is responsible. When this is known a sacrifice is made to the fetish and its owner is asked to stop it troubling the sick man.

When a fetish owner dies, his medicines are preserved until his spirits enter into one of his descendants who will then become a fetish owner in his stead. A man may purchase a fetish from another; the medicine is only the habitation of the fetish spirits who exist apart from it. The Nuer believe that a fetish kills someone because its owner dislikes him.

The Nuer Ghoul

Many of the Nilotic tribes believe in ghouls who feed on the bodies of those recently dead. This belief is found among the Acholi, Anuak, Shilluk, Lango, Dinka and Nuer. The Nuer ghoul is called the *rodh* and is regarded with horror by the people. The practice of ghoulist activities is to some extent hereditary, for the potentiality is found in certain lineages, but a man may become a *rodh* even if he is not a member of such a lineage. Disinterment of the dead is regarded as his most horrible activity.

A *rodh* may be killed by common consent and, although no blood must be spilt, he may be beaten to death with sticks without fear of revenge. This is the only instance among the Nuer of killing which does not demand compensation or vengeance.

LIFE CYCLE

BIRTH

In childbirth a woman is attended by a female relative who is herself already a mother. The child's incisor teeth are removed at the age of eight years.

The birth of twins constitutes a danger to their family; special decorations are worn by the kinsmen, animals are sacrificed, and ritual prohibitions observed. As do other Nilotic groups, the Nuer believe that the parents are safe if the twins are of opposite sexes, for the boy will want to preserve his father and the girl her mother. In spite of the dangers, however, the Nuer are joyful at the birth of twins if they both live. Throughout life, twins are subject to certain ritual observances; before a twin can get married they must both together go through a fictional

(1) Evans-Pritchard, *S.N.R.*, 1935, p.74.

marriage ceremony with partners selected for the purpose, and, in the ceremony, the role of the sexes is reversed.(1)

BURIAL

The grave is dug and the corpse buried as quickly as possible and without ceremony. Young people and age-mates of the deceased do not participate. The grave site is at the left-hand side of a man's hut. All ornaments are removed and the body is buried in a flexed position, one arm being placed under the head and the other over it. The body lies on the right side facing west. Graves are not long remembered, and are not places for ritual. When a leopard-skin chief or a *wut ghok* dies he is buried on a platform and covered with skins.

A few days after death, the *gwan buthni,* the ritual expert of the lineage, makes a sacrifice and cleanses the people of the homestead. The ghost *(joak)* is told not to trouble the living. Some believe that spirits live in the sky, others that they continue to live under the earth the same kind of life as they lived when alive.(2)

Relatives mourn until the mortuary ceremony which is held several months after death. The purpose of this ceremony, the *wocene cuol* or *cuol woc*, is to prevent misfortune which might befall the relatives on account of the death and to cut off the dead from the living.

THE BURUN

GENERAL

The Burun inhabit the regions between the White and Blue Niles in the province of Dar Fung. The country is a flat plain, with rocky hills emerging from it. These jebels are in some cases of considerable size and, wherever there is water in or near them, they have settlements on them. The populations of the hills have been considerably affected by foreign influence over a long period of time and, as a consequence, are very mixed. The Burun-speaking peoples may be divided into two groups:

The Northern Burun, comprising the settlements on hills Maiak, Surkum, Jerok, Mufwa, Kurmuk, Kudul, Ragreig, Abuldugu, Mughaja, and Tullok;

The Southern Burun, comprising the Meban of the southern plains, the dwellers on hills Ulu and Gerwai and the Jumjum on hills Tunya, Terta, Wadega and along Khor Jumjum.

The following account is a brief summary of the information available on the social organisation, cultural features and ritual beliefs and practices of the Burun-speaking people. Each hill community is treated separately for, according to the authorities, each is entirely independent of the rest. Most of the information available is contained in Evans-Pritchard's article in S.N.R., 1932, Vol.XV, Pt.I.

(1) Evans-Pritchard, *Uganda Journal,* 1936, Vol.III, No.3, p.233.
(2) Evans-Pritchard, *African Affairs,* 1949, Vol.48, p.57.

JEBEL ULU

The village of Jebel Ulu is situated on the slopes of the hill amidst boulders and scrub.   It is said to have been the seat of a strong Fung colony before the time of Turkish rule in the Sudan.   Many of the inhabitants of Ulu call themselves Fuin and say that their ancestors came originally from Sennar and settled in various outposts in Burun country, subjugating and taxing the inhabitants.   The prosperity of the community was eventually ruined by the Mahdia, although it appears that even before them the Fung aristocracy was growing weak - perhaps because of the custom of king-killing which diminished their numbers.

The king was always killed in a ritual manner by a relative who wished himself to become king.   The proposed assassination had first to be approved by a family council so that only rulers who alienated their Fuin relatives were in real danger of sudden attack.   The spearing was usually done by a half-brother of the ruler, though the mother's brother's son and the father's brother's son might also perform the killing.   If several brothers united to kill another, it was the eldest who normally took the kingship.   According to Evans-Pritchard it was considered likely that the son of the slain king would, in his turn, kill the slayer of his father.(1)

The killing took the form of an attack on the king by night, or he might be ambushed when alone.   The king went around with an armed bodyguard of slaves and, like the Shilluk *reth*, he regularly changed his sleeping hut so that no-one would know where he was.   He was generally killed with a spear and his wives were inherited by a brother, but not by the slayer.

Age and sickness were not regarded as reasons for killing a ruler, as among the Shilluk, nor was he debarred from taking part in war.   On his accession the king was secluded for seven days in his hut and at the end of that time he was brought out and invested with his new powers, the investiture being the occasion of a feast and the slaying of a bull.   All leopard-skins belong, by right, to the king.   Regicide at Ulu is regarded by the local population as a custom brought by the Fuin from Sennar.(2)

GENERAL CUSTOMS AT ULU

A bridegroom works for several years on his father-in-law's cultivations.   He also makes a payment of bridewealth.   After marriage the bridegroom remains for about a year in his father-in-law's village.   According to Evans-Pritchard a man might marry the daughters of his uncles and aunts on both sides of the family.(3)

In the past the people used to fight the Jumjum and the Meban.

They use the niche grave as the mode of burial, and above the grave they place two big stones at either end and stones round it.   The corpse is wrapped in cloth and placed on its right side, facing east.

(1) Evans-Pritchard, *S.N.R.*, 1932, Vol.XV, Pt.1, p.14.
(2) *Ibid.*, p.15.
(3) *Ibid.*, p.16.

THE MEBAN OF THE SOUTH

The southern or plains Burun occupy the marsh country in the extreme south of the Dar Fung hills, their villages being widely separated from each other. They are circular in shape and comprise 5 to 20 huts unprotected by palisades. Probably the village forms part of a larger political group, which is the unit operating in blood feuds. No compensation is paid for homicide, and the slayer or one of his kin is killed. Mostyn maintains that feuds between villages often continue for years; villages are raided or solitary villagers are ambushed and killed.[1]

GENERAL CUSTOMS

A man works on the cultivations of his father-in-law for some years before his marriage and probably a certain amount of bridewealth is handed over when the marriage is concluded. The bridegroom collects spears, beads, axes, bracelets, pigs and beer, to present to the bride's father. He usually kidnaps the girl in a traditional manner and takes her to his village.[2] A man lives with his wife in his own village from the beginning. There is no mother-in-law avoidance. Widows are inherited by the brothers of the dead husband and property by a man's sons.

RITUAL

A man is buried in a shaft in his own hut. The body is placed on its side and the legs are drawn up, with one hand placed to support the head. Some of the dead man's possessions are placed in the grave.

The Southern Meban name for god is *juon* and they are great believers in witchcraft.[3] The Burun on Khor Yabus regard the rain and the sun as gods, the sun god being most revered. The rain god is called *doam*. According to popular belief the first chief of the Burun, who originally founded the tribe, became a spirit and has always looked after them and guarded them.[4]

THE JUMJUM

The Jumjum live to the south east of Jebel Ulu, at the foot of hills Tunya, Terta and Wadega, and along Khor Jumjum. They themselves maintain that they come from the west, and claim to be related to the Burun of Ulu, though Arabs told Evans-Pritchard that they were of Dinka origin.[5]

Each village consists of a number of homesteads separated from each other by some 100 yards. Each homestead has two or three huts for living in, a granary, and huts for sheltering pigs and goats. The Jumjum of Khor Jumjum occupy one straggling village and one to three villages at Jebel Tunya. Virtually nothing is known of their political organisation. They appear to have an hereditary rain-maker who undergoes a special ceremony of investiture; his hut is regarded as a sanctuary. "He also seems

(1) Mostyn, *S.N.R.*, 1921, Vol.IV, p.211.
(2) *Ibid.*, p.210.
(3) Wedderburn-Maxwell, *S.N.R.*, 1936, Vol.XIX, p.183.
(4) Mostyn, *loc.cit.*, pp.209-10.
(5) Evans-Pritchard, *S.N.R.*, 1932, p.21.

to exercise functions of a political nature, as well as of a religious
nature and may be regarded as political-religious chief of the type which
is common in the Nuba hills."(1)

GENERAL CUSTOMS

The Jumjum have exogamous clans. Leviratic marriage is practised, a
man taking the wife of his deceased brother. A man will work for several
years on the cultivations of his future father-in-law and his relatives
will assist him in this labour. Bridewealth consists of cows, goats,
spears and other miscellaneous objects, but this appears to be less important than the labour which the man is expected to perform. A wife goes
straight to her husband's home on marriage.

A man guilty of homicide flees but, after a short time, compensation
of 5 cows or 20 goats is paid on his behalf and he returns unmolested.

RITUAL

A man is buried facing south. His broken spear, hoe and ornaments
are placed in the grave. Later, branches are placed on top and a few
stakes are driven in. Offerings are made at the grave.

The Jumjum at Wadega have a rain-maker called *mun nial* or *mun dyong* -
'man of rain' or 'man of god'; the two names refer apparently to the same
man. At Khor Jumjum there is no *mun nial*, but only a *mun dyong*. On the
death of a rain-maker the office goes to one of his sons, not necessarily
the eldest. Rainstones are used for obtaining rain; the rain-maker has
a shrine consisting of a piece of raised ground, like a miniature watershed, with a branched post at the back of it - if a generalisation can be
made from Evans-Pritchard's reference to the rain-maker of Wadega. The
washing of the rainstones and the sacrifice of a goat, the blood of which
is allowed to drip on the stones is supposed to bring rain, in appropriate
ritual circumstance.

The name for god is *Dyong*, and he is thought of as living in the sky
though he may sometimes come to earth. He is like a man, has a beard and
sits on a horse. He is sometimes said to reside at the top of Jebel
Tunya where no-one goes. Witches are called *ammu* and their powers are
hereditary.

THE NORTHERN BURUN

Each of the hills of the Northern Burun appears to be a political unit
having its own distinctive name and its own chiefs; feuds between neighbouring communities seem to have been frequent.

GENERAL CUSTOMS

It appears to be the custom on each hill for a bridegroom to work in
the gardens of the father-in-law before marriage and to pay a certain
amount of bridewealth. The length of the period of work, and the amount

(1) Evans-Pritchard, *S.N.R.*, 1932, p.26.

paid vary in the different communities.   If a man dies, his brother will
take his widow.   A man may not marry the daughters of his father's brother
or his mother's brother.   A mock battle between relatives of bride and
relatives of groom occurs at the wedding.   The people of Kurmuk and of
Mughaja observe similar customs.

RITUAL

Each community appears to have rain-makers.   There is also an association between the firmament and the idea of a supreme being.   The words
for sun and god are not identical, as in other languages of this area,
but there seems nevertheless to be an association.   Mostyn writes that
on Jebel Maiak the sun is a big god but each jebel is believed to have a
god of its own who lives in the rocks.   Bad years are believed to be a
sign that the god is angry with the inhabitants.[1]   The people of
Mughaja call god *djok* and say *djok nial* - 'god is in the firmament'.

Witchdoctors are known on every jebel and appear to perform their
usual functions of curing illness.

THE PARI

The Pari of Lafon hill in Equatoria Province live in terraced villages.   Land in the neighbourhood of the hill, which rises out of a
plain, is utilised for cultivation and grazing grounds.   As there is no
water on the hill itself, it has to be fetched from the pools close by.

There has been considerable controversy regarding the origin of
this people.   Walsh points out that one of the Pari villages consisted
originally of Acholi but he believes that the whole tribe migrated from
Anuak country.[2]   Driberg confirms this statement, pointing out that
the Pugeri claim to be Shilluk from the north, while the Boi and Kor
claim to be Anuak from the north-east.[3]   The exact connection between
the Anuak, the Shilluk and the Pari is not known but facts point to the
closest connection between them in the past.

ORGANISATION OF THE PARI

All the Pari villages are built on the hill and the entire population is divided into 6 villages and three sections, Pugeri, Boi and Kor.
Two of the sections, the Boi and Kor, trace descent from the mythological
ancestor, Ochudho, who appears to be identical with the ancestor of the
noble clan of the Anuak.

According to one authority, the fighting men live round the foot of
the hill, the older people higher up.   The population is governed and
led in war by a chief whose office is hereditary, brothers succeeding
each other in order of seniority.   After the death of the youngest
brother the succession passes to the eldest son of the eldest brother and
so on through his family.   The chief has the task of settling disputes.

(1) Mostyn, *S.N.R.*, 1921, p.209.
(2) Walsh, *S.N.R.*, 1922, Vol.V, p.47.
(3) Driberg, *S.N.R.*, 1925, Vol.VIII, p.49.

For deliberate murder the punishment is death; for homicide resulting from a quarrel the offender must hand over a boy to the family of the deceased. Compensation (a cow, 5 sheep and 5 hoes) is paid to the husband by an adulterer. People work on the cultivations of the chief.

GENERAL CUSTOMS

There are early betrothals; the bridegroom pays a number of sheep every year until his fiancée reaches marriageable age and the ceremony is then celebrated by a beer feast. Widows are inherited by the dead husband's brother.

Nalder states that there is an age-class association, each age set extending over the whole community.[1]

RITUAL

The Pari have rain-makers. To get rain a bull and a goat are eaten and some blood is collected on a grinding-stone and placed in the chief's hut. When the meal is over, the rain-makers dip their hands in water and shake them over the burning embers of the fire on which the bull was cooked. Clouds of steam arise and immediately all rush to their huts and remain quiet until the sun rises. Shrines can be seen near every hut and sheep are killed over the grave of an ancestor.

THE BELANDA

The Belanda occupy the areas in the neighbourhood of the Wau, Sueh and Bo rivers in the Bahr el Ghazal. As previously stated, (see above p. 9) the Belanda consist of two peoples of different origins, the Nilotic Bor and the Ndogo Biri.

THE DIVISIONS OF THE BOR BELANDA

According to Santandrea, the Nilotic section of the Belanda, the Bor, admit a broad division into two sections: the Jo-ku-nam, the people of the river, and the Jo-Ugot, the people of the hill to the north of them. Their nicknames originated from the fact that the former used to live on the banks of the river Sueh, while the others lived on the rocky hills of the neighbourhood.[2]

There seems to be an important distinction at present between the two halves of the Bor, and this is explained by Evans-Pritchard in terms of their history. M.J.W. mentions the ruling tribes, the Fujiga and Kamun.[3] He states that the Fujiga can speak the Jo Luo dialect and have some cultural features in common with them. There are traditions among the people themselves that they originally split off from the Jo Luo and joined the Bor, who were living in the hill region to the west of the Sueh. Here they gained ascendancy and grafted themselves on to the people as an aristocracy; it was this Fujiga aristocracy which organised resistance to the Zande invasion and finally led the Bor northwards across the Bo river.

(1) Nalder, *A Tribal Survey of Mongalla Province*, 1937, p.144.
(2) Santandrea, *Anthropos*, 1942, p.233.
(3) M.J. Wheatley, *S.N.R.*, 1923, Vol.VI, No.2, p.251.

The section of the Bor which came under the migrating Fujiga had previously been ruled over by a tribe called Kamun.   These assert that they
inhabited the country before the Bor and, three generations ago, ruled
over four sub-tribes whom they eventually absorbed.[1]   The Bor, and
later the Biri, joined them;   family quarrels and Zande pressure caused
them to move northwards and eastwards, following in the steps of the
Fujiga withdrawal from their hilly country.[2]   Evans-Pritchard sums up:
"what little information we possess points to successive waves of
Shilluk southwards, each representing a typical Nilotic breakaway from the
amalgam of Shilluk-speaking tribes.   The Kamun were probably an early
wave of this southward rolling tide, the Amberidi and Fujiga were later
waves."

Santandrea considers that the Bor were better organised than the Biri
and that the Bor chiefdom appears to have been predominant.[3]   He also
states that the Bor have the same units as the Jo Luo, namely: the tribe
(kodi), the clan (fa), and the lineage (dendot).

RITUAL

There are certain characteristics of the Bor which suggest their
Nilotic origins.[4]   They believe that sickness and death are due to the
spirits of dead men rather than to witchcraft or magic;   this belief is
typical of the Nilotes and is in contrast to the beliefs of the Azande and
the southern and western tribes, who maintain that witchcraft is the main
source of evil.   Santandrea asserts that at the bottom of all the religious beliefs and practices of the Biri there lies the idea of *sini*
(*cyen* of the Luo-Shilluk) and this belief is undoubtedly borrowed from the
Nilotic Bor.[5]

The word for god or spirit in Bor is *jok*;   in the Biri dialect it is
joki.

---

(1)   M.J.W., *S.N.R.*, 1923, Vol.VI, No.2, p.252.
(2)   Evans-Pritchard, *S.N.R.*, 1931, Vol.XIV, Pt.1, pp.17-18.
(3)   Santandrea, *Anthropos*, 1942, p.235.
(4)   Evans-Pritchard, *op.cit.*, p.23.
(5)   Santandrea, *Anthropos*, 1924, p.234.

THE   LUO   TRIBES   OF   THE
BAHR   EL   GHAZAL

In the Bahr el Ghazal province there are a number of small and apparently diverse tribes, all of which, however, are of Nilotic origin. These are the Dembo or Bwodho, the Shatt or Thuri, and the Shilluk or Luo, - the first name being that by which they are known to foreigners, the second, their own name for themselves.

THE DEMBO

The Dembo live north of the river Kpango and are divided into two groups: the Kapango and the Kyom Dembo. The Kapango live mainly near Kpango river and are now under the Shilluk-Luo chief; the Kyom Dembo live on both sides of the Khor Kyom (though mainly to the north of it) and are under the authority of the chief of the Dembo.

The chiefs of the Dembo group, the *kyom Dembo*, all belong to a special lineage of a single clan, the Pakeer. The most famous of the chiefs was Kwomo. His staff has been kept, and orders are sent out with it, fights are stopped, and rain is made. The Pakeer clan is divided into a number of sub-clans which, according to Santandrea, may almost be said to be independent clans.(1)

Clans of the Dembo include the Briere, Pakeer, Burpiom, Birbiam, Agwara and Fijulu clans. There are no sacred spears among the Dembo but the royal staff, as an emblem of power, and the rainstones, suggest a combination of temporal, ritual and mystic power.(2)

GENERAL CUSTOMS

According to Santandrea the marriage procedure of the Dembo is essentially the same as that of the Jo Luo.

Wooden posts with notches carved on them commemorate men famous for having killed people in war or for having killed big game.

THE SHILLUK-LUO

The Shilluk-Luo live together with the Dembo, and to the north of them, between the Kuru and the Kpango rivers. They are divided into two main groups: the Northern Shilluk-Luo, and the Southern Shilluk-Luo, living north and south of the Kpango river respectively.

The founder of the famous Wadelmak dynasty of the Shilluk-Luo was the chief Yamo Kon. He brought all the neighbouring Luo and Dembo under his sway and the Shatt clans also acknowledged him. He was backed by the Dinka, with whom he was on friendly terms, and he had little to fear from the slave-traders who were busy in that area before British occupation. At the height of his prestige he was given the Arabic name Wadelmak, which was also given to the dynasty which he founded. Wadelmak claimed direct

(1)   Santandrea, *S.N.R.*, 1938, p.278.
(2)   Santandrea, *Annali Lateranensi*, 1944, Vol.VIII, p.101.

descent from Dimo from whom his ancestors had inherited the sacred spear in
the possession of his family.   It was supposed to have a double power:
rain-making and war magic.   Wadelmak's power ended at the time of Kara-
mallah's invasion and he was put to death for rallying to Dem Zubeir with
other chiefs.[1]   He was succeeded by his brother Aweya, but the power of
the Shilluk-Luo chieftainship waned as the Dinka began to dominate their
smaller neighbours.   Though the Dinka made a friendly use of their powers,
the Shilluk-Luo chiefs inevitably lost much of their independence.

SOCIAL   ORGANISATION

1.   *The Northern Shilluk-Luo*

Before British intervention, the Northern Shilluk-Luo had as chief a
man of the Wadelmak lineage.   He was believed to be endowed with extraordinary powers, and was a divine king after the style of the *reth* of the
Shilluk, although on a smaller scale because his people were less important
in numbers and prestige.[2]   The spirit of Dimo, the great founding ancestor of the group, was supposed to dwell in him.   This spirit was regarded as the spirit of life and every effort was made to keep it, and have
it transmitted to an heir.   Thus, when the chief was ill and dying, his
elderly counsellors and relatives were brought to him and would kill him
ritually.

The Shilluk-Luo chief had charge of Dimo's ancient spear and used it
both as a war charm and also to obtain rain on behalf of his people.   Ceremonies in which the spear was used were performed by a lineage of the same
clan as that of the chief or by the chief himself.   Two events are believed to have brought about the downfall of the Wadelmak dynasty: the
abandonment of the traditional custom of violent death, and the loss of
Dimo's sacred spear which was seized by a Dinka raiding band.   The Wadel-
maks are still looked on with respect and the head of the survivors is
reverenced;   "he often performs the duty of priest-king, especially where
the rain-making ceremony is concerned."[3]

2.   *The Southern Shilluk-Luo*

The Southern Shilluk-Luo seem to have had a similar organisation to
that of the northern group.   Chiefs have always belonged to the Demöi
clan, though all admit that the southern chiefs were far inferior to the
Wadelmak whose power extended into their sphere.

CLANS

Tha clans are exogamous except in the Demoi clan, where intermarriage
is allowed among some of the more widely separated branches - probably between the most distant maximal lineages.

TOTEMISM

They possess only a slight form of totemism.   The Demöi have the

(1)   Santandrea, *S.N.R.*, 1938, Vol.XXI, pt.II, p.280.
(2)   Santandrea, *Annali Lateranensi*, 1944, Vol.VIII, p.98.
(3)   Santandrea, *S.N.R.*, 1938, p.283.

keno, a sort of pumpkin, as a totem and this is shared by all branches of the Demöi, even those that intermarry. Certain ceremonies are performed with the *keno* at the time of a child's birth. One of the most important clans of the Shilluk-Luo, the Dediä, has a tree as a totem. They call it *kwer* (taboo); reverence is paid to it and its leaves are used in ritual. The other clans likewise have totems.

THE JO LUO

The Jo Luo is the largest and the best known tribe of the Luo group in the Bahr el Ghazal province. Most of the information about them is derived from various publications of Father Santandrea.

The Jo Luo are divided into two parts:

1. The North-West Jo Luo, who live in the neighbourhood of Kpango mission.

2. The South-East Jo Luo, who live on the right bank of the River Jur.

ORGANISATION

Santandrea states that the headman was called *ja*, but that now he is named the *ruoth* (plur. *ruodhen*).[1] It appears from his account, however, that he may have failed to distinguish between the Jo Luo headmen, sub-chiefs and chiefs. A chief, when dying, calls a trusted elder who does not belong to the same clan and names his successor who will not necessarily be his son.[2] After the funeral all the people assemble at the house of the deceased headman or chief in commemoration of his death. The elder in whom he had confided brings a small mat *(belo)* and a hippopotamus-hide whip; he leads the man designated as successor to the mat and puts the whip in his hands. He does likewise with two other men chosen as the leaders of the elders' council.

If a new chief or headman is to be elected by common consent, the elders *(jo dono)* discuss the matter and, when the choice has been made, the people proceed to the hut of the elected man bearing gifts with them. The chief designate is lifted up and then placed on the ground again - a procedure which is reminiscent of the installation of the Dinka spear-chief. At the same time an elder strikes the ground with the whip three times, to show how the chief will punish those who disobey him. The chief then puts on a leopard-skin and is placed on some ashes. For a headman or a lesser chief, a cob's skin is used.

When a headman is to be discharged, the decision is reached in secret, then the skin of a *dikdik* or cob is placed against the door of his hut at night. The headman next morning finds it and takes it to the customary meeting-place in the village. He is asked whether he found anything by

(1) Santandrea, *Annali Lateranensi*, 1944, Vol.VIII, p.97.
(2) *Ibid.*, p.96.

his door and is told to leave the skin with the elders.   By this procedure it is understood that he must relinquish his office.

Headmen are easily recognisable for they alone wear clothing, their
usual garment consisting of an antelope's skin with a hole in the middle
for the head to pass through.   The *ja* is assisted in his duties by the
elders *(jo dono)* and some strong and reliable men carry out police duties.
These men are called *woden* (sing. *wodo* or *woro*).   Santandrea also mentions sub-chiefs, small petty chiefs, living in a semi-dependent position
and often calling on their chiefs for support 'but doing alone their
smaller home business'.[1]   Powers of leadership, ability in settling
disputes fairly and tact in handling people give the *ja* his ascendancy,
according to Santandrea, and, if he is really popular, a son may inherit
his father's position.   Chiefs and headmen do not collect tribute, and
proceeds from court cases are their sole means of obtaining financial aid.

Some chiefs seem to have been fairly well known and to have acted as
intermediaries in dealings with other tribes.   Minor chiefs and headmen
have smaller spheres of influence and they seek the support of the more
powerful chiefs and headmen.[2]

JO LUO TRIBAL SECTIONS AND CLANS

Santandrea states that the Jo Luo tribe is split into groups of
clans.[3]   Each group or sub-tribe has a common name and each clan in a
sub-tribal territory has its own name.   Clans belonging to the same sub-
tribal group live in a closer relationship with each other than with clans
of other sub-tribal groups.   They have a common stock of usages and traditions and, in fights, acts of vengeance and similar occurrences, they
are likely to join forces.   Santandrea somewhat ambiguously remarks that
the clans of one sub-tribe are all grouped, 'as a rule, in one continuous
territory though they may be scattered far and wide.[4]   It is probable
that the Jo Luo have an association of dispersed clans and territories
similar to the other Nilotes.

The Western Jo Luo are divided into two sub-tribes: the Amec and
Logo, each having a certain number of clans associated with the tribal
territory.[5]   All chiefs are said to belong to the Amec.

The Eastern Jo Luo form a congeries of sub-tribes: the Aluro,
Athiiro, Abut, Akwer and Yau, each sub-tribe having a number of clans associated with it as among the Western Jo Luo.[6]

Jo Luo clans are strictly exogamous.   Each clan is sub-divided into
numerous *dhe uot* (lineages) and there seems to have been a regular process
of clan bifurcation in the past.   Clan and lineage names are usually preceeded by the prefix *ya*, meaning 'people'; some have the prefix *piny*
meaning 'land', others the prefix *par* meaning 'home'.   Close bonds link
together members of the same clan and the different *dhe uot* of a clan.
In the case of blood fines all the *dhe uot* may be called on to contribute

(1) Santandrea, *Annali Lateranensi*, 1944, Vol.VIII, p.98.
(2) *Ibid.*   (3) *Ibid.*, p. 103.
(4) *Ibid.*, p. 104.   (5) *Ibid.*
(6) *Ibid.*, p. 105.

and all may assist in taking vengeance.   Game is also shared among the
che wot according to fixed rules.[1]

The relative importance of the lineage system and the hierarchy of
officials is a question which arises from the literature on the Jo Luo but
unfortunately it is not yet possible to reach any satisfactory conclusion
about it.

LEGAL PROCEDURE

Cases of civil disputes and crimes are heard by the chief or sub-chief
or, in their absence, by any of the elders of the village.[2]   The accused,
the plaintiff and the witnesses, as well as all who are interested, attend
the court of settlement.   Only fines are imposed.   Ghawi states that
courts have many ways of executing their judgements;   for example, if a
debtor should fail to pay his debt, he is compelled to deliver an unmarried
sister or daughter as security.   Whether Ghawi's account describes the
result of European influence is not certain, but it does seem that the Jo
Luo method of settling disputes is more formalised than would be expected
of a Nilotic society, especially one without even an outstanding chief or
king.   In addition there is no mention of the blood feud which is characteristic of all other Nilotic tribal groups.

Ordeals

Several ordeals are practised among the Jo Luo.   Among the Northern
Jo Luo the ordeal by boiling water was the most popular, particularly in
cases of adultery.   Among the Eastern Jo Luo the most common ordeal was
that of drinking a poison called *kwir*.[3]

Fines

A fine of 200 *malodas* (iron hoes) is paid for murder in the areas east
of Wau;   200 *malodas*, one cow and one bull are paid in the west.   The compensation is given to the next of kin of the deceased.   In cases of acci-
dental homicide, half these amounts are paid.   Less is paid for killing a
woman if she has born children, while 50 *malodas* are paid for a slain
child.[4]

AGE ORGANISATION

Most Jo Luo practise the Dinka form of scarification, and the ceremony
is usually performed by Dinka experts.   There are no indigenous age classes and, where the Dinka system is copied, there is only a bond of friendship among age mates.   According to Santandrea a youth enters public life
by taking part in dances;   he also acquires a new name *(nyin twot)* which is
given by an old man of the house without any ceremony.   Only relatives of
the same clan call a man by his real name, the others call him by his *twot*
name and this applies even to stepmothers.   *Twot* names are given to girls
at about the same age.[5]

(1)   Santandrea, *Annali Lateranensi*, 1944, Vol.VIII, p.107.
(2)   Ghawi, *S.N.R.*, 1924, Vol.VII, p.71.
(3)   Stubbs, *S.N.R.*, 1942, Vol.XXV, Pt.I, p.135.   (4)   Ghawi, *op.cit.*, p.77.
(5)   Santandrea, *Annali Lateranensi*, 1945, Vol.IX, p.254.

MARRIAGE

The Jo Luo are polygynous; a prosperous man has two or more wives but the majority have only one. The most important men have three, though this is rare.

A man is forbidden to marry into his own or his mother's clan.

Bridewealth

Bridewealth is paid in instalments and the bridegroom is assisted by his father and male relatives. There are fixed rates; normally 200 *malodas* and two bulls are paid but for chiefs and wealthy people the amount is greater.[1] The bridewealth goes to the bride's father and brothers. A woman is usually paired with one of her brothers on the day of her birth so that the bridewealth, which will one day be received for her, can be used for him to obtain a wife. The bridewealth instalments should all be paid off before the marriage is completed, and during the period of engagement the bridegroom has to send presents to his bride consisting of meat, fish and cloth, etc.

Besides paying the ordinary bridewealth, the bridegroom works on the girl's mother's cultivations and is sometimes helped in this by near relatives and friends. All kinds of work in the parents-in-law's fields may be requested.

Marriage Ceremonies

When a young man has decided whom he wishes to marry he proceeds with his friends and relatives to the girl's house to gain her consent. If she accepts, the suitor ties a bead necklace round her neck and may give her a token present. According to Santandrea the ceremony of tying on the beads marks the final acceptance and the actual betrothal.[2]

The suitor's parents and relatives now call on his fiancée's family to discuss terms. When marriage is definitely decided on by both parties, avoidance is observed, the paying of the bridewealth begins and the suitor starts to work for his future parents-in-law. When the bridewealth has been fully or nearly paid, the marriage arrangements are made.

According to Santandrea, two forms of marriage existed side by side. The regular form consists of a public assembly of the relatives at the bride's home on an appointed day and the performance of certain ceremonies. The father's eldest brother explains her new duties to the bride, blesses her, wishes her prosperity and offspring, and ties an *apwobo* rope round her neck. All the elders likewise bless her. The bride with her relatives and friends is then escorted to her husband's home under the leadership of her paternal aunt. A feast takes place at the husband's house and celebrations may last for several days; marriage usually takes place at the beginning of a new year after the millet harvest.

(1) Ghawi, *S.N.R.*, Vol.VII, 1924, Pt.II, p.73.
(2) Santandrea, *Annali Lateranensi*, Vol.IX, 1945, p.223.

The second form is marriage by abduction *(tin nyarkov)* and it usually occurs when the bridegroom is tired of waiting until he has paid all the bridewealth. After the abduction a settlement between the husband and the girl's parents is effected by the payment of a large instalment of the bridewealth. If the abduction fails to secure a settlement the man may be brought before the courts and fined for seduction.

Avoidance

From the moment a marriage is agreed on, ceremonial avoidance is an obligation. Avoidance_extends chiefly to the girl's mother, mother's brothers, half-brothers, sisters and half-sisters, and also to the father, his half-brothers, brothers, sisters and half-sisters. The couple also avoid each other; they do not speak directly to each other in public,[1] but communicate through intermediaries.

After marriage, avoidance is practised but in a limited way. A man will not eat with his parents-in-law or with their brothers and sisters.

Sexual Offences

For seduction a fine of 60 hoes is paid to the parents of the girl. For adultery, 60 hoes are paid to the husband and a purifying ceremony takes place in which each party sacrifices a goat. The actual amounts paid vary according to region.

Sexual intercourse with someone of the same clan is regarded as a sin and if it is discovered a special ceremony *(adual)* is carried out, in which an animal is divided in two halves and the parties each seize one half and hurry away with it in opposite directions. A child born of such a union belongs to the husband of the woman and not to its real father.[2]

Divorce

If a man divorces his wife, he takes back nearly all the bridewealth he originally paid. If children have been born he will only take back part of the bridewealth. Cattle are left for the maintenance of the children who remain with their mother until they are 9 years old, in the case of boys, and 7 years old, in the case of girls.[3] A woman may leave her husband if she wishes and her parents then have to pay back the bridewealth, keeping back 40 to 60 hoes in consideration of his having cohabited with her.

Widow Inheritance

A man's wives belong to his heirs, his brothers and sons. Widows are usually allotted to the brothers and half-brothers of the dead husband, but young widows are inherited by the mature sons to whom they had originally been step-mothers. Santandrea states that "all the children of widows, either born before or after the death of their first husband, even after

---

(1)   Santandrea, *Annali Lateranensi*, 1945, Vol.IX, p.221.
(2)   *Ibid.*, p.236.
(3)   Ghawi, *S.N.R.*, 1924, Vol.VII, Pt.II, p.76.

long years, are counted to him: he purchased them with his own means." [1]

Widows are handed over to the heirs on *calca* day - after the feast held in honour of the dead man. The word *ger* denotes taking a widow, while to marry a woman in a regular way is *nywom*. No bridewealth is paid for a widow because she remains the wife of the dead husband, but a small ceremony takes place in which a sacrifice is made to avert the danger of the heir supplanting the dead man and taking his position. Old widows settle with their eldest son. If a widow is not wanted and is not very old she may become a prostitute or concubine.

RITUAL AND OTHER CULTURAL FEATURES

TOTEMISM

Totemism seems to be strongly established among the Jo Luo. Totems include birds, snakes and all sorts of animals and plants; beliefs associated with them are in many respects similar to those of the Dinka. Totem beliefs are explained in myths of twin births - the ancestor of the clan being born with the totem animal - and by various miraculous occurrences in the past. The totem plant or animal is called 'our relative' by those possessing it, and such totems are reverenced by being carefully handled and used. They may not be eaten or misused and are appeased and included in ritual ceremonies.

A husband is bound to observe his wife's taboos, and totems as well as his own, and children and grandchildren observe both. If a man is tired of observing these taboos he will send a goat to his wife's parents for the purpose of releasing himself and his children.

Very large trees are never cut for they are supposed to be possessed by a *jwok* (spirit). [2] Any extraordinarily big thing is thought to be possessed of a *jwok*.

SORCERY

It is thought that death may be due to sorcery. The man or woman held to be responsible is charged with murder and, if he admits the charge, is fined half the amount fixed for intentional murder; if he denies it he undergoes an ordeal and pays 200 hoes if proved guilty. If not guilty he receives 30 to 40 iron hoes from the plaintiff. [3]

A sorcerer is believed to go to the house of his enemy at night, and kill the occupant by throwing blood into the room. A special class of sorcerer uses the roots of trees known to have medical properties. The Jo Luo also believe in the evil eye. All cases of death from snake bites are attributed to acts of magic. [4]

(1) Santandrea, *Annali Lateranensi*, 1945, Vol.IX, pp.237-8.
(2) Santandrea, *Annali Lateranensi*, 1944, Vol.VIII, p.117.
(3) Ghawi, *S.N.R.*, 1924, Vol.VII, p.78.
(4) *Ibid.*, p.79.

If not due to sorcery death may be caused by the evil spirit of a dead man. A ritual is carried out in which some of the earth from the grave of the suspected man is used; if this fails the dead man is exhumed and one of his teeth is pulled out and worn round the neck of the sick person. If the dead man is a relative of the sufferer the nearest of his descendants is asked to perform a ritual to take away sickness. If he is not a relative, the witchdoctor may be called in for assistance.

LIFE CYCLE

BIRTH

A woman is assisted by one or two trained helpers who adjure her to confess the names of all the men with whom she has had relations since her marriage; if she should omit to do this it is believed that the child will die. The men named are fined for adultery.

Twins

At the birth of twins, special rules and taboos are observed and special names are given to them. Eating bird meat, bathing in hot water, having relations with the father and so forth, are all forbidden. When the twins can walk a feast is held at which the mother dances a twins' dance. After this the taboos lapse. Formerly one of twins used to be killed owing to the belief that two children born at once would kill their parents with their powerful evil influence.

The father gives his child a name, usually that of an ancestor, unless extraordinary circumstances accompany the birth. The name is given on the third day after birth for a male child, on the fourth day for a female child. There are certain set names which are given to a child born after the death of a brother or sister, to a child born after twins and to a posthumous child.

DEATH

Adults are generally buried near their huts, babies and twins close to the door. Great men, hunters and chiefs have a drum beaten to announce their death and, later, during the funeral, sham fights take place. A goat is generally killed upon the grave and a common meal taken at which people split into two groups, clansmen and non-clansmen. The first period of mourning lasts three days for a man, four days for a woman. After this period the *can tol* or *can dun* is held; this consists of the ritual burning of the personal belongings of the dead person.

Thirty days after death, on the day known as *calca* day, the customary feast of beer, meat and grain foods is held. Hard, cement-like soil is beaten on the grave; the dead man's inheritance and his wishes as to its disposal are then discussed and his belongings are distributed accordingly.

According to Santandrea the *nade yat* (medicine man) is summoned to perform a ceremony against the *cyen*.[1] *Cyen* is, presumably, the evil spirit

(1) Santandrea, *Annali Lateranensi*, 1945, Vol.IX, p.258.

with which the dead man may plague his descendants if he has died with a
grievance or is annoyed at their behaviour.   After a year or so the *can
gur loro* is celebrated;   this is the day when the grave mound is beaten
and a hard covering of earth is put on it.   There is no distinctive mark
for a great man's grave.   If a man wants successful hunting he may make a
small sacrifice on the grave of his father or his mother, and ask for their
assistance.

THE ALUR

GENERAL

The Alur live in the extreme north east of the Belgian Congo territory extending into Uganda.   They border the north west shores of Lake
Albert and are the western neighbours of the Acholi.   The countryside is
forest savannah with marshes in the low-lying ground and valleys.

ECONOMIC SYSTEM

They are pastoralists and cultivators and are reported to have great
herds of cattle.   Herds of goats are kept and also hens, although the
latter are not eaten and serve as a means of barter.   The people are
diligent cultivators;   they cultivate the same piece of land for two or
three successive harvests and then abandon it for another plot.   When the
land in the neighbourhood of a village is exhausted (after 7 to 10 years'
planting) the whole village moves to a new site.   Plots are often made on
the side of rising ground, and sorghum, maize, eleusine, sesame, millet,
bananas, beans and tobacco are grown.

Hunting is enthusiastically and skilfully pursued and provides an important addition to the diet.   Fishing is not very important except among
those who live along the shores of Lake Albert.

SOCIAL   ORGANISATION   AND
POLITICAL   STRUCTURE

The Alur are divided into a number of groups or tribes, and these are
subdivided into various smaller segments.

THE VILLAGE

A village usually consists of about 10 or 12 huts, with additional
huts used for storing grain and as shelters in which household work may be
performed.   There are miniature huts which are ancestral shrines and in
the middle of the village an old tree to which magical objects and hunting
trophies are attached from time to time.   The village is usually built on
a hill near a water-course and in the neighbourhood of a stretch of forest.
The huts are arranged in a circle, forming an enclosure.   Sometimes a hut
has round it a small enclosure of its own in which the household work is
done and celebrations take place.   Only the chiefs' villages are fortified.   In a chief's village the huts are bigger than those of an ordinary
village and one is set aside for the women and another for his sons.

A village is usually occupied by one extended patrilineal family, rarely by several families.   If a family grows too big, the parent village is not enlarged but a number of small related homesteads are founded near-by.   The sphere of authority of the village headman is thus enlarged and may, if it extends widely enough, become a factor in the political organi-sation.   As many as four villages may acknowledge one sub-chief or headman - *(nyampara)*.(1)

THE RELATION BETWEEN THE KINSHIP SYSTEM AND TERRITORIAL GROUPS

One particular clan seems to be associated with each tribe or tribal segment;   according to information elicited by Breugelmens from various literary sources, clans are localised, each forming a geographical unit and consequently may be considered as identified with the tribe or tribal seg-ment.(2)   As such they form the basis of the social and political organi-sation.   Also, the Alur clans appear to be of two types: either *djuker*, noble or aristocratic clans, or *luak*, commoner or client clans.

The name of a clan is often made up of the name of its founder with the prefix *pa* (man).   The clan organisation has ramifications outside the tribal unit to which it is primarily attached, while the traditions or origin and those relating to the clan's historical development play a vital part in clan solidarity.   The clans are reported to be exogamous and clan members observe the duty of blood revenge.

THE CHIEF

Breugelmens is of the opinion that Alur political organisation is of a decentralised type;   there are numerous small groups, partially independent, under the authority of chiefs and sub-chiefs or of a headman - *(nyampara)*. The chieftainship is hereditary, a chief being succeeded by his eldest son who is designated as successor by the heads of the various families acknow-ledging his father.   If the younger brothers of a chief found new commun-ities they remain subordinates and acknowledge their elder brother.

A chief is distinguished from lesser men in several ways.   His dwell-ing is particularly imposing and if he is powerful he possesses in the villages acknowledging him special houses in which he stays and accommo-dates his followers and to which he invites his guests.   The chief eats alone, being served by women.   He observes certain food taboos and enjoys certain marks of respect.   A chief's prestige is measured by the herds of cattle he possesses and, presumably, the entertainment he is able to afford. Sub-chiefs pay him a certain number of cattle and receive invitations to feasts and celebrations.   The people render their chief tribute, which takes the form of grain, cattle, salt, bark-cloth, iron implements and tobacco after the harvest.   He has the task of organising hunts and of firing the bush.   He also has a right to one tusk of every elephant killed in a hunt and to the skin of every leopard.   Leopard's teeth are reserved for the children of chiefs who alone have the right to wear them as neck-laces.   Every year the chief has the right to first fruits - this is the custom of *adjok* - and on this occasion he gives a great feast.   He has

---

(1) Breugelmans, *Les Alur*, p.24.   (2) *Ibid.*, p.10.

certain rights over the lands of the people who acknowledge him and any stranger wishing to use a tree or to settle on the land must first ask his permission.

The chief has certain judicial functions in which he is assisted by notable elders. The shedding of blood on the chief's territories constitutes an offence and is compensated for by the sacrifice of two goats and the presentation of two more to the chief.(1)

The chief is the rain-maker of the community and consequently an important ritual figure.

LEGAL ASPECTS OF THE ALUR SOCIETY

The chief and the elders deal with difficult cases and, if a satisfactory decision cannot be reached, there is recourse to divination. In a case of theft the goods must be returned and compensation paid. Compensation is paid for injury and for murder.

Property passes from father to son or, failing direct heirs, it goes to a man's nearest agnatic kinsmen. A family has rights in as much land as it can cultivate. When land is abandoned it reverts to the chief who holds all land on behalf of his people.

THE FAMILY

Each family occupies a hut and when the children grow up they leave their father's house and set up homesteads for themselves a short distance away. Every married woman has her own household for herself and her family. Young unmarried women live together in a special hut. As a family group extends so the influence of the family head grows and he may be remembered as the founder of a lineage.

MARRIAGE

A union is regarded as complete only after a number of ceremonies have been held. An agreement between two families that a marriage shall take place is marked by the exchange of gifts between the parents of the man and the girl. The payment of bridewealth then begins and the two families and their respective villages pay a series of visits to each other. Bridewealth consists of a number of cattle, sheep, goats, some iron implements and spears. If the marriage is not concluded the bridewealth is returned. The bride is formally taken by the groom when the bride's mother and her friends and relatives visit the village of the groom's family. Sacrifices are made and feasts are held to mark the occasion. Some time after this the girl adopts the married woman's tail and it is probable that as among other Nilotes the union is regarded as fully complete when a child is born.

A tribal chief may have more than one wife, as also a village chief and the wealthier family heads. At a man's death his wives and herds are taken over by his eldest brother. If a wife dies the husband has the right to ask for her sister. A man will not marry two sisters but will accept

(1) Breugelmans, *Les Alur*, p.89.

one as a substitute for a dead wife.

Fines are paid for various sexual offences such as adultery, rape, and seduction.

RITUAL

DJOK

The religious concepts of the Alur are very similar to those of the Acholi. The name for their supreme spirit, Rubanga has been imported from neighbouring Bantu. They also have the concept of *djok* and it is probable that Rubanga has partially taken over certain attributes which were originally associated with Djok.

All types of spirits are referred to as *djok*, as are certain mystical concepts, the supreme spirit, various minor spirits, the wind, and echoes. The word *djok* is combined with other qualifying terms to express specific aspects of experience, as among the Acholi and Lango.

The *djok* spirits are manifested in large rocks, in mountains, large snakes and rivers. Some of those inhabiting mountains or rivers are known as 'mother of the mountain' and 'mother of the river' respectively. Some sound like the wind and are called *yannu*, which is the Alur word for wind. Some inhabit the forest and others the marsh. The river *djok* are greatly feared. There are a number of especially important *djok*: these include Rubanga, who is sometimes referred to as an aspect of *djok*, is believed to be the creator of the world, and is associated with the sky and possibly with rain-fall. Djok Matar, a white spirit, is *djok* of the Lake; Ukelo is daughter of Rubanga; Adranga is djok of the rivers. The Alur make sacrifices to these various *djok* from time to time, especially when they wish to propitiate a particular aspect of life conceived to be under the influence of a *djok*.

THE ANCESTRAL CULT

Offerings are made to the ancestral spirits at particular shrines, called *kac* or *abila*, constructed in front of the door of a hut in the form of a table on four posts. Miniature huts also are made as temporary dwellings for the ancestral spirits. The spirits are believed to appear in dreams and protest against the negligence of their descendants.

MAGICAL PRACTICES

The Alur have a number of ritual officials including rain-makers and medicine men. Generally the chief is also the rain-maker, though men may be designated by the chiefs to perform this function. A sacrifice is made to *djok* when rain is required and there are various rituals which may be performed to induce rain to fall. Sacrifice may also be made to Rubanga.

The medicine man is reported to have considerable influence - especially in times of war and when his powers of divination are called upon to indicate those guilty of crime and sorcery. He also sells charms as protections against the evil eye and special amulets for twins.

Magicians who communicate with the spirits are known as *ajwaka*.

Sorcery is believed to be practised in secret.

LIFE CYCLE

BIRTH

Birth takes place in the mother's hut with several old women in attendance.   When a woman is having her first child she must name any lovers she had had and the payment of a goat may be demanded from each by her husband.

Twins are welcomed and their birth is associated with *djok*.   Celebrations are held and a special ritual, called *kwar djok*, is observed; without it the Alur think the twins would die.   A dance called *karema* takes place one and a half months after birth.   The names of twins are stereotyped.   Special observances are practised at the death of twins.

DEATH

On the death of a chief the heads of neighbouring families assemble. The eldest son of the deceased is designated as successor and he has the task of burying his father.   The chief's funeral is accompanied by sacrifices of animals on a large scale and by public mourning.   His body is wrapped in skins placed on 3 stones and buried in a hut with offerings of food.   After burial the hut is left.   If the chief is buried in the village enclosure, a hut is constructed over the grave.   Those who dug the grave live in the hut for three days.   Seven days after death a feast is held for the mourners.

The funeral of an ordinary person is simpler.   Fewer animals are killed, the corpse is wrapped in one skin only and is buried either in the hut he used while living or outside it to the right of the doorway.   The body is placed on three stones if a man, four if a woman.   A person struck by lightning is buried behind a hut.   A woman is taken to her parental village for burial.

Men and women who help in the burial bathe afterwards.   Mourning lasts three days for a man and four for a woman.   On the day on which the public mourning ends a feast is held, a goat or cow is killed and the blood if offered on the grave.   Beer is also spilt on the grave, and a woman's utensils or a man's weapons are placed on it.

CONCLUSION

No attempt has been made to present a comparative analysis of the social structure and organisation of the peoples described in Part II of this study because the existing material is unevenly distributed and does

not provide an adequate basis for generalisation. Until detailed studies
of each group have been made no general analysis covering all the groups
can be undertaken.

Nevertheless the material presented in Part II reveals some significant patterns of belief, organisation and structure which support the conclusions reached in Part I. For example, the belief in Jok is almost
universal - only among the Luo of Kenya is the word absent. Among the
Shilluk, Jok is the remote and supreme creator, to be approached through
Nyikang; among the Lango and Acholi Jok is an omnipresent spirit manifested in many different phenomena. Among the Nuer the *joak* is the ghost of
the dead, and among the Dinka the *jok* are the spirits of the dead. In
several tribal groups the witchdoctor is termed 'the man of Jok'. The
concept of *cien*, ghostly vengeance, also prevails in most Nilotic societies. It is significant that magic does not play a very important part
and does not pervade men's lives as among the Azande to the West, nor has
magic the same character. As Evans-Pritchard has pointed out in relation
to Nuer practices, the Nilotes tend to spiritualise their ritual concepts
and magical efficacy is regarded as the result of the operation of a spirit
and not of the innate virtue of a particular substance in a certain ritual
circumstance. Likewise, totemism, where it exists, is spiritualised.
It is generally unimportant - except among the Dinka.

Rain-making and other ritual powers exercised for the material prosperity of the people are of great importance but there does not appear to
be a general pattern. The rain-maker may be the most important person in
a social unit, as among the Dinka; he may combine one of a number of
ritual experts, as among the Nuer. Among the Lango rain-making is in the
hands of the age-sets, and, in particular, the old men of the set.

In various aspects of social life also the Nilotic groups show certain
common features such as observances relating to twins and burial customs,
in which, in most instances, the dead person is buried to one side of the
living hut. In marriage procedures, in the two general forms of marriage
- by abduction and by arrangement - and in the series of ceremonies leading
to the union there is a characteristic similarity. There is reason to
believe that the kinship terms and usages are also comparable.

Naturally these cultural features appear in slightly different forms
in each tribal group and, when more research has been carried out, it will
be interesting to see how far a common pattern exists and what variations,
elaborations and omissions may be found in individual groups, in accordance
with different social settings or historical contexts.

The question arises whether the structures of Nilotic societies have
a genetic relationship and form a general Nilotic pattern. There is some
indication of this in the material available. The concept of divine kingship and the form it takes in the Shilluk *reth* and in some of the hill
communities of the Burun-speaking people, the preponderantly ritual powers
of the *rwodi* of the Acholi, of the nobles of the Anuak and of the spear-
chiefs of the Dinka, are features which arrest attention and suggest, in
their relationship with the structure and organisation in which each is
embedded, some genetic connection.

Each Nilotic group has some ritual office of vital importance to the functioning of the whole social system. Among the more centralised groups, such as the Shilluk, Anuak and Acholi, the ritual figure symbolises the political unit and is the focus of authority, whether the unit is the whole kingdom, as among the Shilluk, or the village or league of villages, as among the Anuak. It is remarkable too, that the same word, or a form of the same word, is used for all the leaders of the main groups described. Thus, there is the Shilluk *reth*, the Acholi *rwot*, the Lango *rwot*. The *jago* is known to all three tribal groups and also to the Anuak. Among those groups which lack a centralised authority, on the other hand, these ritual figures are not generally identified with one particular unit but are strategically placed in the structure of the group and their functions make for the smoother working of the various segments of the whole in relation to one another. Thus, the leopard-skin chief of the Nuer does not symbolise his tribe or village or even the tribal segment or lineage to which he belongs, but is the means by which feuds between lineages or tribal segments may be resolved.

In the more centralised as well as in the acephalous Nilotic societies the lineage system seems to take a similar form. There is a general dispersion of clans (for the most part exogamous) and the importance of the lineage system lies in the fact that a number of lineages, linked together by ties of common residence, kinship, affinity, etc., are associated with a certain territory and that one lineage or clan in particular is regarded as dominant and may have specific ritual functions, a special relationship with the earth and a higher status in relation to the rest. This dominant lineage is the core of the community and the focal point of political and social activities. There is thus reason to believe that the kinship system of the Nilotes, combined with certain forms of territorial grouping, a specific ecology, and social values expressed through ritual offices, forms a type of structure which might be regarded as typically Nilotic. At the same time, it should not be forgotten that pastoral Nilo-Hamitic tribal groups have many of the structural patterns of the Nilotes, and that some aspects of their culture and organisation are similar.

If we consider only the structure of the Nilotic tribal groups it might, at first sight, seem as though there are two different types: the Shilluk, Anuak, Acholi and Lango type, in which there is personal political authority and a centralised office or offices about which the sentiments, values and the allegiance of the people revolve; and the acephalous kinship society of the Nuer, Central Dinka and Luo of Kenya, based on the relationship between lineage segments co-ordinated with territorial segments, and on the principles of opposition between segments on the same level and their fusion in relation to those of a different level in the structure. The structure of the Shilluk type of society does not function in the same way, for, although there are dominant lineages in the social unit, they do not all belong to a dominant clan associated with a tribal territory, as in the Nuer - Dinka - Luo type.

Yet, in spite of the differences between these two extremes, represented by the Shilluk and Nuer, they have a sufficient number of features in common, to be regarded as variations of one type. The Nuer social structure has, if only in an undeveloped form, all the features character-

istic of Shilluk structure.   The Lango appear to be nearly midway between
the two, having a very rudimentary political authority centered in the *jago*
- and in certain circumstances, the *rwot* - and also seemingly being capable
of developing to the same degree as the Nuer, the lineage system in relation to the territorial segments.   More information on the Lango would be
valuable in view of this apparent midway position.

Considering the main Nilotic tribal structure, therefore, we may
tentatively place them in the following order, according to the degree of
centralisation:

Shilluk ⟶ Anuak ⟶ Acholi ⟶ Lango ⟶ Luo ⟶ Dinka ⟶ Nuer

It is obvious that further research will modify the conclusions suggested here, and permit some important generalisations to be made.   Detailed firsthand accounts of tribal groups belonging to the same ethnic group,
rich in variations and elaborations of a common basic pattern, should produce fruitful results anthropologically and provide material for a more
systematic analysis than could be achieved through the study of a number of
peoples of different ethnic groups.

BIBLIOGRAPHY[1]

The following bibliography has been compiled by Professor E.E. Evans-Pritchard and is printed here with his permission.   Certain recently published works have been added.

THE   SHILLUK

Angerer, G.	"Ein Begrabnis bei den Schilluk." *Stern der Neger*, 1923.
Banholzer, W.	"Aus unserer Missionstation Lul." *Bericht Negerkiner*, 1902.
''	"Im Lande der Schilluk." *Die Katholischen Missionen*, 1902-3.
''	"Etwas über Geschichte und Sitten der Schilluk-könige." *La Nigrizia*, 1904.
''	"Come vestone e come s'adornane gli Scilluk." *La Nigrizia*, 1904.
''	"L'incoronazione del nuove Re degli Scilluk." *La Nigrizia*, 1905.
Banholzer, W. and Giffen, J.K.	*The Anglo-Egyptian Sudan*. (Ed. Count Gleichen) ch.VIII, 1905.
Banholzer, W.	"Die Schilluk." *Stern der Neger*, 1906.
''	"Seltsame Anschauungen unter den Schilluk." *Stern der Neger*, 1908.
''	"Der konservative Sinn der Schilluk." *Stern der Neger*, 1908.
''	"Gli indovinelli tra gli Scilluk." *La Nigrizia*, 1909.
''	"Einige Tierfabeln der Schilluk." *Stern der Neger*, 1909.
''	"Favole Scilluk.' ' *La Nigrizia*, 1910.
Beduschi, G.	"I Giudizi del Ret dei Scilluk." *La Nigrizia*, 1902.

(1) *Abbreviations*

J.E.A.U.N.H.S.	-	Journal of the East African and Uganda Natural History Society.
J.R.A.I.	-	Journal of the Royal Anthropological Institute.
J.R.-L.I.	-	Journal of the Rhodes Livingstone Institute.
S.N.R.	-	Sudan Notes and Records.

Beduschi, G.	"La religione degli Scilluk." *La Nigrizia*, 1903.
"	"Idee religiose degli Scilluk." *La Nigrizia*, 1907.
Cann, G.P.	"A day in the life of an idle Shilluk." *S.N.R.*, 1929.
Crazzolara, J.P.	"Beiträge zur Kenntnis der Religion und Zauberei bei den Schilluk." *Anthropos*, 1932.
D(irector). I(ntelligence).	"Conspiracy against the Mek of the Shilluks in 1917." *S.N.R.*, 1922.
Evans-Pritchard, E.E.	*The Divine Kingship of the Shilluk of the Nilotic Sudan.* Frazer Lecture, 1948. (A detailed analysis of the Rethship and its importance in the Shilluk social order and ritual.)
Geyer, F.X.	"Fra gli Scilluk - Osservazioni e impressioni." *La Nigrizia*, 1910.
Hofmayr, W.	"Der Regentanz bei den Schilluk." *Stern der Neger*, 1910.
"	"Zur Geschichte und sozialen und politischen Gliederung des Stammes der Schillukneger." *Anthropos*, 1910.
"	"Religion der Schilluk." *Anthropos*, 1911.
"	"Schillukkalender und Schule." *Stern der Neger*, 1912.
"	"Trauer bei den Schilluk." *Stern der Neger*, 1913.
"	*Die Schilluk. Geschichte, Religion und Leben eines Niloten-Stammes*, 1925. (A general account of the main aspects of Shilluk social organisation, culture and history.)
Howell, P.P.	"The Shilluk Settlement." *S.N.R.*, 1941. (A useful analysis of the structure of the Shilluk Settlement and a detailed account of the age set system.)
"	"Observations on the Shilluk of the Upper Nile. The Laws of Homicide and the Legal Functions of the *Reth*." *Africa*, 1952.
" and Thomson, W.P.G.	"The Death of a Reth of the Shilluk and the Installation of his Successor." *S.N.R.*, 1946. (A detailed account of the procedure of installation and its relevance to the social structure and organisation and the history of the Shilluk people.)

Kohnen, B. "Trattenimento cogli Scilluk." *La Nigrizia*, 1904.

" "Kriegerischer Sinn der Schilluk." *Bericht Negerkinder*, 1908.

Maggio, A. "Seltsame Zeremonien." *Bericht Negerkinder*, 1905.

" "Fra gli Scilluk." *La Nigrizia*, 1906.

Meroni, P. "Relazione sugli Scilluk." *La Nigrizia*, 1906.

Munro, P. "Installation of the Ret of the Chol (King of the Shilluks)." *S.N.R.*, 1918.

Mutwakil, H. "Types of Dura used by Shilluk and Dinka." *S.N.R.*, 1947.

Ohrwalder, J. "Im Lande der Schilluk." *Stern der Neger*, 1901.

Oyler, D.S. "Nikawng's Place in the Shilluk Religion." *S.N.R.*, 1918.

" "Nikawng and the Shilluk Migration." *S.N.R.*, 1918.

" "The Shilluk's belief in the Evil Eye. The Evil Medicine Man." *S.N.R.*, 1919.

" "The Shilluk's belief in the Good Medicine Man." *S.N.R.*, 1920.

" "The Shilluk Peace Ceremony." *S.N.R.*, 1920.

" "Shilluk Notes." *S.N.R.*, 1926.

Oyler, Mrs. D.S. "Examples of Shilluk Folk-Lore." *S.N.R.*, 1919.

P.C. "Matrimonio fra gli Scilluk." *La Nigrizia*, 1912.

Pschorn, E. "Il popolo Scilluk." *La Nigrizia*, 1933.

Pumphrey, M.E.C. "Shilluk 'royal' Language Conventions." *S.N.R.*, 1937.

" "The Shilluk Tribe." *S.N.R.*, 1941.
(An account of the various territorial units and types of clans of the Shilluk and also an account of marriage and certain lineage inter-relationships based on marriages between them.)

Seligman, C.G. "The Cult of Nyikang and the Divine Kings of the Shilluk." *Report of the Wellcome Tropical Research Laboratories*, 1911.

Seligman, C.G. & B.Z. *Pagan Tribes of the Nilotic Sudan.* Chs. II & III, 1932.

Stang, I.   "Welchen Nutzen die Schilluk aus der Viehzucht ziehen."   *Stern der Neger*, 1914.

"   "Meine Erlebnisse am Hofe des Schillukkönigs Fadiet."   *Stern der Neger*, 1932/1933.

Tappi, C.   "Notes Ethnologiques sur les Chillouks."   *Bull. Soc.Khediv.de Géographie*, 1903.

"   "Le Pays des Chillouks."   *Bull.Soc.Khediv.de Géographie*, 1904.

Thomson, W.P.G.   "Further Notes on the Death of a Reth of the Shilluk (1945)" *S.N.R.*, 1948.

Westermann, D.   *The Shilluk People.   Their Language and Folklore.* 1912.
(An analysis of the Shilluk language accompanied by a number of texts in the original and with the translation. The book contains a useful general outline of the life of the people.)

THE ANUAK

Bacon, C.R.K.   "Kingship amongst the Anuak."   *S.N.R.*, 1921.

"   "The Anuak."   *S.N.R.*, 1922.
(An account of certain cultural features of the Anuak.)

"   "The Investiture of an Anuak Nyeya or Sultan."   *S.N.R.*, 1924.

Cummins, A.G.   "Anuak Fable."   *Man*, 1915.

Evans-Pritchard, E.E.   *The Political System of the Anuak of the Anglo-Egyptian Sudan*, 1940.
(A detailed analysis of the Eastern political system based on the struggle of the nobles for the emblems and of the Western political system based on headmanship. It includes an account of the various aspects of the Anuak villages and of the ritual and symbolic nature of the competition for the emblems.)

Evans-Pritchard, E.E.   "Folk Stories of the Sudan."   *S.N.R.*, 1940/1941.
(and Beaton, A.C.
and Myners, T.H.B.)

Evans-Pritchard, E.E.   "Further Observations on the Political System of the Anuak."   *S.N.R.*, 1947.

Smith, G.L. Elliot.   "Spear-rest and other Tribal Heirlooms."   *Man*, 1935.

Sudan Intelligence Reports	No.200, March 1911. "Note on the Anuak Country (Western Abyssinia)", compiled mainly from a report by Mr. B.H. Jessen, and information supplied by Mr. J.M. Clayton; No.202, May 1911, "Further information *re* the Anuak country", supplied by an English elephant-hunter; No.216, July 1912, "Notes on the Anuaks of the Gila River", by Capt. H.D. Pearson, R.E.; No.217, August 1912, "Notes on the Anuak Country", by Capt. H.G. Kelly, R.E.
Whalley, R.C.R.	"Note on the Adonga Anuak." *S.N.R.*, 1936.

THE   ACHOLI

Anywar, R.	"The Life of Rwet Ibyraim Awich." *Uganda Journal*, 1948.
Rere, R.M.	"Acholi Dances (Myel). Note on the Origin of the Payera Acholi. Acholi Hunts." *Uganda Journal*, 1934.
"	"The Nature and Characteristics of the Supreme Being Worshipped among the Acholi of Uganda." *Uganda Journal*, 1939.
"	"An Outline of Acholi History." *Uganda Journal*, 1947.
"	"Awich - A Biographical Note and a Chapter of Acholi History." *Uganda Journal*, 1946.
Boccassino, R.	"Una raccolta di oggetti etnografici degli Acioli dell'Uganda." *Annali del R. Istituto Superiore Orientale di Napoli*, 1937.
"	"La figura e le caratteristiche dell'Essere Supremo degli Acioli dell' Uganda." *Atti del XIX Congresso Internationale degli Orientalisti*, (1935) 1937. (See Uganda Journal April 1939.)
"	"La Mitologia degli Acioli dell' Uganda sull' Essere Supremo, i primi tempi e la caduta dell' uomo." (con testi). *Anthropos*, 1938.
"	"La preghiera degli Acioli dell' Uganda." (con testi). *Annali Lateranensi*, 1949.
Calegari, G.	"Malattie, Medicine, Stregonerie." *La Nigrizia*, 1936/1937.
Cosner, F.	"Attraverso gli Acioli di Mongalla (Sudan)." *La Nigrizia*, 1923.

Crazzolara, J.P.	"Tierfabeln der Atscholi."	*Stern der Neger*, 1914.

"	"The African Explains Witchcraft."	*Africa*, 1935.

"	*A Study of the Acooli Language*, 1938.
(Introduction contains a certain amount of information on Acholi chiefs, kingdoms, clans and lineages)

Cunningham, J.F.	*Uganda and its Peoples*, 1905.

Delmé-Radcliffe, C.	"Surveys and Studies in Uganda."	*Geographical
Journal*, 1905.

De Marchi, E.	"Reminiscenze bibliche tra gli Acioli."	*La
Nigrizia*, 1925.

Fiocco, A.	"Il camaleonte porta-fortuna e porta-sventura."
La Nigrizia, 1931.

Gray, J.M.	"Rwot Ochama of Payera."	*Uganda Journal*, 1948.

Grove, E.N.T.	"Customs of the Acholi."	*S.N.R.*, 1919.
(A general account of the Acholi)

Johnston, H.H.	*The Uganda Protectorate*, Vol.II, 1902.

Kitching, A.L.,	"The Acholi Country."	*The Church Missionary
Lloyd, A.B. and	Intelligence*, 1904.
Cook, A.R.

Kitching, A.L.	*On the Backwaters of the Nile*, 1912.

Landra, G.	*Nuovi dati sulla biologia degli Acioli dell'
Uganda*.

Lucian Upper Nile	"Out with an Acholi Hunt."	*African Affairs*, 1946.

Lloyd, A.	*Uganda to Khartoum, Life and Adventure on the Upper
Nile*, 1907.

Malandra, A.	"Culto degli Antenati presso gli Acioli."
La Nigrizia, 1938/1939.

"	"The Ancestral Shrine of the Acholi."	*Uganda
Journal*, 1939.

"	"Gli anziani narrane Tradizioni storiche tagli
Acioli."	*La Nigrizia*, 1940.

"	"Tradizioni steriche di alcuni gruppi della
tribù Acioli."	*Annali Lateranensi*, 1943.

Nalder, L.F. (Ed.)	*A Tribal Survey of Mongalla Province*, 1937.

Seligman, C.G. & B.Z.   *Pagan Tribes of the Nilotic Sudan*, Ch.III, 1932.

Stigler   "Ethnographische und anthropologische Mitteilungen über einige wenig bekannte Volksstämme Ugandas." *Mitteilungen der Anthropologischen Gessellschaft in Wien*, 1922/1923.

Usher-Wilson, L.C.   "An Acholi Hunt." *Uganda Journal*, 1947.

Wright, A.C.A.   "Some Notes on Acholi Religious Ceremonies." *Uganda Journal*, 1936.

"   "The Supreme Being among the Acholi of Uganda - Another Viewpoint." *Uganda Journal*, 1940.

THE LANGO

Cox, T.R.F.   "Lango Proverbs," *Bull.Uganda Soc.*, 1945.

"   "Lango Proverbs," *Uganda Journal*, 1946.

Crazzolara, J.P.   "Eine Reise nach Foweira zu den Lango." *Stern der Neger*, 1913.

Driberg, J.H.   *The Lango*, 1923.
(A detailed survey of the main aspects of Lango history, religion, culture and social organisation and the only account available on the age set system which has since died out.)

"   "Some Aspects of Lango Kinship." *Sociologus*, 1932.

Hayley, T.T.S.   "The Power Concept in Lango Religion." *Uganda Journal*, 1940.

"   "Changes in Lango Marriage Customs." *Uganda Journal*, 1940.

"   "Wage Labour and the Desire for Wives among the Lango." *Uganda Journal*, 1940.

"   *The Anatomy of Lango Religion and Groups*, 1947.
(An analysis of various Lango social groups, ritual beliefs and practices, including details concerning the Etogo groups.)

Nalder, L.F. (Ed.)   *Tribal Survey of Mongalla Province*, 1937.

Olyech, Erimayo   "The Anointing of Clan Heads among the Lango." *Uganda Journal*, 1937.

Tarantino, A.G.   "Il matrimonio tra i Lango anticamente e al presente." *Anthropos*, 1940/1941.

| Tarantino, A.G. | "The Origin of the Lango." *Uganda Journal*, 1946. |

Tarantino, A.G.   "The Origin of the Lango." *Uganda Journal*, 1946.

"   "Notes on the Lango." *Uganda Journal*, 1949.

"   "Lango Wars." *Uganda Journal*, 1949.

"   "Lango Clans." *Uganda Journal*, 1949.

THE LUO

Dobbs, C.M.   "Fishing in Kavirondo Gulf, Lake Victoria." *J.E.A.U.N.H.S.*, 1927.

Evans-Pritchard, E.E.   "Luo Tribes and Clans." *J.R.-L.I.*, 1949. (An analysis of the structure and organisation of the Luo tribes and related features.)

"   "Marriage Customs of the Kenya Luo." *Africa*, Vol.XX, 1950.

"   "Ghostly Vengeance among the Kenya Luo." *Man.* Vol.L. July, 1950.

Hartmann, H.   "Some Customs of the Luwo (or Nilotic Kavirondo) living in South Kavirondo." *Anthropos*, 1928.

Hobley, C.W.   "Kavirondo." *The Geographical Journal*, 1898.

"   "Eastern Uganda." *Occasional Papers of the R.A.I.*, 1902.

"   "Anthropological Studies in Kavirondo and Nandi." *J.R.A.I.*, 1903.

Johnston, H.H.   *The Uganda Protectorate*, Vol.II, Ch.XVIII, 1902.

Marquordt, F.   "Bericht über die Kavirondo." *Zeitschift für Ethnologie.* 1909.

Millikin, A.S.   "Burial Customs of the Wa-Kavirondo of the Kisumu Province." *Man.*, 1906.

Northcote, G.A.S.   "The Nilotic Kavirondo." *J.R.A.I.*, 1907.

Nyangweso   "The Cult of Mumbo in Central and South Kavirondo." *J.E.A.U.N.H.S.*, 1930.

Owen, W.E.   "Food Production and Kindred Matters amongst the Luo." *J.E.A.U.N.H.S.*, 1934.

Odede, W.   "Luo Customs with regard to animals. (With particular reference to cattle.)" *J.E.A.U.N.H.S.*, 1942.

Roscoe, J.   *The Northern Bantu: An account of some Central African Tribes of the Uganda Protectorate.* Pt.VI, 1915.

Shaw, K.C.   "Some Preliminary Notes on Luo Marriage Customs.' *J.E.A.U.N.H.S.*, 1932.

Stam, N.   "The Religious Conceptions of the Kavirondo." *Anthropos*, 1910.

THE DINKA

Anon.   "Peace Making Ceremony of the Raik Dinka, Bahr el Ghazal Province." *S.N.R.*, 1924.

Anon.   "The reason for the Beir's hatred of the Dinka." (Extract from M.I.R., No.134, Sept. 1905.) *S.N.R.*, 1921.

Bedri, Ibrahim.   "Notes on Dinka Religious Beliefs in their hereditary Rain-makers." *S.N.R.*, 1939.

"   "More Notes on the Padang Dinka." *S.N.R.*, 1948. (An account of Dinka beliefs in connection with Nialich and a description of the Installation of the Spear Chief. Also includes an account of various other rituals.)

Beltrame, G.   "Brevi cenni sui Denca e sulla loro origine." *Rivisti Orientale*, 1867.

Lienhardt, G.   "Some notions of witchcraft among the Dinka." *Africa*, 1951.

Beltrame, G.   "Le Stagioni presso i Denca e lore denominazioni." *Bull.Soc.Geog.Ital.*, 1868.

Bloss, J.F.E.   "Notes on a Dinka Game Trap." *S.N.R.*, 1939.

"   "The Sudanese Angler." *S.N.R.*, 1945.

Boccassino, R.   "Alcune Notizie sui Dinka (Sudan Anglo-Egiziano) particolarmente sulla loro religione." *Annali del R. Instituto Superiore Orientale di Napoli*, 1935.

Consorti, F.   "Sepolto vive: Morte da Re." *Strenna delle Missioni Africane*, 1940.

Cummins, S.L.   "Sub-Tribes of the Bahr-el-Ghazal Dinka." *J.R.A.I.*, 1904.

Fergusson, V.H.   "The Holy Lake of the Dinka." *S.N.R.*, 1922.

Fergusson, V.H.   "Mattiang Goh! Witchcraft."   *S.N.R.*, 1923.

Gleichen, Count   *The Anglo-Egyptian Sudan*, Ch.VI, 1905.

Howell, P.P.   "The Zeraf Hills."   *S.N.R.*, 1945.

Hirschberg, J.E.C.   "Die Dinka und Nuer in der Sammlung Franz Binder." (Museum Paper), 1935/1936.

Johnston, R.T.   "The Religious and Spiritual Beliefs of the Bor Dinka."   *S.N.R.*, 1934.

Mackrell, J.E.C.   "The Dinka Oath on Ashes."   *S.N.R.*, 1942.

Mills, W.L.   "A Dinka Witchdoctor."   *S.N.R.*, 1919.

Nebel, A.   "Wau in the Dinka Folk-lore."   *The Messenger*, 1936.

"   "Life History of a Dinka."   *The Messenger*, 1937.

"   "Sulla Vita dei Denka - Note etnografiche." *La Nigrizia*, 1940, 1941.

Nunn, N.   "A Dinka Public Health Measure."   *S.N.R.*, 1942.

Olivetti, P.   "Fra una tribu di Giganti," 1933.

O'Sullivan, H.   "Dinka Laws and Customs."   *J.R.A.I.*, 1910.

Raimondi, G.   "Lo Stregone Denka."   *La Nigrizia*, 1936.

Richards, M.G.   "Medical Treatment by Bor Witch-Doctors." *S.N.R.*, 1927.

"   "The Truth Diviner (Amongst the Agar Dinkas)." *S.N.R.*, 1924.

Seligman, C.G. & B.Z.   *Pagan Tribes of the Nilotic Sudan*, Ch.IV and V, 1932.

Shaw, A.   "Dinka Animal Stories."   (Bor Dialect) *S.N.R.*, 1919.

"   *Akokol Fables*, 1930.

"   "Dinka Songs."   *Man.*, 1915.

Sorur, D.   "I Denka."   *La Nigrizia*, 1899.

Stubbs, J.M.   "Notes on Beliefs and Customs of the Malwal Dinka of the Bahr el Ghazal Province." *S.N.R.*, 1934.

Stubbs, J.M. &
Morrison, C.G.T.

"The Western Dinkas, their Land and their Agricul-
ture."   *S.N.R.*, 1938.
(A full account of the crops and methods of cultivation of the Dinka and the co-ordination of a
pastoral and an horticultural economy.)

Tappi, C.

"Fra gli accampamenti estivi dei Denka."
La Nigrizia, 1902.

Titherington, G.W.

"Magicians, etc., among the Raik Dinka."   *S.N.R.*,
1925.

"

"Burial Alive among Dinka of the Bahr el Ghazal
Province."   *S.N.R.*, 1935.

"

"The Raik Dinka of the Bahr el Ghazal Province."
S.N.R., 1937.
(A general account of the organisation, culture,
economy etc.)

THE   NUER

Alban, A.H.

"Gweks' Pipe and Pyramid."   *S.N.R.*, 1940.

Capri, P.

"I Nuer - una tribù indomita."   *Le Missioni
del Comboni*, 1938/1939.

Coningham.

Sudan Intelligence Reports, 1910.

Coriat, P.

"The Gaweir Nuers."   Appendix to H.C. Jackson's
articles, (see below) when reissued as a monograph.

Crazzolara, J.P.

"Die Gar-Zeremonie bei den Nuer."   *Africa*, 1932.

"

Outlines of a Nuer Grammar, Introduction and
Appendix, 1933.

"

"Pygmies on the Bahr el Ghazal."   *S.N.R.*, 1933.

Crazzolara, J.P.   "Die Bedeutung des Rindes bei den Nuer." *Africa*,
                        1934.

    "   "A Nuer Story: Goor Kene Nyaang."   *The Messenger*,
                        1937.

Coriat, P.   "Gwek, the Witch-doctor and the Pyramid of
                        Dengkur."   *S.N.R.*, 1939.

Evans-Pritchard, E.E.   "The Nuer, Tribe and Clan."   *S.N.R.*, 1933/1935.

    "   The Nuer Age-Sets."   *S.N.R.*, 1936.

    "   "Customs relating to Twins among the Nilotic
                        Nuer."   *Uganda Journal*, 1936.

    "   "Daily Life of the Nuer in Dry Season Camps."
                        *Custom is King.   A Collection of Essays in honour
                        of R.R. Marett*, 1936.

    "   "Some aspects of Marriage and the Family among the
                        Nuer."   *Zeitschrift fur Rechtswissenschaft*, 1938.

    "   "Economic Life of the Nuer."   *S.N.R.*, 1937/1938.

    "   "Nuer Time-Reckoning."   *Africa*, 1939.

    "   *The Nuer.   A Description of the Modes of Liveli-
                        hood and Political Institutions of a Nilotic
                        People*, 1940.

    "   "The Nuer of the Southern Sudan."   *African
                        Political Systems*, 1940.

    "   "Nuer Bridewealth."   *Africa*, 1946.

    "   "Bridewealth among the Nuer."   *African Studies*,
                        1947.

    "   "Nuer Marriage Ceremonies."   *Africa*, 1947.

    "   "A Note on Courtship among the Nuer."   *S.N.R.*,
                        1947.

    "   "A Note on Affinity Relationships among the Nuer."
                        Man., 1948.

    "   "Nuer modes of Address."   *Uganda Journal*, 1948.

    "   "The Nuer Col Wic."   *Man.*, 1949.

    "   "Burial and Mortuary Rites of the Nuer."   *African
                        Affairs*, 1949.

Evans-Pritchard, E.E.   "Nuer Rules of Exogamy and Incest."   *Social Structure.*   *Essays presented to A.R. Radcliffe-Brown,* 1949.

     "   "Some Nuer Ritual Concepts."   *Man.,* 1949.

     "   "Nuer Totemism."   *Annali Lateranensi,* 1949.

     "   "The Nuer Family."   *S.N.R.,* Vol.XXXI, 1950.

     "   "Kinship and Local Community among the Nuer." *African Systems of Kinship and Marriage* (ed. Forde and Radcliffe-Brown), 1950.

     "   "Some features and forms of Nuer Sacrifices." *Africa,* 1951.

Fergie, Bey,   *The Story of.*   1930.

Fergusson, V.H.   "The Nuong Nuer."   *S.N.R.,* 1921.

     "   "Nuer Beast Tales."   *S.N.R.,* 1924.

Gordon, H.   *Sudan Intelligence Reports,* 1903.

Hawkes, G.   *Sudan Intelligence Reports,* 1902.

Howell, P.P.   "A Note on Elephants and Elephant Hunting among the Nuer."   *S.N.R.,* 1945.

     "   "On the Value of Iron among the Nuer."   *Man.* 1947.

     "   "The Age-Set System and the Institution of 'Nak' among the Nuer."   *S.N.R.,* 1948.

Howell, P.P. and Lewis, B.A.   "Nuer Ghouls; A Form of Witchcraft."   *S.N.R.,* 1947.

Huffman, R.   *Nuer Customs and Folklore,* 1931.

Jackson, H.C.   "The Nuer of the Upper Nile Province."   *S.N.R.,* 1923.

Kingdon, F.D.   "The Western Nuer Patrol 1927-28."   *S.N.R.,* 1945.

Kohnen, B.   "Mein erster Besuch bei den Nuer."   *Bericht Negerkinder,* 1905.

Mlakic, S.   "Nuer Religion."   *The Messenger,* 1943/1944.

Maxse, F.J.   *Sudan Intelligence Reports,* 1899.

O'Sullivan Bey   *Sudan Intelligence Reports,* 1910.

Prina, M.	"Il Segno distintive nazionale dei Nuer. *La Nigrizia*, 1935.
Redaelli, E.	"Fra i Nuer." *La Nigrizia*, 1926.
Stigand, C.H.	"Warrior Classes of the Nuers." *S.N.R.*, 1918.
"	"The Story of Kir and the White Spear." *S.N.R.*, 1919.
Struve, K.C.P.	*Sudan Intelligence Reports*, 1907.
Westermann, D.	"The Nuer Language." Introduction and Part II. (Folklore) *Mitteilungen des Seminars für Orientalische Sprachen zu Berlin*, 1912.
Willis, C.A.	"The Cult of Deng." *S.N.R.*, 1928.
Wilson, H.H.	*Sudan Intelligence Reports*, 1905.

THE SHILLUK-LUO PEOPLES OF THE BAHR EL GHAZAL

Briani. G.	"Cerimoniale Giur atterno neonato." *La Nigrizia*, 1936.
Colombaroli, A.	"La corte d'assise fra i Giur." *La Nigrizia*, 1909/1910.
Geyer, F.X.	"Eine Fahrt auf dem Djur." *Die Katholischen Missionem*, 1904/1905.
Ghawi, J.B.	"Notes on the Law and Custom of the Jur Tribe in the Central District of the Bahr el Ghazal Province." *S.N.R.*, 1924.
Maffei, G.B.	"Ceremonie d'imposizione del nome." *La Nigrizia*, 1916.
"	"Curiosità dei Giur." *La Nigrizia*, 1920.
Magagnotto, F.S.	"Alcune note sui Giur." *La Nigrizia*, 1915, 1916, 1917, 1919, 1921, 1924.
"	"Il sentimento religioso dei Giur." *La Nigrizia*, 1925/26.
"	*Dal Fiume delle Gazzelle - Il sentimento religioso tra i Giur*, 1926.
"	"Il capro espiatorio." *La Nigrizia*, 1944.
Santandrea, S.	"The Shilluk Hordes in the Bahr el Ghazal - The Jur and Belanda." *The Messenger*, 1934.

Santandrea, S.   "Il Totemismo nelle Tribù minori del Bahr el Ghazal." *La Nigrizia*, 1937.

"   "Costumi fra i Giur." *La Nigrizia*, 1937.

"   "Minor Shilluk sections in the Bahr el Ghazal." *S.N.R.*, 1938.

"   "The Shilluk-Luo tribes in the Bahr el Ghazal - Jo Luo (Jur) and Boor (Belanda)." *Anthropos*, 1942.

"   "The Luo of the Bahr el Ghazal." *Annali Lateranensi*, 1945 and 1948.
                         (This includes an account of the tribal organisation, culture and various customs of the Jo Luo)

Stubbs, J.M.   "The Ordeal by Boiling Water." *S.N.R.*, 1938.

Tappi, C.   "Nel paese dei Giur." *La Nigrizia*, 1904/1905.

"   "Civiltà Africana - Saggio di studio sui Giur del sud-est di Wau." *La Nigrizia*, 1913/1914. *Bull.Soc.Khediv.Geographie*, 1917.

"   "Essai sur les Djour du sud-est de Waou." *Bulletin de la Societé Sultaniel de Géographie*. Tome VIII, 1917.

Vokenhuber, S.   "Die Djur." *Stern der Neger*, 1906.

THE   BELANDA   (BOR)

Evans-Pritchard, E.E.   "The Mberidi and Mbegumba of the Bahr el Ghazal." *S.N.R.*, 1931/1932.

Michelon, K.   "Note ethnografiche." *La Nigrizia*, 1917.

"   "Costumi Belanda." *La Nigrizia*, 1919.

Nebel, A.   "Una Nuova Tribù; I Manangeer." *La Nigrizia*, 1939.

Santandrea, S.   "The Belanda, (Ndogo, Bai and Sere) in the Bahr el Ghazal." *S.N.R.*, 1933.

"   "Shilluk Luo Tribes in the Bahr el Ghazal." *Anthropos*, 1942/1945.

"   "Superstition." *The Messenger*, 1943.

Struck, B.   "An Unlocated Tribe on the White Nile."
                            J.Afr.Soc., 1908.

Tucker, A.N.   "The Tribal Confusion around Wau."   *S.N.R.*,
                            1931.

Wheatley, M.J.   "The Belanda."   *S.N.R.*, 1923.
                            (Points out the fact that the term 'Belanda'
                            covers two groups of different origins.)

THE   BURUN-SPEAKING   PEOPLES

Evans-Pritchard, E.E.   "Ethnological Observations in Dar Fung."   *S.N.R.*,
                            1932.
                            (Analysis of the various Burun-speaking peoples
                            on the basis of language - with some details of
                            culture and organisation.)

Mostyn, J.P.   "Some Notes on Burun Customs and Beliefs."
                            S.N.R., 1921.

Stigand, C.H.   "Notes on the Burun."   *S.N.R.*, 1922.

Vallance, D.J.   "Notes on the Ethnographical Specimens collected
                            by Dr. A. MacTier Pirrie."   *Report of the Well-
                            come Research Laboratories*, 1908.

Watersten, D.   "Report upon the Physical Characters of some of
                            the Nilotic Negroid Tribes."   *Report of the
                            Wellcome Research Laboratories*, 1908.   (Based
                            on Dr. A. MacTier Pirrie's measurements.)

Wedderburn-Maxwell,   "The Maban of Southern Fung."   *S.N.R.*, 1936.
H.G.

THE   PARI

Crazzolara, J.P.   "The Lwoo People."   *Uganda Journal*, 1937.

Driberg, J.H.   "Lafon Hill."   *S.N.R.*, 1925.

Evans-Pritchard, E.E.   "The Relationship between the Anuak and the Föri
                            (Sudan)."   *Man.*, 1940.

Walsh, R.H.   "The Beri, or more correctly Pari."   *S.N.R.*,
                            1922.

Zambonardi, C.   "La Tribù dei Lokorong."   *La Nigrizia*, 1934.

THE ALUR

Breugelmans, R.   "Les Alur" Unpublished M.S.   Musée du Congo Belge.   Institut Royal Colonial Belge.   Centre de Documentation Ethnographique.

Colombaroli, A.   "Amministrazione della giustizia tra gli Aluro." *La Nigrizia*, 1912.

De Marchi, E.   "Matrimonio tra gli Alur." *La Nigrizia*, 1930/31.

P.C.   "Quando gli Alur vogliono cercare il colpevole." *La Nigrizia*, 1945.

Vanneste, M.   "De getallen in De Alur-taal." *Congo*, 1934.

"   "De Benaningen der Familie betrekkingen Bij de Alur." *Congo*, 1936.

"   "Regels der welluidenheit in de Alur-taal. (Mahagi)." *Congo*, 1925.

Vignato, A.   "Fra gli Alure." *La Nigrizia*, 1914.

GENERAL

Bryan, M.A. and Tucker, A.N.   *Distribution of the Nilotic and Nilo-Hamitic Languages of Africa.*   London: Oxford University Press for the International African Institute, 1948.

Crazzolara, J.P.   *The Lwoo*.   Part I. Lwoo Migrations, 1950. Part II. Lwoo Traditions, 1951.   Verona, Missioni Africane (Museum Combonianum).

Hamilton, J.A. de C. (Ed.)   *The Anglo Egyptian Sudan from Within*, 1935.

Hurst, H.E. and Phillips, P.   *The Nile Basin*, Vol.I, 1931.

Macmichael, Sir H.   *The Anglo-Egyptian Sudan*, 1934.

Seligman, C.G. & B.Z.   *Pagan Tribes of the Nilotic Sudan*, 1932.

Tucker and Myres   "A Contribution to the Anthropology of the Sudan." *J.R.A.I.*, 1910.

For Product Safety Concerns and Information please contact our EU
representative GPSR@taylorandfrancis.com
Taylor & Francis Verlag GmbH, Kaufingerstraße 24, 80331 München, Germany